ANCESTORS
and
DESCENDENTS *of*
THOMAS LEACH
of
Maryland,

NORTH CAROLINA, AND NORTHWEST ARKANSAS

ANCESTORS
and
DESCENDENTS *of*
THOMAS LEACH
of
Maryland,

NORTH CAROLINA, AND NORTHWEST ARKANSAS

George Leach

iUniverse LLC
Bloomington

Ancestors and Descendents of Thomas Leach of Maryland, North Carolina, and Northwest Arkansas

iUniverse books may be ordered through booksellers or by contacting:

iUniverse LLC
1663 Liberty Drive
Bloomington, IN 47403
www.iuniverse.com
1-800-Authors (1-800-288-4677)

Because of the dynamic nature of the Internet, any web addresses or links contained in this book may have changed since publication and may no longer be valid. The views expressed in this work are solely those of the author and do not necessarily reflect the views of the publisher, and the publisher hereby disclaims any responsibility for them.

Any people depicted in stock imagery provided by Thinkstock are models, and such images are being used for illustrative purposes only.
Certain stock imagery © Thinkstock.

ISBN: 978-1-4917-0004-4 (sc)
ISBN: 978-1-4917-0005-1 (ebk)

Printed in the United States of America

iUniverse rev. date: 08/26/2013

To help clarify and identify each individual listed herein I have decided to use the following code to identify Leach decendants. The oldest known Leach in our family line is Richard Leach, Sr. The oldest child of Richard would be #1-1. His second child will be #1-2. His third child #1-3. This would signify: First the generation #1, second the child number in that generation. The oldest child of Richard's oldest child will be #2-1-1. The second child of Richard's oldest child will be #2-1-2. This should identify what generation and which child. I am sure I will not have all ages or descendants correct but will list them as my records reflect.

To further clarify the numbering system. Using the number #3-4-2-5. this would be the third generation of Richard Leach, Sr.'s fourth child, John H. Leach. Then, second child of John H. Leach, Elizabeth Leach. Then Elizabeth's fifth child, Mary "Polly" Leach. The same identification system will be used for all other families herein until they become Leach descendants, then the Leach numbering system will be used.

THE LEACH FAMILY IN NORTHWEST ARKANSAS, THEIR ANCESTORS, DESCENDANTS AND KINDRED

The first Leach to settle in Northwest Arkansas was Thomas Leach, #1-3. Thomas came to Washington County, Arkansas, with his wife, Ruth Renshaw, their five sons and daughter, settling on Bush Creek, South of Lincoln about 1828. Thomas was the son of a North Carolina Planter, Richard Leach, Sr., who was born in Maryland in the 1750's. Early Maryland records are scarce, many courthouses having been burned by the invading British army in the War of 1812. There was, however, a short family history written by Zadock Leach VI, a North Carolina resident, when he was in his eighties. In making his two page history sound creditable he says his Grandfather Zadock, Leach, IV, had in his possession the Leach family German Bible when he came to North Carolina but that it was later lost or destroyed. Zadock Leach, IV, was a brother to Richard Leach, Sr. In the history Zadock, VI, stated that the Leach family sailed from Scotland to Germany in the 1600's. That shortly after 1700 they sailed from Germany to what is now the United States, settling on the Potomac River in Maryland twelve miles from what is now Washington D.C. His history reports that the father of the Leach family died and was buried at sea during the crossing. Based on Zadock, VI, short history, The father of Richard Leach, Sr., would have been Zadock Leach, III. Since only fifty years passed between the time the father of the Leach family died at sea and the birth of Zadock Leach, IV, The name of the father of the Leach family who died at sea was probably Zadock, but that can not be determined with any certainty.

The earliest Maryland record I find for Richard Leach, Sr., is his service in the Maryland Militia during the American Revolution. Richard's service was in the 7th Co., Middle Battalion of the Montgomery County Militia. The second record is his marriage to Elizabeth Hulen, 31 January 1784, Wilkes County, North Carolina. Richard Leach, Sr., Homesteaded property on the Yadkin River in Rowan County North Carolina in 1785, after that date records of Richard are plentiful.

Other Leach families who homesteaded property contiguous to Richard were his brothers James, Benjamin and Zaddoch, IV. Richard and his three brothers each named a son John. This would probably be a good research key in looking for a recent common ancestor, his name would no doubt be John. The portion of Rowan County where Richard Leach lived became Davie County before his death.

Elizabeth Hulen, #1-2, who married Richard Leach, Sr., was the daughter of William Hulen, born 20 January 1730 in Bristol Parish, Virginia, and Elisibeth Beckneil born about 1753 in Virginia. William Hulen died 25 October 1785, Wilkes County, North Carolina.

Children of William Hulen and Elisabeth Beckneil

#1-1.	Milly Hulen born about 1765 in Wilkes County, North Carolina, married William Leach, 14 June 1781.
#1-2.	Elizabeth Hulen, born about 1768 Wilkes County, North Carolina, married Richard Leach, Sr.#1-2.
#1-3.	Ambrose Hulen, born 1768, Wilkes County, North Carolina.
#1-4.	Mary "Polly" Hulen, born 30 January 1775, Wilkes County, North Carolina.
#1-5.	John Hulen, born about 1777, Wilkes County, North Carolina.
#1-6.	Sarah Hulen, born about 1783, Wilkes County, North Carolina, and
#1-7.	Thomas Hulen, both about 1785, Wilkes County, North Carolina.

RICHARD LEACH, SR.

Richard Leach, Sr., born in the 1750's in Maryland died 9 November1841, Davie County, North Carolina. It's exciting to imagine the life and times of Richard and the people he no doubt came in contact with daily. One of the neighbors owning property adjoining

Richard was Squire Boon, the father of Daniel Boon. One can but imagine the conversations that might have occurred at community gatherings regarding Daniel's travels and adventures. Most researchers put the death of Elizabeth Hulen as being some time in the later part of 1841. Both Richard and Elizabeth were buried in Davie County, North Carolina. Most information on the family of Richard Leach, Sr., would have been difficult, if not impossible, to find had it not been for the probate of his will in Davie County, North Carolina.

Children of Richard Leach, Sr., and Elizabeth Hulen

#1-1.	Sarah Leach, born about 1785, Rowan County, North Carolina, married Henry Helfer.
#1-2.	Mildred Leach, born 1789, Rowan County, North Carolina, married James Renshaw.
#1-3.	Thomas L. Leach, born 14 September 1789, Rowan County, North Carolina, married Ruth Renshaw.
#1-4.	John H. Leach, born 1791, Rowan County, North Carolina, married Hulda Baxter.
#1-5.	Rebecca Leach, born in 1793, Rowan County, North Carolina, married Francis Renshaw.
#1-6.	Elizabeth Leach, born 1798, Rowan County, North Carolina, married Britian Owings.
#1-7.	Mary Leach, born 1799 Rowan County, North Carolina, married Henry F. Wilson.
#1-8.	Richard L. Leach, Jr., Born 1807, Rowan County, North Carolina, married Elizabeth Sims.
#1-9.	Temperance Leach, born 1809, Rowan County, North Carolina, married Mumford Bean.

SECOND GENERATION

#1-1   SARAH LEACH

Sarah and her husband, Henry Helfer, were married before 1810 and had only one child. Henry was born about 1785. Both Sarah and Henry died between the time when the 1820 and 1830 census was taken; they were living on the Forks of the Yadkin Township, Rowan County, North Carolina. Sarah is mentioned in Richard's will as a deceased daughter, with her share of his estate going to her daughter.

Child or Sarah Leach and Henry Helfer

#2-1-1.   Rachel Helfer, born 1810, Rowan County, North Carolina.

#1-2   MILDRED LEACH

Mildred Leach born 1787, Rowan County, North Carolina, married James Renshaw, 1 March 1809, Rowan County, North Carolina, James was born about 1775, Rowan County, North Carolina and died in 1837, Davie County, North Carolina, Mildred and James lived their entire lives in Rowan County, now Davie County, North Carolina. Mildred died there in 1848.

Children of Mildred Leach and James Renshaw

#2-2-1.   Mary Ann Renshaw, born about 1813, Rowan County, North Carolina, married William Nendricks

#2-2-2.   Arthur Renshaw, born April 4, 1813, Chatham County, North Carolina, married Margarew W. Wilson.

#2-2-3.	Sarah Renshaw, born 1817, Rowan County, North Carolina, married Denton Hendren.
#2-2-4.	Rebecca Renshaw, born 1822, Rowan County, North Carolina, married Abraham Bessent.
#2-2-5.	Elizabeth Renshaw, born 1824, Rowan County, North Carolina, married John D. Hall.
#2-2-6.	John B. Renshaw, born 1825, Rowan County, North Carolina, married Lamira C.

#1-3   THOMAS L. LEACH

Thomas L. Leach born 14 September 1789, Rowan County, North Carolina. Little is known about the early years of Thomas' life. During the War of 1812 he served in active duty with the North Carolina Militia. After the war Thomas married Ruth Renshaw, 25 October, 1814. Ruth was the daughter of Elijah Renshaw. The Renshaw's were neighbors to Richard Leach, Sr. After the birth of their first child in 1815, Thomas and Ruth moved to Rutherford County, Tennessee, where other family members had previously settled. Thomas, Ruth and their three sons moved on to Jackson County, Alabama about 1822. In 1828, Thomas and Ruth moved again, this time to Arkansas. Their family had now grown to five sons and one daughter. Thomas' family came to Northwest Arkansas by Steamboat. They came up the Arkansas River to Van Buren. At Van Buren they went North across the mountain where a roadway had just recently been opened by way of Post, then on to Bush Valley South of Lincoln where Thomas homesteaded in 1829. One of Ruth's Sisters, Elizabeth Renshaw West and her husband Thomas West, who had been in Jackson County, Alabama, when Thomas and Ruth were there, homesteaded in Washington County not too far from Thomas and Ruth. It is not known if they came to Northwest Arkansas with Thomas and Ruth or not. Ruth was born, 22 February 1795 Rowan County, North Carolina and died, 31 August 1848, Washington County, Arkansas. Thomas died 27 August 1879 in Benton County. after the death of Ruth, Thomas married Delila (Taylor) Culberson. Thomas was a Methodist and a Mason.

Children of Thomas L. Leach and Ruth Renshaw

#2-3-1.	Richard L. Leach, born 1 August 1815, Rowan County, North Carolina, married Eliza Hewitt.
#2-3-2.	Ambrose Leach, born 1818, Rutherford County, Tennessee, married Mary L. Scott #5-1-2-2-2.
#2-3-3.	Elijah Leach, born 1819 Rutherford County, Tennessee, Married Nancy Emily (Dyer) Sear.
#2-3-4.	Thomas L. Leach, Jr., born 14 July 1820, Jackson County, Alabama, married Catharine Turner.
#2-3-5.	Tempie Leach, born 27 August 1822, Jackson County, Alabama, married John Morrow.
#2-3-6.	John M. Leach, born 1828, Jackson Alabama, married Christina Scott.

Children of Thomas L. Leach and Delila (Taylor)Culberson

Thomas L. Leach married Delila (Taylor) Culberson, 4 November 1849, Washington County, Arkansas. Delila was a young widow with three children, she was born in Missouri, 12 October 1825. Delila died in Benton County, Arkansas 16 August, 1871, and was buried at the Hico Cemetery, Siloam Springs, Arkansas.

Children

#2-3-7.	Nathan West Leach, born 8 June 1851, Washington County, Arkansas, married Frances (Fanny) Butler.
#2-3-8.	William W. Leach, b. December 1853, Washington County, Arkansas, married R. E. Sarah Jones.
#2-3-9.	Redmond Boyd Leach, born 20 August 1855, Washington County, Arkansas, married Sarah Alice Sitton.
#2-3-10.	Joseph H. Leach, born October 1858, Benton County, Arkansas, married Nancy Elizabeth Rogers.

#2-3-11.	Flora Belle Leach, born 20 December 1859, Benton County, Arkansas, married Bailey N. Hogan.
#2-3-12.	Laura Alice Leach, born 10 June 1862, Benton County, Arkansas, married George Agustus Sitton.

#1-4   JOHN H. LEACH

John H. Leach born 1791, Rowan County North, Carolina, married Hulda Baxter 10 December 1815, Rowan County, North Carolina. Hulda was a Rowan County, North Carolina native, having been born there in 1792. After marriage John and Hulda moved to Warren County, Tennessee, where they made their home for about five years. John and Hulda move on to new land being opened up in West Illinois, which later became St. Clair County. Another John Leach, a cousin, had settled there previously. John and Hulda remained in St. Clair County, Illinois, until John's death prior to 1838. After John's death Hulda married James Taylor in St. Clair County, Illinois.

Children of John H. Leach And Hulda Baxter

#2-4-1.	Diana Leach, born 28 February 1818, Warren County, Tennessee, married first Abraham J. Gooding, second William Lierle.
#2-4-2.	Elizabeth Leach, born 1820, Warren, Tennessee, married Robert Leach.
#2-4-3.	Temperence Leach, born 1822, St. Clair County, Illinois, married John Leach, Jr.
#2-4-3.	Richard Leach, born 1824, St Clair County, Illinois, married Elizabeth Lierle.
#2-4-5.	Eliza Ann Leach, born 1824, St Clair County, Illinois, died 1839, St Clair County, Illinois.

Rebecca Leach born 1793, Rowan County, North Carolina, married Francis Renshaw August19, 1816, Rowan County, North Carolina. Francis was the son of Elijah Renshaw and his first wife Ann. He was born in 1791, Rowan County, North Carolina. Frances was the brother of Ruth Renshaw who married Thomas L. Leach. In 1820, Francis and Rebecca moved to Jackson County Alabama where the Indian land had just been opened for settlement and made their home there the rest of their lives. Francis was probably the wealthiest of the Renshaws at the time of his death. Rebecca died in 1850, Jackson County, Alabama. After Rebecca's death Frances married Agnes Sargant, 15 October 1851. Frances died July 1, 1860. Papers filed in the probate of Francis's Estate say he had no heirs which was completely erroneous.

Children of Rebecca Leach and Francis Renshaw

#2-5-1.	Tempa M. Renshaw, born 1817, Rowan County, North Carolina, married William H. Green.
#2-5-2.	Belinda Anna Louisa Renshaw, born 1818, Rowan County, North Carolina, married Carson.
#2-5-3.	Ambrose D. Renshaw, born 1819, Rowan County, North Carolina, married Lucinda C. Taylor.
#2-5-4.	Elizabeth H. Renshaw, born 1824, Jackson County, Alabama, married Edward H. Kyle.

#1-6   **ELIZABETH LEACH**

Elizabeth Leach was born 1789, Rowan County, North Carolina. She married Britian Owings 4 March 1822, Rowan County, North Carolina. Britain was born in 1789, in North Carolina. Around 1827, Elizabeth and Britian moved to St Clair County, Illinois, where Elizabeth's brother and cousins had previously settled. Britian must have been well trusted and respected. When a dispute rose over the Richard Leach, Sr., Estate his nieces and nephews located in Illinois all appointed him power of attorney to represent them in the Court hearings. Elizabeth and Britian remained in St Clair County the rest of their lives, both dying before 1880.

Children Of Elizabeth Leach And Britian Owings

#2-6-1.	Norman Henry Owings, born 1823, Rowan County, North Carolina, married Mary.
#2-6-2.	Mary Owings, born 1823, Rowan County, North Carolina, married Drury Leach.
#2-6-3.	Martha Owings, born 1826, Rowan County, North Carolina, married Lewis Holcomb.
#2-6-4.	Maria Catherine Owings, born 1828, St Clair County, Illinois, married Richard Pulliam.
#2-6-5.	Elizabeth M. Owings, born 1829, St Clair County, Illinois, married Mr. Ballard.
#2-6-6.	Thomas Phelps Owings, born 1830, St Clair County, Illinois, Married Frances Arabella Goodrich.
#2-6-7.	John Owings, born 1832, St Clair County, Illinois.
#2-6-8.	Mildred Emily Owings, born 1835, St Clair County, Illinois.
#2-6-9.	Rebecca Jane Owings, born 1837, St Clair County, Illinois, married William Simmons.
#2-6-10.	Sarah Temperance Owings, born 1839, St Clair County Illinois.

#1-7   MARY LEACH

Mary Leach born 1799, Rowan County, North Carolina. Mary married Henry F. Wilson 18 September 1819, in Rowan County, North Carolina. The Wilson name was often spelled with two L's in early days. Little is known about the family of Mary and Henry F. Wilson. They moved their family to Kaufman County, Texas, prior to the 1850's. Henry was born in North Carolina in 1801.

Children of Mary Leach and Henry F. Wilson

#2-7-1.	Ambrose M. Wilson, born 1831, North Carolina.
#2-7-2.	William D. Wilson, born 1836, North Carolina.
#2-7-3.	Francis M. Wilson, born 1843, North Carolina.

#1-8   RICHARD LEACH, JR.

Richard L. Leach, Jr., born 1807, in Rowan County, North Carolina, married three times. He married his first wife, Elizabeth Maxwell, 12 March 1825, Rowan County, North Carolina. His second marriage was to Elizabeth Linebarrier 14 February 1850, Rowan County, North Carolina. Richard and Elizabeth were living with Elizabeth's sister at the time of the 1850 census. His occupation was listed as laborer. The 1860 censuses is the only time I find Richard with any assets. He was a farmer and had $150.00 real property and $50.00 personal property. Richard's third marriage was to Barbara Simpson 27 August 1860, Rowan County, North Carolina. Richards only children were born to his first marriage.

Children of Richard Leach, Jr., and Elizabeth Maxwell

| #2-8-1. | Amanda Leach, born 1836, Davie County, North Carolina. |
| #2-8-2. | Louisa Leach, born 1841, Rowan County, North Carolina. |

#1-9   TEMPERANCE LEACH

Temperance Leach born 1809, Rowan County, North Carolina, married Mumford Bean 3 March 1829, Rowan County, North Carolina. Mumford was born 1808, Rowan County, North Carolina and died in 1865, Davie County, North Carolina. Mumford was a cabinet maker and must not have impressed his father in law. In Richard Leach, Sr.'s will all property to the benefit of Temperance was left to a guardian to administer use and distribution. Temperance later challenged this in the

Probate Court and got it changed. Temperance and children were still in Davie County in 1870.

Children of Temperance Leach and Mumford Bean

#2-9-1.   Malinda Bean, born 1848, Davie County, North Carolina.
#2-9-2.   Anderson Bean, born 1850, Davie County, North Carolina.
#2-9-3.   Mariah Bean, born 1852, Davie County, North Carolina.
#2-9-4.   John Bean, born 1855, Davie County, North Carolina.
#2-9-5.   Jefferson Bean, born, 1860 Davie County, North Carolina.

THIRD GENERATION

#2-1-1   RACHEL HELFER

Rachel Helfer born 1810, Rowan County, North Carolina, Married David Earnest 8 June 1830, Rowan County, North Carolina. Rachel and David moved from Rowan County to Union County, Illinois, where they lived out their lives and raised their children. Rachel Earnest died in 1845, Union County, Illinois. After her death David married Sarah Hinkle 17 August 1845, Union County, Illinois. An 1835 special census held in Union county showed two sons under the age of ten years. These two sons were not living at home during the 1850 census, so they have been omitted. David Earnest was born 1810, Rowan County, North Carolina, and died in 1858, Union County, Illinois. Both Rachel and David are buried in the Jonesboro Cemetery, Union County, Illinois.

Children of Rachel Helfer And David Earnest

#3-1-1-1.	Daniel Earnest born, 1837, Union County, Illinois, married Rebecca Keller.
#3-1-1-2.	Temperance Earnest, born 1839, Union County, Illinois, married Temperance Karraker.
#3-1-1-3.	Saran Earnest, born 1841, Union County, Illinois, married Meredith Keller.
#3-1-1-4.	Jacob Earnest, born 1845, Union County, Illinois, married Elizabeth Ridenhour.

David Earnest and Sarah Hinkle had the following Children according to the 1850 census, Union County, Illinois.

1.	Louisa Earnest, born 1848, Union County, Illinois, married James M. Keller, 6 June 1867 Union County, Illinois.

2.   Nancy Earnest, born 1848, Union County,
                          Illinois, married William R. Hoffner 16 May
                          1867, Union County, Illinois,

#2-2-1   MARY ANN RENSHAW

Mary Ann Renshaw, born 1813, Rowan County, North Carolina,
married William Hendricks 18 July, 1830, Rowan County, North
Carolina. Mary and William were in Davie County, North Carolina,
with their children for the 1850 census. Mary was in Kaufman County,
Texas, with their children for the 1860 census. William died between
1850 and 1860 but I couldn't determine if it was in North Carolina or
Texas. Mary died in 1885, Kaufman County, Texas.

Children of Mary Ann Renshaw and William Hendricks

#3-2-1-1.   James Franklin Hendricks, born 1832, Rowan
                       County, North Carolina.
#3-2-1-2.   William Hendricks, born 1837, Davie County,
                       North Carolina.
#3-2-1-3.   Elijah Renshaw Hendricks, born 1840, Davie
                       County, North Carolina.
#3-2-1-4.   Richard L. Hendricks, born 1842, Davie County,
                       North Carolina.
#3-2-1-5.   Elenor Hendricks, born 1844, Davie County,
                       North Carolina.
#3-2-1-6.   Sarah Hendricks, born 1846, Davie County,
                       North Carolina.
#3-2-1-7.   Mary Hendricks, born1849, Davie County,
                       North Carolina.

#2-2-2   ARTHUR RENSHAW

Arthur Renshaw, born 14 April 1813, Chatham County, North Carolina,
Married Margaret Wilson, probably in North Carolina. Margaret was
born in 1825, North Carolina and died between 1855 and 1860 in

Kaufman County, Texas, to where Author and Margaret had moved from Davie County, North Carolina about 1845. Arthur died in 1885, Kaufman County, Texas. Arthur farmed throughout his lifetime.

Children of Arthur Renshaw and Margaret Wilson

#3-2-2-1.	James Renshaw, born 1841, Rowan County, North Carolina.
#3-2-2-2.	Henry L. Renshaw, born 1844, Rowan County, North Carolina.
#3-2-2-3.	John B. Renshaw, born 1846, Kaufman County, Texas.
#3-2-2-4.	Mary A. Renshaw, born 1851, Kaufman County, Texas.
#3-2-2-5.	Samuel D. A. Renshaw, born 1853, Kaufman County, Texas.
#3-2-2-6.	Ambrose Renshaw, born 1855, Kaufman County, Texas.

#2-2-3   SARAH RENSHAW

Sarah A. Renshaw born 1817 Davie County, North Carolina, married Denton Hendren about 1836. Denton Hendren was born 1816 in Davie County, North Carolina. Both Sarah and Denton lived and raised their family in Davie County, Denton farmed and Sarah was a bookkeeper. The last record I find of Sarah or Denton is the 1870 Davie County census. They probably died before the 1880 census.

Children of Sarah A. Renshaw and Denton Hendren

#3-2-3-1.	Arthur Hendren, born 1837, Davie County, North Carolina.
#3-2-3-2.	Rebecca Hendren, born 1839, Davie County, North Carolina.
#3-2-3-3.	Margaret Hendren, born 1844, Davie County, North Carolina.

#3-2-3-4.	Mary Hendren, born 1848, Davie County, North Carolina.
#3-2-3-5.	Linville Hendren, born 1851, Davie County, North Carolina.
#3-2-3-6.	Agessia E. Hendren, born 1854, Davie County, North Carolina.
#3-2-3-7.	Emuren B. Hendren, born 1857 Davie County, North Carolina

#2-2-4   REBECCA RENSHAW

Rebecca Renshaw born 1822, Rowan County, North Carolina, married Abraham N. Bessent around 1845, Davie County, North Carolina. Abraham was born 1825, North Carolina and died before 1880, Dyer County, Tennessee, where Rebecca and Abraham had moved about 1850. By trade Abraham was a Cooper, according to the 1860 census taker. Rebecca was living with her son, William Bessent in 1880. Her occupation at that time was Knitting.

Children of Rebecca Renshaw and Abraham Bessent

#3-2-4-1.	Margaret Bessent, born 1847, Davie County, North Carolina.
#3-2-4-2.	R. P. Bessent, born 1851, Dyer County, Tennessee.
#3-2-4-3.	M. S. Bessent, born 1854, Dyer County, Tennessee.
#3-2-4-4.	William Bessent, born 1857, Dyer County, Tennessee.

#2-2-5   ELIZABETH RENSHAW

Elizabeth Renshaw born 1824, Davie County, North Carolina, married John D. Hall prior to 1850, probably in Davie County, North Carolina. Elizabeth and John followed the lead of other of Elizabeth's family and moved to Kaufman County, Texas about 1852. Elizabeth died before

1860 and John had remarried Narcissa, who was born in Texas about 1833. John was born Davie County, North Carolina in 1825.

Children of Elizabeth Renshaw and John D. Hall

#3-2-5-1.	John Hall, born 1851, Davie County, North Carolina.
#3-2-5-2.	Nuly Hall, born 1853, Kaufman County, Texas.
#3-2-5-3.	Mary Hall, born 1853, Kaufman County, Texas.

#2-2-6   JOHN B. RENSHAW

John B. Renshaw born 1825, Davie County, North Carolina, married Lamira C. in 1850, North Carolina. John was single and living with his sister, Elizabeth, when the 1850 census were take, later in 1850 he and his wife Lamira C. conveyed property. In 1851, John and Lamira were living in Tennessee. In 1860, Lamira was living in Kaufman, County, Texas, married to A. A. Love.

Child of John B. Renshaw and Lamira C.

#3-2-6-1.	Arthur Renshaw, born 1851, Tennessee.

#2-3-1   RICHARD L. LEACH

Richard L. Leach, born 1 August, 1815 Rowan County, North Carolina, first married Eliza Hewitt about 1835. Early Arkansas records of marriage depend somewhat on the reliability of the person performing the marriage to record same. You did not purchase a license or post a marriage bond as in many states but instead the person performing the marriage wrote out on a slip of paper that he performed the wedding of naming the persons and the date and they were married. It was left to the person performing the marriage to record the marriage. Unfortunately Richard was not married by a responsible person on either marriage. Richard homestead property in Crawford County, North of what is now Natural Dam, Arkansas. When Richards father,

Thomas L. Leach moved to Benton County. Arkansas, he deeded his Washington County homestead to Richard. At that time Richard began living in Washington County. After the death of Eliza, Richard married Jane Scott,#5-1-2-6-1. Richard died 27 December 1889, Washington, County Arkansas. Eliza Hewitt was born 17 November 1818, and died 22 November 1841, at barely 23 years of age. Both Richard and Eliza are buried in Bethesda Cemetery, Washington County, Arkansas.

Children of Richard L. Leach and Eliza Hewitt

#3-3-1-1.   Mary J. Leach, born 1837, Washington County, Arkansas.
#3-3-1-2.   Nathan W. Leach, born 4 November 1838, Washington County, Arkansas.
#3-3-1-3.   Richard Robert Leach, born 22 November 1841, Washington County, Arkansas.

Children of Richard L. Leach and Jane Scott

Richard and Jane were married about 1842. Jane was the daughter of Joseph Scott and Ede Peeler. Both Scotts and Peelers will be covered later.

Jane was born 18 March 1828, Crawford County, Arkansas and died 29 December 1912, in Washington County, Arkansas. Jane and Eliza are buried side by side. Children of Richard and Jane:

#3-3-1-4.   John Leach born, 17 February 1844, Washington County, Arkansas. John died 19 February 1959, Washington County, Arkansas and is buried in the Bethesda Cemetery.
#3-3-1-5.   Martha Adora Leach, born 4 July 1846, Washington County, Arkansas.
#3-3-1-6.   Ruth Ann Leach, born 4 September 1848, Washington County, Arkansas.
#3-3-1-7.   Samantha Jane, Leach born 4 August 1850, Washington County, Arkansas.

#3-3-1-8.	Jamima Leach, born January 1855, Washington County, Arkansas.
#3-3-1-9.	James Thomas Leach, born 22 July 1858, Washington County, Arkansas.
#3-3-1-10.	Robert Calvin Leach, born 2 January 1860, Washington County, Arkansas.
#3-3-1-11.	Arthur Zedick Leach, born June 1864, Washington County, Arkansas.

#2-3-2   AMBROSE LEACH

Ambrose Leach born1818, Rutherford County, Tennessee, married Mary L. Scott around 1840. Mary was born 20 March 1820, Gallatin County, Illinois and died 19 November 1885, Washington County, Arkansas. After the death of Mary Ambrose married Plumey Davis 22 February 1888, Benton County, Arkansas. According to my Grandfather, George N. Leach, Plumey was able to get all of the assets of Ambrose transferred to her, then abandoned him and left him alone and penniless probably in Oklahoma City. Two of Ambrose's nephews went after him and returned him to Arkansas where he lived out the rest of his life. He is probably buried next to Mary in Bethesda Cemetery, Washington County, Arkansas, but his grave is not marked. Ambrose served in the Union Army during the Civil War and scouted for the advanced units when they invaded Washington County. In 1904, additional paperwork was filed in Ambrose's application for pension. It's strange because Ambrose had died before 1900 census. I wonder if Plumey had came back for more. The application was signed with Ambrose's name. Ambrose couldn't write. It's also strange why two of Ambrose's nephews would have gone after him when he had living sons.

Children of Ambrose Leach and Mary L. Scott

| #3-3-2-1. | Margaret Christina Leach, born 20 March 1842, Washington County, Arkansas. |
| #3-3-2-2. | Thomas Frank Leach, born June 1844, Washington County, Arkansas. |

#3-3-2-3.	Laura Temperance Leach, born December1854, Washington County, Arkansas.
#3-3-2-4.	Eliza Jane Leach, born 1848 Washington County, Arkansas, died 1910 Tulare County, California.
#3-3-2-5.	James Andrew Leach, born 18 April 1851, Washington County, Arkansas.
#3-3-2-6.	George Washington Leach, born 11 May 1853, Washington County, Arkansas, died June 12, 1853.
#3-3-2-7.	Ambrose Decatur Leach, born 8 September 1858, Washington County, Arkansas.

#2-3-3   ELIJAH R. LEACH

Elijah Leach born 1819, Rutherford County, Tennessee, Died November 13, 1864, in Cane Hill, Washington County, Arkansas. Elijah was hanged by elements of the Union Army that had invaded Cane Hill. Elijah had on 2 May 1847, married a widow with three daughters, named Nancy Emily (Dyer) Seay. He was guardian for her daughters. When he learned that the Union Army was about to invade he hid the girls money. When he refused to disclose the hiding place to the soldiers they hung him, together with an old man named Whinery. The night after the hanging three young girls crawled out on the arch over the gate where they had been hanged and cut them dawn. Elijah and Mr. Whinery were buried by the girls in shallow graves in Cane Hill Cemetery. The graves have no markers. Nancy died in 1867, in Washington County, Arkansas.

Children of Elijah R. Leach and Nancy Emily (Dyer) Seay

#3-3-3-1.	Melvina Leach, born 1849, Washington County, Arkansas.
#3-3-3-2.	Myra Alis Leach, born 4 August 1851, Washington County, Arkansas, died 8 August 1857, Washington County, Arkansas. Myra is buried in the Bethesda Cemetery.

Thomas L. Leach born 14 May 1820 Jackson County, Alabama, married Catharine Turner about 1847 probably in North Carolina. A dispute occurred in the Richard L. Leach Estate in North Carolina, Thomas was sent to the hearings to represent his father's interest in the estate. When Thomas returned, he returned with a wife, Catharine. Thomas was a farmer and a Methodist Minister. He was the first white man to pay a fine for striking a black man in Lincoln, Arkansas, after the emancipation. The black called him Tom instead of Mr. Tom. Catharine died 31 October 1865, Washington County, Arkansas. After the death of Catharine, Thomas married a widow, Louise (Crocket) Woods.

Children of Thomas L. Leach, Jr. and Catharine Turner

#3-3-4-1.	Samuel Turner Leach, born and died in Washington County, Arkansas, dates unknown. Samuel is buried in Bethesda Cemetery, Washington County, Arkansas.
#3-3-4-2.	Mary Clementine Leach, born 27 August 1849, Washington County, Arkansas.
#3-3-4-3.	Cornelia Jane Leach, born 24 August 1851, Washington County, Arkansas.
#3-3-4-4.	E. Pauline Leach, born 1852, Washington County, Arkansas, died 5 February 1855, Washington County, Arkansas. E. Pauline is buried in the Bethesda Cemetery, Washington County, Arkansas.
#3-3-4-5.	Florence T. Laura Leach, born 1853, Washington County, Arkansas
#3-3-4-6.	Leonare R. Leach, born 1855, Washington County, Arkansas.
#3-3-4-7.	Lovenia (Christina) Leach, born 1856, Washington County, Arkansas.
#3-3-4-8.	Margaret Florence Leach, born 1857, Washington County, Arkansas.
#3-3-4-9.	Norris Thomas Leach, born 1859, Washington County, Arkansas.

#3-3-4-10.   Albert Ernert Leach, born 27 June 1861, Washington County, Arkansas.

Child of Thomas L. Leach, Jr., and Louisa (Crocket) Wood

The Second wife of Thomas L. Leach, Jr., was Louisa (Crocket) Woods, born 3 June 1827, in Virginia. Louisa and Thomas were married 6 August 1869, Washington County, Arkansas. Louisa died 24 June 1916, Delaware County, Oklahoma and was buried in the Ralston Cemetery. Thomas was a Royal Arch Mason.

Child

#3-3-4-11.   Lenora Leach, Born 1870, in Washington County, Arkansas.

#2-3-5   TEMPIE LEACH

Tempie Leach born 27 August 1822, Jackson County, Alabama, first married John Morrow around 1843. From all appearances John abandoned her and the marriage was dissolved. John was born 21 September 1821, Washington County, Arkansas and died November 18 1844. Tempie then married James Green Walker. James Walker was born 30 September 1811, Monroe County, Illinois. He had previously been married to Luvica, who died 16 March 1848. James was a Methodist Minister and a physician. Tempie and James moved to Graceland County, Texas, in the fall of 1964. Tempie never recovered from seeing her brother Elijah Leach being dragged from his home near Cane Hill, Arkansas and hanged by union soldiers on an arch over a gate near the house and the death of her brother John Leach who was killed in the Civil War. Tempie died 17 April 1904, in Guadalupe County, Texas and is buried in the San Geronimo Cemetery.

Child of Tempie Leach and John Morrow

#3-3-5-1.   George Thomas Morrow, born 4 August 1844, Washington County, Arkansas.

#3-3-5-2.	Samantha Ann "Annie" Walker, born in 25 June 1849, Washington County, Arkansas.
#3-3-5-3.	Levi Reese Walker, born 7 October 1851, Washington County, Arkansas.
#3-3-5-4.	Richard Leach "Dick" Walker, born 28 April 1854, Washington County, Arkansas.
#3-3-5-5.	Evan Jones Walker, born 4 December 1856, Washington County, Arkansas.
#3-3-5-6.	Netter Walker, born 1 August 1858, Washington County, Arkansas.
#3-3-5-7.	Lovely "Lovie" Walker, born 10 April 1861, Washington County, Arkansas. He never married and died single 21 April 1918, Williamson County, Texas.

#2-3-6   JOHN M. LEACH

John M. Leach born 1828, Jackson County, Alabama, married Louisa Scott 20 September 1855 in Washington County, Arkansas. John died 23 December 1864, while a member of Captain Shannon's Company of Stan Waite's command, during the Civil War. Upon hearing of John's death, Louisa and a neighbor woman traveled by ox and sled from Cane Hill Arkansas to Ft. Gibson, Oklahoma, and recovered John's body. Some one had built a picket fence around the body. It was in good condition except for being decapitated by a bullet to the head and his ring finger having been cut off, probably to steal his Masonic ring, which he was always known to wear.

John Leach was shot on a prior occasion by a member of his own unit. They were back in Washington County at the time. The other soldier named Pieatte stepped out from behind a tree as he approached, and shot him presumably to steal his horses. John fell back in his wagon, his team spooked from the shot and ran home Louisa nursed him back to health. The Pieatte who shot him was killed in Cane Hill, when the Northern army came in. The rest of John's unit retreated and sought refuge at John's house but Pieatte could not go there and tried to hide in Cane Hill. One story that John told about the war was that he was walking down a road where a battle had been fought and several dead bodies remained. He heard voices nearby and there was no place to go, so he laid down in a ditch with the bodies. John must have been fat. As the union soldiers passed one of them said "Look at how that old Reb is swollen'. The other one said "I'm going to shoot him in the bully to let the gas out". The first soldier told him not to, he would stink to bad.

John homesteaded between the homestead of his father, Thomas L. Leach, Sr., and his brother, Thomas L. Leach, Jr. The homestead of John contained a cave called Leach Cave. All the neighbors hid their supplies there during the occupation by the Northern Army. Also on his homestead is Leach Spring, which was the location of the old stage stop.

The date of Louisa's death is unknown. Both Thomas and Louisa are buried in the Cane Hill Cemetery in unmarked graves.

Children of John Leach and Louisa Scott

#3-3-6-1.	Louis M. Leach, born 1857, Washington County, Arkansas, died 2 April 1872, Washington County, Arkansas. Buried Cane Hill Cemetery, no marker.
#3-3-6-2.	George Nimrod Leach, born 18 January 1858, Washington County, Arkansas.
#3-3-6-3.	Frances (Fanny) Leach born, March 1861, Washington County, Arkansas, married Hyram King 28 April 1901, Washington County, Arkansas, died 1960 Washington County, Arkansas, buried Lincoln Cemetery, Lincoln, Arkansas.
#3-3-6-4.	Samuel R. Leach, born June 1862, Washington County, Arkansas.

#2-3-7 NATHAN WEST LEACH

Nathan West Leach, the oldest son of the second Thomas L. Leach, Sr., and Delila (Taylor) Culberson, was born 8 June 1851, Washington County, Arkansas. Nathan married Frances (Fannie) Mary Butler 19 December 1871, Benton County, Arkansas. Frances was born 26 May 1851, in Georgia and died 5 April 1912, Benton County, Arkansas. Nathan owned and operated a mercantile store in Logan, Benton County, Arkansas. Nathan died 2 October 1919, Benton County, Arkansas. Both Nathan and Frances are buried in the Fairmont Cemetery.

Children of Nathan West Leach and Frances (Fannie) Mary Butler

#3-3-7-1. Bela West Leach, born 7 December, 1874, Benton County, Arkansas.

#3-3-7-2. John Alvin Leach, born 4 March 1876, Benton County, Arkansas.

#3-3-7-3. Orella Leach, born 2 January 1879, Benton County, Arkansas.

#3-3-7-4. Arthur James Leach, born 9 January 1881, Benton County, Arkansas.

#3-3-7-5. Leavey Belle Leach, born 5 May 1887, Benton County, Arkansas.

#3-3-7-6. Lula Leach, born 8 February 1889, Benton County, Arkansas.

#2-3-8 WILLIAM L. LEACH

William L. Leach was born in December of 1853, in Washington County, Arkansas. On 31 March 1872, he married R. E. "Sarah" Jones Benton County, Arkansas. Sarah was born 1854, in Georgia. After the 1900 census William moved with his family to Custer County, Oklahoma. In 1910 they moved on to Baca County, Colorado where they remained about five years, then on to Prowers County, Colorado, where William died ten years later, 6 October 1924. Sarah died 12 March 1936 Prowers County, Colorado. Both William, and Sarah are buried in the Riverside Cemetery, Lamar Colorado. The Cemetery record shows Sarah's name to be Sarah Rheu Leach.

Children of William L. Leach and R. E. "Sarah" Jones

#3-3-8-1.	Ollie F. Leach, born December 1876, Benton County, Arkansas, married Minnie I. Adams 16 February 1911, Springfield, Colorado. He died 20 February 1929.
#3-3-8-2.	Laura Leach born, 1878, Benton County, Arkansas.
#3-3-8-3.	Mary Ann Leach, born 1881, Benton County, Arkansas.
#3-3-8-4.	Emma Leach, born April 1881, Benton County, Arkansas.
#3-3-8-5.	Loula Leach, born March 1883, Benton County, Arkansas.
#3-3-8-6.	Myrtle Leach, born December 1886, Benton County, Arkansas.

#2-3-9   REDMAN BOYD LEACH

Redman Boyd Leach, born 20 August 1855, Benton County, Arkansas, married Sarah Alice Sitton 8 September, 1880, at Decatur, Benton County, Arkansas. Sarah was born 30 October 1861, in Eljay, Georgia and died 11 August 1940, Brawley, California.

In the 1850 and 1860 census Redman Boy was Edmond Boyd. On the 1880 census he was Boyd. In 1900 and 1920 census he was Redmond. On his death certificate he was Redman Boyd. Redman farmed for a living. He died 11 April 1931, Benton County, Arkansas. Both Redman and Sarah are buried in the Springtown Cemetery, Benton County, Arkansas.

Children of Redman Boyd Leach and Sarah Alice Setton

#3-3-9-1.	Thomas Benjamin Leach, born September 1881, Benton County.
#3-3-9-2.	Flora Alice Leach, born 12 September 1883, Benton County.
#3-3-9-3.	Maley Ester Leach, born August 1885, Benton County, Arkansas.
#3-3-9-4.	Jason Agustus Leach, born 7 August 1888, Benton County, Arkansas.
#3-3-9-5.	Florence Angeline Leach, born 3 March 1899, Benton County, Arkansas.

#2-3-10   JOSEPH H. LEACH

Joseph H Leach born October 1858, Washington County, Arkansas, married Nancy Elizabeth Rogers 3 September 1876, Washington County, Arkansas. Nancy was born 3 April 1856, Washington County, Arkansas and died 8 March 1914, Benton County, Arkansas. Joseph farmed throughout his lifetime in Benton County, Arkansas, where he died in 1905. Joseph was buried in Flint Cemetery. The 1900 census show Nancy as the mother of 10 children with 6 living. After the death of Joseph, Nancy married J. F. Scott.

Children of Joseph H. Leach and Nancy Elizabeth Rogers

#3-3-10-1.	N. A. "Nettie" Leach, born about 1882, Benton County, Arkansas.
#3 3 10 2.	William L. Leach, born November 23, 1883, Benton County, Arkansas.
#3-3-10-3.	Melvin Franklin Leach, born November 23, 1883, Benton County Arkansas.
#3-3-10-4.	Delila J. "Lila" Leach, born January 6, 1886, Benton County Arkansas.
#3-3-10-5.	Thomas Clifford Leach, born December 25, 1888, Benton County, Arkansas.

| #3-3-10-6. | Joseph Omers Leach, born February 16, 1892, Benton County, Arkansas, died March 18, 1916 Joplin, Jasper County, Missouri. |

#2-3-11   FLORA BELLE LEACH

Flora Belle Leach born 30 December 1859, Benton County, Arkansas married Bailey N. Hogan 6 November, 1880, Benton County, Arkansas. Bailey was born 13 December 1855, Benton County, Arkansas and died 1 March 1898, Custer County, Oklahoma Territory. Bailey is buried in the Summit Cemetery. About 1905 Flora married Joel Benham. In the 1930 census Flora was living in Henryetta with two Granddaughters, Katherine and Justiana Moss. Flora died 31 October 1940, Henryetta, Oklahoma and is buried in the West Lawn Cemetery.

Children of Flora Belle Leach And Bailey B. Hogan

#3-3-11-1.	Maude Lee Hogan, born October 1882, Benton County, Arkansas.
#3-3-11-2.	Mabel E. Hogan, born 1884, Benton County, Arkansas.
#3-3-11-3.	George J. Hogan, born May 1885, Benton County, Arkansas.
#3-3-11-4.	Frank W. Hogan, born July 1887, Benton County, Arkansas.
#3-3-11-5.	Alonzo A. Hogan, born 17 November 1891, Ardmore, Oklahoma Territory.
#3-3-11-6.	Commodore Hogan, born 17 November 1891, Ardmore, Oklahoma Territory.
#3-3-11-7.	Blanche Ethil Hogan, Born October 1894, Oklahoma Territory.

#2-3-12   LAURA ALICE LEACH

Laura Alice Leach, born 10 June 1862, Benton County, Arkansas, married George Agustus Sitton 19 September 1880, Benton County,

Arkansas. Laura and George were farmers. They lived in Benton County throughout their lives, are buried there and many of their descendants live there today. Laura died 7 November 1939. George was born in Gilmer, Georgia, 22 June 1859, and died in Benton County, Arkansas, 29 September 1922.

Children of Laura Alice Leach and Augustus Sitton

#3-3-12-1.	Council B. Sitton, born 10 June 1881, Benton County, Arkansas.
#3-3-12-2.	Adolphus J. Sitton, born Septemner 1882, Benton County, Arkansas.
#3-3-12-3.	Grover A. Sitton, Born March 1885, Benton County, Arkansas.
#3-3-12-4.	Lucy A. Sitton, born July 1888, Benton County, Arkansas.
#3-3-12-5.	George Conner Sitton, born January 1891, Benton County, Arkansas.
#3-3-12-6.	Beula M. Sitton, born 11 July 1893, Benton County, Arkansas.
#3-3-12-7.	Walter Booker Sitton, born 15 March 1897, Benton County, Arkansas.
#3-3-12-8.	Loma Gladys Sitton, born 9. October 1900, Benton County, Arkansas.
#3-3-12-9.	Paul Marrion Sitton, born January 16, 1907, Benton County, Arkansas.

#2-4-1   DIANA LEACH

Diana Leach, born 24 February 1818, Warren County, Tennessee, married William Lierle 30 May 1844, St Clair County, North Carolina. William was the father of Elizabeth Lierle who married Richard Leach, Diana's younger brother. William Lierle was born 25 September 1796, Montgomery County, North, Carolina and died 13 February 1870, Adams County, Illinois. Diana died 18 November 1891, Adams County, Illinois. William was a farmer. His marriage to Diana was his second marriage.

#3-4-1-1.	Amanda Lierle, born 2 May 1881, Adams County, Illinois.
#3-4-1-2.	Jacob Lierle, born 24 March 1847, Adams County, Illinois.
#3-4-1-3.	William Lierle, Jr., born 1848, Adams County, Illinois.
#3-4-1-4.	Hulda A. Lierle, born 1849, Adams County, Illinois.
#3-4-1-5.	Silas Lierle, born 30 October 1848, Adams County, Illinois.
#3-4-1-6.	Richard Lierle, born 1 January 1852, Adams County, Illinois.
#3-4-1-7.	James Willis Lierle, born 27 December 1853, Adams County, Illinois.
#3-4-1-8.	Huldianna Lierle, born 1855, Adams County, Illinois.

#2-4-2   ELIZABETH LEACH

Elizabeth Leach, born 1820, Warren County, Tennessee, married Robert Leach. Elizabeth and Robert were related but the exact degree of kindred is unknown. Their fathers were first cousins from the Hulins and some relation from the Leach family. The exact extent of which is unknown. Elizabeth and Robert were married in 1839, Missouri. This was a second marriage for Elizabeth, her name at the time of the marriage was Elizabeth Cleveland. Elizabeth and Robert lived and farmed in Gasconade County, Missouri. They both apparently died before the1880 census.

Children of Elizabeth Leach and Robert Leach

#3-4-2-1.	Diana Leach, born 1839, Gasconade County, Missouri.
#3-4-2-2.	John T. Leach, born 1841, Gasconade County, Missouri.

#3-4-2-3.	Malinda Leach, born 20 May 1842, Gasconade County, Missouri.
#3-4-2-4.	Hulda Leach, born 28 February 1844, Gasconade County, Missouri.
#3-4-2-5.	Mary "Polly" Leach, born 9 March 1846, Gasconade County, Missouri.
#3-4-2-6.	Angeilina Leach, born 2 March 1850, Gasconade County, Missouri.
#3-4-2-7.	Ambrose H. Leach, born 21 October 1852, Gasconade County, Missouri.
#3-4-2-8.	Thomas Leach, born 1855, Gasconade County, Missouri.
#3-4-2-9.	James M. Leach, born 1855, Gasconade County, Missouri.

#2-4-3   TEMPERENCE LEACH

Temperence Leach born 1822, Warren County, Tennessee, married John Leach, Jr., 22 September 1842 in St Clair County, Illinois. Temperence was a sister of Elizabeth Leach who married Robert Leach and John was the brother of Robert Leach. Temperence and John made their home in Gasconade County, Missouri until after 1860 census. In 1870 they were living Crawford County, Missouri. They apparently died before the 1880 census. John was a prosperous farmer. John was born in St Clair County, Illinois in 1820.

Children of Temperence Leach and John Leach, Jr.

#3-4-3-1.	Richard Leach, born 1843, St Clair County, Illinois.
#3-4-3-2.	Robert T. Leach, born 1845, Gasconade County, Missouri.
#3-4-3-3.	Joseph Leach, born 1847, Gasconade County, Missouri.
#3-4-3-4.	Elizabeth Leach, born 1849, Gasconade County, Missouri.

#3-4-3-5.	Marian Lemuel Leach, born 10 January 1852, Gasconade County, Missouri.
#3-4-3-6.	William Leach, born 1855, Gasconade County, Missouri.
#3-4-3-7.	Louis Leach, born 1857, Gasconade County, Missouri.

#2-4-4   RICHARD LEACH

Richard Leach born 1824, St Clair County, Illinois, married Elizabeth Lierle 30 May 1844, St Clair County, Illinois. Elizabeth was born in 1825, Union County, Illinois. Richard died in 1848, Adams County, Illinois. After the death of Richard, Elizabeth married Jeremiah Cox 27 December 1849, Adams County, Illinois.

Child of Richard Leach and Elizabeth Lierle

| #3-4-4-1. | Sarah Leach, born 1845 Adams County, Illinois. |

#2-4-5   ELIZA ANN LEACH

Eliza Ann Leach, born in 1824 St Clair County, Illinois, died in 1839 in St Clair County, Illinois.

#2-5-1   TEMPA M. RENSHAW

Tempa M. Renshaw, born 1817, Rowan County, North Carolina, married William H. Green 14 January 1840, Jackson County, Alabama. William was born in North Carolina in 1812 and died 24 February 1890, Holmes County, Mississippi. William was a prosperous farmer. Tempa died in Holmes County, Mississippi in 1960. After Tempa's death William married Abigail E.

Children of Tempa M. Renshaw and William H. Green

#3-5-1-1.	Mary E. Green, born 1843, Holmes County, Mississippi.
#3-5-1-2.	Martha Green, born 1846, Holmes County, Mississippi.
#3-5-1-3.	William Green, born 1848, Holmes County, Mississippi.
#3-5-1-4.	Frank Green, born 1850, Holmes County, Mississippi.
#3-5-1-5.	Catherine Greene, born 1853, Holmes County, Mississippi.
#3-5-1-6	James Green, born 1856, Holmes County, Mississippi.

#2-5-2   BELINDA ANNA LOUISA RENSHAW

Belinda Anna Louisa Renshaw, born 1818, Rowan County, North Carolina, married Carson about 1839, Jackson County, Alabama.

Child of Belinda Anna Louisa Renshaw and Carson

#3-5-2-1.	Belinda Anna Louisa Carson, born 1846, Jackson County, Alabama.

#2-5-3   AMBROSE D. RENSHAW

Ambrose D. Renshaw born 1819, Rowan County, North Carolina, married Lucinda C. Taylor about 1846. After being raised in Jackson County, Alabama, Ambrose moved to Wood County, Texas, with his wife and first child shortly after the 1850 census were taken. Lucinda was born in Tennessee in 1827. Both Ambrose and Lucinda were still living in Woods County in1880. Like his father, Ambrose was a farmer.

#3-5-3-1.	Mary Jane Renshaw, born 1847, Jackson County, Alabama.
#3-5-3-2.	Francis W. Renshaw, born 1849, Jackson County, Alabama.
#3-5-3-3.	Ambrose Duane Renshaw, born 1852, Wood County, Texas.
#3-5-3-4.	John E. Renshaw, born 31 August 1854, Wood County, Texas.
#3-5-3-5.	Elizabeth D. Renshaw, born 1856, Wood County, Texas.
#3-5-3-6.	Rebecca A. Renshaw, born 1858, Wood County, Texas.
#3-5-3-7.	James T. Renshaw, born 1859, Wood County, Texas.
#3-5-3-8.	Lucinda Catherine "Caty" Renshaw, born 1862, Wood County, Texas.
#3-5-3-9.	Robert Renshaw, born 1870, Wood County, Texas.
#3-5-3-10.	Amelia Renshaw, born 1870, Wood County, Texas.
#3-5-3-11.	Nancy T. Renshaw born 12 January 1874, Wood County, Texas.

#2-5-4 ELIZABETH H. RENSHAW

Elizabeth H. Renshaw born 1824, Jackson County, Alabama, married Edward H. Kyle. Edward was born in 1828 in Alabama. Elizabeth and Edward were married prior to the 1850 census. In 1850 Edward was farming in Jackson County, Alabama. In 1860 Elizabeth and Edward were both in the School of Medicine, Guntersville, Marshal County, Alabama. They had no children.

#3-6-1   NORMAN OWINGS

Norman Owings born 1823, Rowan County, North Carolina, migrated to St Clair County, Illinois with his parents about 1827.

#2-6-2   MARY M. OWINGS

Mary M. Owings, born 15 April 1823, St Clair County, married Drury C. Leach 3 September 1844, St Clair County, Illinois. Drury was a farmer. Mary died 28 July 1849, St Clair County, Illinois, and is buried in the Owings Cemetery. After the death of Mary Drury married Elizabeth Davis 29 February 1852, St Clair County, Illinois. Drury was born 1n 1814, St Clair County, Illinois, and died in Jersey County, Illinois 24 April 1887. He is buried in the Oak Grove Cemetery.

Children of Mary M. Owings and Drury C. Leach

#3-6-2-1.	Martha J. Leach, born 1845, St Clair County, Illinois.
#3-6-2-2.	Robert W. Leach, born 1849, St Clair County, Illinois.

#2-6-3   MARTHA ANN OWINGS

Martha Ann Owings born 1826, Tennessee, married Lewis Holcomb 30 March 1848, St Clair County, Illinois. Lewis was a farmer, who was born in Illinois in 1823. Martha died shortly after the 1850 census. After the death of Martha, Lewis Married Elila Stoakey.

Child of Martha Ann Owings and Lewis Holcomb

#3-6-3-1.	Silas Franklin Holcomb, born 1849, St Clair County, Illinois.

Maria Catherine Owings, born 1828, St Clair County, Illinois, married Richard C. Pulliam 16 October 1849, St Clair County, Illinois. Richard was a farmer, born in Illinois and died in Jefferson County, Illinois, after the 1870 censes. Maria and Richard lived in St Clair County until between 1860 to 1870 when they moved to Jefferson County, Illinois. Maria was still living in Jefferson County in 1880.

Children of Maria Catherine Owings and Richard C. Pulliam

#3-6-4-1.	Elizabeth D. Pulliam, born November 1850, St Clair County, Illinois.
#3-6-4-2.	Oscar J. Pulliam, born 1853, St Clair County, Illinois.
#3-6-4-3.	Walter J. Pulliam, born 1855, St Clair County, Illinois.
#3-6-4-4.	Laura M. Pulliam, born Sept 1859, St Clair County, Illinois.
#3-6-4-5.	Albert R. Pulliam, born April 1864, St Clair County, Illinois.
#3-6-4-6.	Nora Pulliam, born 1869, St Clair County, Illinois.

#2-6-5   ELIZABETH M. OWINGS

Elizabeth M. Owings, born 1829, St Clair County, Illinois, married Harry Ballard, a Physician. In 1870 they were living in Adams County, Illinois. Harry Ballard was born 1811, Kentucky; in 1880 he was still living in Adams County, alone.

Child of Elizabeth M. Owing and Harry Ballard

#3-6-5-1.	Charles S. Ballard, born 1862, Illinois.

Thomas Phelps Owings born November 1830, St Clair County, Illinois, married Frances Arabella Goodrich 31 July 1860, St Louis Missouri. Thomas and Frances farmed in St Clair County, Illinois, until after 1880 when they moved to LeRoy, Coffey County, Kansas. Frances was born in New York, 20 November 1840, and died in Coffey County, Kansas, 18 June 1919. Thomas died 16 October 1907, Coffey County, Kansas.

Children of Thomas Phelps Owings and Frances Arabella Goodrich

#3-6-6-1.	Edgar Leach Owings, born 7 June 1861, St Clair County, Illinois.
#3-6-6-2.	John Warren Owings, born 13 March 1863, St Clair County, Illinois.
#3-3-6-3.	Allen G. Owings, born 10 March 1865, St Clair County, Illinois.
#3-6-6-4.	Ida L. Owings, born 14 September 1867, St Clair County, Illinois.
#3-6-6-5.	Clara Belle Owings, born 18 October 1870, St Clair County, Illinois.
#3-6-6-6.	Stella Owings, born 8 December 1872, St Clair County, Illinois.
#3-6-6-7.	Birdie Owings, born 21 February 1875, St Clair County, Illinois.
#3-6-6-8.	Orlando D. Owings, born 16 September 1879, St Clair County, Illinois died 10 October 1879, St Clair County, Illinois.

#2-6-7   **JOHN H. L. OWINGS**

John Henry L. Owings born 18 October 1932, St Clair County, Illinois, married Mildred R. Mildred was born 6 April 1835, and died 6 September 1862, St Clair County, Illinois. John died 19 August 1862, St Clair County, Illinois. Both John and Mildred are buried in the Owings Cemetery, Millstadt, St Clair County, Illinois.

Mildred Emily Owings born 1835, St Clair County, Illinois

#2-6-9   REBECCA JANE OWINGS

Rebecca Jane Owings born 12 October 1837, St Clair County, Illinois, married William Simmons 2 April 1863, St Clair County, Illinois. William was born in March 1834, St Clair County, Illinois. In 1880 William was farming in St Clair County, between 1880 and 1900 William and Rebecca and moved to Arkansas City, Kansas where William was a Clerk in a Drug Store. William died in 1905. Rebecca died 7 April 1928, Kansas City, Jackson County, Missouri and is buried in the Mt Washington Cemetery.

Children of Rebecca Jane Owings and William Simmons

#3-6-9-1.	Harry L Simmons, born February 1864, Illinois.
#3-6-9-2.	George Simmons, born 1877, Illinois.

#2-6-10   SARAH TEMPERANCE OWINGS

Sarah Temperance Owings, born 1839 St Clair County, Illinois, married Russell H. Mace 25 December 1866, St Clair County, Illinois. Russell was a dentist born 1845, Illinois. Sarah and Russell were still living in St Clair County in 1880 but do not appear in the 1900 census.

Children of Sarah Temperance Owings and Russell H. Mace

#3-6-10-1.	Marquis Mace, born 1868, St Clair County, Illinois.
#3-6-10-2.	Bessie Mace, born 1874, St Clair County, Illinois.

FOURTH GENERATION

#3-1-1-1   DANIEL EARNEST

Daniel Earnest, born February 1837, Union County, Illinois, married Rebecca Keller 8 October 1858, Union County, Illinois. Rebecca was born in November 1840, North Carolina. After marriage, Daniel and Rebecca moved to Potosi, Linn County, Kansas, where they farmed until their deaths between 1910 and 1920. According to the 1900 census Rebecca was the mother of 10 children with 6 of them living.

Children of Daniel Earnest and Rebecca Keller

#4-1-1-1-1.	Mariah Earnest, born 1862, Linn County, Kansas.
#4-1-1-1-2.	John H. Earnest, born 1865, Linn County, Kansas.
#4-1-1-1-3.	Mary A. Earnest, born 1870, Linn County, Kansas.
#4-1-1-1-4.	Tempa Earnest, born 1873, Linn County, Kansas.
#4-1-1-1-5.	Amanda Earnest, born October 1878, Linn County, Kansas.
#4-1-1-1-6.	Manta Earnest, born April 1881, Linn County, Kansas.
#4-1-1-1-7.	Charlie Earnest, born Mar 1894, Linn County, Kansas.

#3-1-1-2   TEMPERANCE EARNEST

Temperance Earnest born 1839, Union County, Illinois, married John W. Karriker 4 March 1858, Union County, Illinois. John was born in South Carolina, in 1835. The 1860 Union County, Illinois, census lists John's occupation as "farming".

#4-1-1-2-1.   Mary Karriker. Born 1859, Union County, Illinois.

#3-1-1-3   SARAH EARNEST

Sarah Earnest was born 1841, Union County, Illinois. She married Meredith Keller also born in Union County, Illinois. Meredith farmed in Union County for over fifty years. Sarah died about 1864, Union County, Illinois. After her death Meredith married Susan Emaline.

Child of Sarah Earnest and Meredith Keller

#4-1-1-3-1.   Henry Keller, born 1859, Union County, Illinois.

#3-1-1-4   JACOB EARNEST

Jacob Earnest born 1845, Union County, Illinois, married Elizabeth Ridenhour born 1850, Illinois. In 1860 Jacob and Elizabeth were farming in Union County, Illinois.

#3-2-1-1   JAMES FRANKLIN HENDRICKS

James Franklin Hendricks born 1832, Rowan County, North Carolina, married Emma Christine Rebecca Chambers 13 September 1868. Emma was born 17 June 1847, in Scott County, Mississippi and died 4 January 1925 in Oakland, Marshall County, Oklahoma. James died 29 September 1885, Johnson County, Texas. James was a farmer.

#4-2-1-1-1.	Sarah Emma Catherine Hendricks, born 4 November 1869, Kaufman County, Texas.
#4-2-1-1-2.	Mary Alice Hendricks, born 12 January 1872, Kaufman County, Texas.
#4-2-1-1-3.	William D. Hendricks, born 1 January 1874, Kaufman County, Texas.
#4-2-1-1-4.	Lacy M. Hendricks, born 30 January 1877, Texas.

#3-2-1-3   ELIJAH RENSHAW HENDRICKS

Elijah Renshaw Hendricks born 1840, Davie County, North Carolina, married Harriet Elizabeth Byrd 17 November 1869, Kaufman County, Texas. Harriet was born in 1849, Arkansas. Elijah died in Hugo, Choctaw County, Oklahoma after 1900. Elijah was a farmer.

Children of Elijah Renshaw Hendricks and Harriet Elizabeth Byrd

| #4-2-1-3-1. | Mildred Elizabeth Hendricks, born November 1871, Kaufman County, Texas. |
| #4-2-1-3-2. | Roy Neely Hendricks, born 1 October 1878, Kaufman County, Texas. |

#3-2-2-1   JAMES RENSHAW

James Renshaw born July1841, Rowan County, North Carolina, married Mary Elizabeth Norton 5 May 1864, Kaufman County, Texas. Mary was born April 1841, Louisiana. James and Mary farmed in Kaufman and Grayson County, Texas. James died in Dougherty, Murray County, Oklahoma between 1900 and 1910. Mary died after the 1910 census still living in Dougherty, Murray County, Oklahoma.

Children of James Renshaw and Mary Elizabeth Norton

#4-2-2-1-1.	Alexander Renshaw, born 1864, Kaufman County, Texas.
#4-2-2-1-2.	Sarah J. Renshaw, born 1865, Kaufman County, Texas.
#4-2-2-1-3.	John Renshaw, born 1868, Kaufman County, Texas.
#4-2-2-1-4.	William A. Renshaw, born in Texas, 1870
#4-2-2-1-5.	Laura F. Renshaw, Born 1873, Texas.
#4-2-2-1-6.	James F. Renshaw, born 1875, Texas
#4-2-2-1-7.	Belle Renshaw, born March 1881, Grayson County, Texas.

#3-2-2-2   HENRY F. RENSHAW

Henry F. Renshaw born October 1844, Rowan County, North Carolina, married Martha J. Shaw 29 February 1872, Kaufman County, Texas. Martha was born in Texas, 1856. Henry and Martha farmed their entire lifetimes in Texas. Martha died about 1891. After Martha's death Henry married Mary M. in 1892. Henry died in Hunt County, Texas after the 1900 census.

Children of Henry F. Renshaw and Mary J. Shaw

#4-2-2-2-1.	Jesse A. Renshaw, born January 1873, Kaufman County, Texas.
#4-2-2-2-2.	Maggie Renshaw, born 1875, Kaufman County, Texas.
#4-2-2-2-3.	Henry F. Renshaw, Jr., born November 1876, Kaufman County, Texas.
#4-2-2-2-4.	Robert L. Renshaw, born December 1878, Kaufman County, Texas.
#4-2-2-2-5.	Charley Renshaw, born February 1880, Kaufman County, Texas.
#4-2-2-2-6.	Margret J. Renshaw, born October 1882, Kaufman County, Texas.

#3-2-2-3   JOHN B. RENSHAW

John B. Renshaw born March 1846, Kaufman County, Texas, married Mary M. Williams about 1872. Mary was born in Texas. In 1880 census John and Mary were living in Kaufman County, Texas and his occupation was listed as a farmer. In 1900 he was in Hunt County, Texas, listed as a widower and his occupation was carpenter.

Children of John B. Renshaw and Mary M. Williams

#4-2-2-3-1.	Theodocia Renshaw, born 1874, Kaufman County, Texas.
#4-2-2-3-2.	John D. Renshaw, born 1876, Kaufman County, Texas.

#3-2-2-5   SAMUEL D. A. RENSHAW

Samuel D. A. Renshaw, born October 1852, Kaufman County, Texas, married Elizabeth V. Shaw 16 September 1874, Kaufman County, Texas. Elizabeth was born in August 1843, Alabama. Samuel was a farmer. In 1880 they were living in Hunt County, Texas. In 1900 they were living in Hopkins County, Texas. Elizabeth died after the 1910 census in Hopkins County, Texas. Samuel died after the 1920 census in Hunt County, Texas.

Children of Samuel D. A. Renshaw and Elizabeth V. Shaw

#4-2-2-5-1.	Sarah Electus Renshaw, born 1877, Texas.
#4-2-2-5-2.	Amanda Renshaw, born 1879, Texas.
#4-2-2-5-3.	John E. Renshaw, born June1880, Texas.
#4-2-2-5-4.	Mamie Renshaw, born March 1882, Texas.
#4-2-2-5-5.	Oirgile C. Renshaw, born August 1883, Texas.

#3-2-3-1   ARTHUR HENDREN

Arthur Hendren, born 1837, Davie County, North Carolina, married Sarah N. "Sallie" Warren 11 September 1856, Davie County, North Carolina. Sallie was born in North Carolina. Arthur and Sallie farmed in Davie County, North Carolina until just before 1880 when they moved to Dyer County, Tennessee.

Children of Arthur Hendren and Sarah N. "Sallie" Warren

#4-2-3-1-1.   Ra Jas. Denton Hendren, born 1858, Davie County, North Carolina.

#4-2-3-1-2.   Jane Hendren, born, 1860, Davie County, North Carolina.

#4-2-3-1-3.   John Garland Hendren, born 1865, Davie County, North Carolina.

#4-2-3-1-4.   William Lee Hendren, born 1869, Davie County, North Carolina.

#4-2-3-1-5.   Sidney J. Hendren, born 1871, Davie County, North Carolina.

#3-2-3-2   REBECCA J. HENDREN

Rebecca J. Hendren, born 1839, Davie County, North Carolina, married W. C. Warren. W. C. Warren was born in 1833, North Carolina and apparently died before 1870. W. C. was a farmer according to 1860 census.

Child of Rebecca J. Hendren and W. C. Warren

#4-2-3-2-1.   Sarah A. F. Warren, born 1858, Davie County, North Carolina.

#3-2-3-3   MARGARET M. HENDREN

Margaret M. Hendren, born 1844, Davie County, North Carolina, married Wesley D. Leach. Wesley was born in North Carolina in 1850. According to 1870 census Margaret was a bookkeeper. Margaret and Wesley were living with Margaret's parents in Davie County, North Carolina in 1870.

#3-2-3-5   LINVILLE T. HENDREN

Linvelle T. Hendren, born October 1850, Davie County, North Carolina, Married Mary E., in 1871. Mary E. was born in March 1847, North Carolina. Linville and Mary Farmed in Davie County, North Carolina, until their deaths after 1910.

Children of Linville T. Hendren and Mary E.

#4-2-3-5-1.	Austin N. Hendren, born November 1871, Davie County, North Carolina.
#4-2-3-5-2.	Hall D. Hendren, born 1873, Davie County, North Carolina.
#4-2-3-5-3.	Mary O. Hendren, born 1875, Davie County, North Carolina.
#4-2-3-5-4.	Willie L. Hendren, born 1878, Davie County, North Carolina.

#3-2-4-1   MARGARET BESSENT

Margaret Bessent, born 1847, Davie County, North Carolina. The 1880 census reflected that Margaret was a school teacher and had never been married.

#3-2-4-2   R. P. BESSENT

R. P. Bessent, born 1851, Dyer County, Tennessee, married Mills after 1870 census and died before the 1880 census.

Child of R. P. Bessent and Mills

#4-2-4-2-1.   Mary B. Mills, born 1873, Dyer County, Tennessee.

#3-2-4-3   M. S. "KITTIE" BESSENT

M. S. "Kittie" Bessent, born 1854, Dyer County, Tennessee, married James T. Capell. James was a Blacksmith, born January 1844, Tennessee. Kittie and James lived their entire lives in Dyer County, Tennessee. Kittie died about 1887. In 1888, James married Bettie Blakemore. James died after 1900.

Children of M. S. Bessent and James T. Capell

#4-2-4-3-1.   Claudia M. Capell, born, 1872 Dyer County, Tennessee.
#4-2-4-3-2.   William E. Capell, born 1875, Dyer County, Tennessee.
#4-2-4-3-3.   Lester S. Capell, born September 1877, Dyer County, Tennessee.
#4-2-4-3-4.   Harris Capell, born December 1886, Dyer County, Tennessee.

#3-2-4-4   WILLIAM BESSENT

William A. Bessent, born 1857, Dyer County, Tennessee, married Mary about 1877. William and Mary farmed their entire lifetimes in Dyer County, Tennessee. Both William and Mary died after 1910. Mary was born in Tennessee, 1861.

Children of William Bessent and Mary

#4-2-4-4-1.	Cora Bessent, born 1879, Dyer County, Tennessee.
#4-2-4-4-2.	Ben T. Bessent, born December 1882, Dyer County, Tennessee.
#4-2-4-4-3.	Kittie L. Bessent, born April 1886, Dyer County, Tennessee.
#4-2-4-4-4.	Cecil H. E. Bessent, born December 1894, Dyer County, Tennessee.

#3-2-5-1   JOHN HALL

John D. Hall, born 1851, Davie County, North Carolina, married Alice. Alice was born 1862 in Texas. John was a farmer.

Child of John D. Hall and Alice

#4-2-5-1-1.	Marion Hall, born 1879, Kaufman County, Texas.

#3-3-1-1   MARY J. LEACH

Mary J. Leach, born 1837, Washington County, Arkansas, married John W. Perkins 23 May 1858, Washington County, Arkansas. John was a farmer, born in Tennessee. Both Mary and John died in Benton County, Arkansas of milk feaver before 1880.

Children of Mary J. Leach and John W. Perkins

#4-3-1-1-1.	Thomas Perkins, born 1859, Washington County, Arkansas and died before 1880, Benton County, Arkansas.
#4-3-1-1-2.	John Creed Perkins, born 6 January 1873, Benton County, Arkansas.

#4-3-1-1-3.   Elzona Perkins, born 1876, Benton County, Arkansas.

#3-3-1-2   NATHAN W. LEACH

Nathan W. Leach, born 4 November 1838, Arkansas, married Nancy G. Breedlove 15 November 1860, Washington County, Arkansas. Nathan died 14 April 1887, from Pneumonia resulting from fighting a wild fire on his farm at Odell, Crawford County, Arkansas. Nathan was a farmer and was buried on his farm. Nancy was born 13 February1842, Green County, Missouri and died 24 January 1898, Sequoyah County, Oklahoma, where she is buried.

Children of Nathan W. Leach and Nancy G. Breedlove

#4-3-1-2-1.   William Henry Leach, born 8 March 1862, Crawford County, Arkansas.
#4-3-1-2-2.   Lee Francisco Leach, born 3 May 1865, Washington County, Arkansas.
#4-3-1-2-3.   Alice Louise Leach, born 15 January 1868, Crawford County, Arkansas.
#4-3-1-2-4.   Tony Gilbert Leach, born 3 June 1874, Union Town, Crawford County, Arkansas.
#4-3-1-2-5.   Iva Jane Leach, born 1 January 1879, Arkansas.

#3-3-1-3   RICHARD H. LEACH

Richard H. Leach, born 22 November 1841, Washington County, Arkansas, married Martha J. Breedlove, 1860, Washington County, Arkansas. Martha was born 11 October 1840, Greene County, Missouri and died 26 June 1898, Sequoyah County, Oklahoma Territory. Martha is buried in the Memorial Gardens Cemetery, Muldrow, Oklahoma. After the death of Martha, Richard married, Naomi Jane Parker about 1899. Richard was a Farmer. Naomi was born 16 November 1875, Pope County, Arkansas and died 14 December 1955. Richard died 5

October 1831, both he and Naomi are buried in the Memorial Gardens Cemetery, Muldrow, Sequoyah County, Oklahoma.

Children of Richard H. Leach and Martha J. Breedlove

#4-3-1-3-1.	Cameron "Camma" Cisco Leach, born 15 October 1866, Van Buren, Crawford County, Arkansas.
#4-3-1-3-2.	Cassie Leach, born Arkansas.

Children of Richard H. Leach and Naomi Jane Parker

#4-3-1-3-3.	Raymond Frederick Leach, born 15 May 1900, Muldrow, Cherokee Nation, Indian Territory of Oklahoma.
#4-3-1-3-4.	James Richard Leach, born 25 January 1901, Muldrow, Cherokee Nation, Indian Territory of Oklahoma.
#4-3-1-3-5.	John Wesley Leach, born 30 December 1904, Muldrow, Cherokee Nation, Indian Territory of Oklahoma.
#4-3-1-3-6.	Wilbur Julian Leach, born 6 February 1907, Muldrow, Sequoyah County, Oklahoma.

#3-3-1-5   MARTHA ADORA LEACH

Martha Adora Leach, born 4 July 1846, Washington County, Arkansas, married Charles Maitland Stout 12 November 1866, Washington County, Arkansas. Charles was born 24 November 1837, Washington County, Arkansas and died 24 February 1904, Guthrie, Oklahoma. Martha and Charles farmed in Cherokee County, Kansas most of their married life. They are both buried at Guthrie, Oklahoma.

Children of Martha Adora Leach and Charles Maitland Stout

#4-3-1-5-1.	James Richard Stout, born 25 October 1867, Washington County, Arkansas.

#4-3-1-5-2.	Charles Fletcher Stout, born 21 March 1869, Washington County, Arkansas. Charles died Cherokee County, Kansas, 25 June 1886.
#4-3-1-5-3.	Mary Jane Stout, born 21 October 1871, Baxter Springs, Kansas.
#4-3-1-5-4.	Lenora Ann Stout, born 12 February 1874, Cherokee County, Kansas.
#4-3-1-5-5.	Ida Stout, born 2 March 1877, Cherokee County, Kansas. Ida died before the1880 census.
#4-3-1-5-6.	Carrie Stout, born 2 March 1877, Cherokee County, Kansas. Carrie died before the 1880 census.
#4-3-1-5-7.	Elmer Bertram Stout, born 25 April 1878, Cherokee County, Kansas.
#4-3-1-5-8.	Alice Christine Stout, born 15 March 1881, Cherokee County, Kansas and died 12 November 1891, Cherokee County, Kansas.
#4-3-1-5-9.	Albert Louise Stout, born 23 April 1885, Cherokee County, Kansas.

#3-3-1-6   RUTH ANN LEACH

Ruth Ann Leach, born 4 September 1848, Washington County, Arkansas, married James Morris 14 March 1878, Washington County, Arkansas. James was born 5 March 1847, North Carolina and died 20 April 1923, Benton County, Arkansas. Ruth and James farmed in Benton County, Arkansas, their entire lives together. Ruth died 25 December 1920, Benton County, Arkansas. Both Ruth and James are buried in the Highfield Cemetery.

Children of Ruth Ann Leach and James Morris

#4-3-1-6-1.	Aleck Julius Morris, born 14 January 1879, Benton County, Arkansas.
#4-3-1-6-2.	William Oric Morris, born 1 November 1880, Benton County, Arkansas.

#4-3-1-6-3.	John R. Morris, born 25 September 1883, Benton County, Arkansas.
#4-3-1-6-4.	Laura Jane Morris, born 14 November 1886, Benton County, Arkansas.

#3-3-1-7   SAMANTHA JANE LEACH

Samantha Jane Leach, born 4 August 1850, Washington County, Arkansas, married James Isom Chesney 31 October 1872, Washington County, Arkansas. James was born 1844, Illinois. Samantha died 6 June 1898, Jackson County, Illinois. James was a Coal Miner.

Child of Samantha Jane Leach And James Isom Chesney

#4-3-1-7-1.	Alonzo Theadore Chesney, born 1876, Tamaria, Perry County, Illinois.

#3-3-1-8   JEMIMA LEACH

Jemima Leach born January 1855, Washington County, Arkansas, married William H. Lillard 26 October 1890, Washington County, Arkansas. William was a Hotel Keeper in Muskogee, Creek Nation, Indian Territory of Oklahoma in the 1900 census. He and Jemima had no children. William was born in September of 1838, Missouri.

#3-3-1-9   JAMES THOMAS LEACH

James Thomas Leach, born 22 July 1858, Washington County, Arkansas, married Mary Ellen Smith 10 February 1881, Washington County, Arkansas. Mary was born 28 November 1858, Washington County, Arkansas and died 18 September 1946, Washington County, Arkansas. James and Mary were lifetime farmers in Washington County, Arkansas. James died 23 May 1919, Washington County, Arkansas. Both James and Mary are buried in the Sugar Hill Cemetery, Washington County, Arkansas.

Children of James Thomas Leach and Mary Ellen Smith

#4-3-1-9-1.	Donna Alice Leach, born June 1885, Washington County, Arkansas.
#4-3-1-9-2.	Samantha "Oma" Leach, born 28 February 1886, Washington County, Arkansas.
#4-3-1-9-3.	William Audman Leach, born 5 October 1889, Washington County, Arkansas.
#4-3-1-9-4.	Rowena Leach, born February 1892, Washington County, Arkansas.
#4-3-1-9-5.	Velma Hope Leach, born 1901, Washington County, Arkansas.

#3-3-1-10   ROBERT CALVIN LEACH

Robert Calvin Leach, born 2 January 1860, Washington County, Arkansas, married Dora Alice Bates 8 August 1886, Washington County, Arkansas. Dora was born 6 August 1865, Texas and died 17 January 1947, Wagoner County, Oklahoma. Robert was a grave stone salesman. He died 27 December 1899, in the Creek Nation, Indian Territory of Oklahoma. Both Robert and Dora are buried in the Elmwood Cenetery, Wagoner, Oklahoma.

Children of Robert Calvin Leach and Dora Alice Bates

#4-3-1-10-1.	Conner Leach, born 2 October 1888, Washington County, Arkansas, died 4 August 1889, Washington County, Arkansas.
#4-3-1-10-2.	Bessie Leach, born April 1890, Creek Nation, Oklahoma Indian Territory.
#4-3-1-10-3.	Alex Leach, born October 1891, Creek Nation, Oklahoma Indian Territory.
#4-3-1-10-4.	Rufus E. Leach, born 5 September 1892, Creek Nation, Oklahoma Indian Territory.

#4-3-1-10-5.	Walter Leach, born June 1894, Creek Nation, Oklahoma Indian Territory.
#4-3-1-10-6.	Susie Leach, born December 1896, Creek Nation, Oklahoma Indian Territory.
#4-3-1-10-7.	James C. Leach, born December 1897, Creek Nation, Oklahoma Indian Territory.
#4-3-1-10-8.	Anna Leach, born 3 April 1899, Creek Nation, Oklahoma Indian Territory.

#3-3-1-11   ARTHUR ZEDICK LEACH

Arthur Zedick "Art" Leach, born June 1864, Washington County, Arkansas, married Emma Helen Chandler 21 September 1890, Washington County, Arkansas.

Emma was born October 1864, Arkansas and died 4 October 1947, Washington County, Arkansas. Art and Emma farmed near Dutch Mills, Washington County, Arkansas. Art died 6 June 1944, both he and Emma are buried in the Bethesda Cemetery, Washington County, Arkansas.

Children of Arthur Zedick Leach and Emma Helen Chandler

#4-3-1-11-1.	Raymond Luther Leach, born 14 June 1891, Washington County, Arkansas.
#4-3-1-11-2.	Ola Jane Leach, born 13 March 1893, Washington County, Arkansas.
#4-3-1-11-3.	Charles Alex Leach, born 17 March 1894, Washington County, Arkansas.
#4-3-1-11-4	Ruth Ann Leach, born 10 October 1897, Washington County, Arkansas.
#4-3-1-11-5.	Paul P. Leach, born 4 March 1899, Washington County, Arkansas, died 29 August 1901, Washington County, Arkansas.
#4-3-1-11-6.	Marie Frances Leach, born 1905, Washington County, Arkansas.

#3-3-2-1   MARGARET CHRISTINA LEACH

Margaret Christina Leach, born 20 March 1842, Washington County, Arkansas, married James Beadley Milton Smith 5 January 1859, Washington County, Arkansas. James was born 5 January 1859, Philips County, Arkansas and died after the 1880 census. James was a farmer. The family moved often, to-wit: In 1860 they were in Benton County, Arkansas, 1865 in Sadan, Chautauqua, Kansas, 1870 on Cove Creek, Washington County, Arkansas, 1880, Cane Hill, Washington County, Arkansas and 1892 in the State of Washington. Margaret died 4 May 1924, Fall City, King County, Washington.

Children of Margaret Christina Leach and James Beadley Milton Smith

#4-3-2-1-1.	Reuben A. Smith, born October 1859, Benton County, Arkansas.
#4-3-2-1-2.	Violet F. Smith, born 1865, Sedan, Chautauqua County, Kansas.
#4-3-2-1-3.	Mary F. Smith, born 1867, Sedan, Chautauqua County, Kansas.
#4-3-2-1-4.	Walter Travis Smith, born October1869, Sedan, Chatauqua County, Kansas.
#4-3-2-1-5.	Getty M. Smith, born November1872, Washington County, Arkansas.
#4-3-2-1-6.	Daniel E. Smith, born May 1973, Washington County, Arkansas.
#4-3-2-1-7	Emma Alice Smith, born 15 February 1875, Washington County, Arkansas.
#4-3-2-1-8.	Asa P. Smith, born 30 November 1882, Washington County, Arkansas.

#3-3-2-2   THOMAS FRANK LEACH

Thomas Frank Leach, born 21 June 1844, Washington County, Arkansas, first married, Catherine Crozier 6 September 1868, Washington County, Arkansas. During Thomas's marriage to Catherine he worked at several job as a farm laborer in Washington and Benton County, Arkansas. Catherine was born 1 December 1842, Kentucky and died 4 February 1880, Benton County, Arkansas. Catherine is buried in Bethesda Cemetery, Washington County, Arkansas. After the death of Catherine Thomas Married Martha Garrett 26 August 1880, Benton County, Arkansas. Martha was born in Georgia 22 March 1853, and died in Tillman County, Oklahoma, 21 February 1928. During Thomas' marriage to Martha he farmed at Prairie Grove, Washington County Arkansas until after 1890, after which he farmed in Payne County, Oklahoma Territory. Thomas died 25 January 1901, Pawnee, Pawnee County, Oklahona Territory. Both Thomas and Martha are buried in Pawnee County, Oklahoma.

Children of Thomas Frank Leach and Catherine Crozier

#4-3-2-2-1.	Monroe Leach, born 1 July 1869, Washington County, Arkansas.
#4-3-2-2-2.	Ida Leach, born 1871, Washington County, Arkansas.
#4-3-2-2-3.	Carry Leach, born 1872, Washington County, Arkansas.
#4-3-2-2-4.	Charley Leach, born 5 December 1873, Washington County, Arkansas, died 6 December 1874, Washington County, Arkansas.
#4-3-2-2-5.	John Leach, born 1874, Washington County, Arkansas, died about 1890, Washington County, Arkansas.
#4-3-2-2-6.	Maggie Leach, born 18 January 1876, Washington County, Arkansas, died 17 April 1890 Washington County, Arkansas.
#4-3-2-2-7.	Berty Leach, born 7 July 1880, Washington County, Arkansas, died young and is buried at Bethesda Cemetery, Washington County, Arkansas.

Children of Thomas Frank Leach and Martha Garrett

| #4-3-2-2-8. | Arthur Leach, born January 1882, Washington County, Arkansas. |

#4-3-2-2-9.	Elmina Leach, born 1 January 1883, Washington County, Arkansas.
#4-3-2-2-10.	Dolphus Leach, born 9 September 1884, Washington County, Arkansas, died 9 September 1887, Washington County, Arkansas.
#4-3-2-2-11.	Zetta Leach, born April 1886, Washington County, Arkansas
#4-3-2-2-12.	Effie Leach, born March 1890, Washington County, Arkansas.

#3-3-2-3 LAURA TEMPERANCE LEACH

Laura Temperance Leach, born December 1854, Washington County, Arkansas, married Napoleon C. Moore 11 December 1872, Washington County, Arkansas. Napoleon was born May 1847, Washington County, Arkansas and died 6 September 1930, Benton County, Arkansas. Napoleon farmed and was a poultry dealer in Washington and Benton County. Laura died 1 October 1937, Benton County, Arkansas.

Children on Laura Temperance Leach and Napoleon C. Moore

#4-3-2-3-1.	Cora M. Moore, born 1874, Washington County, Arkansas.
#4-3-2-3-2.	Maud Mandlie Moore, born 1879, Washington County, Arkansas, died 2 February 1896, Benton County, Arkansas.
#4-3-2-3-3.	Bula P. Moore, born January 1882, Washington County, Arkansas.
#4-3-2-3-4.	Conrad Moore, born October 1892, Benton County, Arkansas.

#3-3-2-4 ELIZA JANE LEACH

Eliza Jane Leach, born 1848, Washington County, Arkansas, married George Amos Etter about 1867. George was born in Missouri, 1845. Eliza moved frequently in their early marriage in 1868 they were in

Douglas County, Kansas, from 1870 to 1873 they were in Platte County, Missiori, then to Benton County, Arkansas, from 1876 to 1884, then on to Tulare County, California where they finally settled for the remainder of their lives. George was a farmer. Eliza died in 1910 in Tulare County, Califotnia and George in 1925.

Children of George Amos Etter and Eliza Jane Leach

#4-3-2-4-1.	Frank Etter, born March 25, 1868, Douglas County, Kansas.
#4-3-2-4-2.	Edna Etter, born May 10, 1970, Platte County, Kansas.
#4-3-2-4-3.	Melvin Etter, Born October 12, 1873, Platte County, Kansas.
#4-3-2-4-4.	Albert Etter, born September 20, 1876, Benton County, Arkansas.
#4-3-2-4-5.	George Etter, born May 19, 1879, Benton County, Arkansas.
#4-3-2-4-6.	Lena Etter, born August 12, 1881, Benton County, Arkansas.
#4-3-2-4-7.	Rolla Etter, born February 6, 1884, Benton County, Arkansas. Died April 29, 1901 Potterville, Tulare County, California.
#4-3-2-4-8.	Leonard Etter, born January 17, 1887, Lindsay, Tulare County, California.
#4-3-2-4-9.	Inez Etter, born July 4, 1890, Tulare County, California.
#4-3-2-4-10.	Donald Cameron Etter, born September 14, 1894, Tulare County, California.

#3-3-2-5 JAMES ANDREW LEACH

James Andrew "Jim" Leach, born 18 April 1851, Washington County, Arkansas, married Sarah Elizabeth King 21 March 1869, Washington County, Arkansas. Sarah was born 28 January 1850, in Arkansas and died 18 October 1921. Jim liked to tell the story of when he talked to Sarah's father about marrying his daughter he objected because they were to young for the marriage to last. The marriage lasted 52 years until their deaths. Jim was a lifetime farmer in Washington County. Jim served as mayor of Lincoln, Arkansas, for many years. He died 16 July 1921. Both Jim and Sarah are buried in Cox Cemetery, Washington County, Arkansas.

Children of James Andrew Leach and Sarah Elizabeth King

#4-3-2-5-1.	Alice A. Leach, born June 1870, Washington County, Arkansas.
#4-3-2-5-2.	Margie Leach, born 23 September 1871, Washington County, Arkansas, died 18 March 1872, Washington County, Arkansas.
#4-3-2-5-3.	George Alvin Leach, born 6 August 1873, Washington County, Arkansas, died 28 September 1892, Washington County, Arkansas.
#4-3-2-5-4.	Samuel Henry Leach, born August 1875, Washington County, Arkansas.
#4-3-2-5-5.	Etta N. Leach, born May 1876, Washington County, Arkansas.
#4-3-2-5-6.	Earl Leach, born 13 May 1879, Washington County, Arkansas.
#4-3-2-5-7.	Emma Leach, born 24 May 1881, Washington County, Arkansas.
#4-3-2-5-8.	John Leach, born 20 March 1882, Washington County, Arkansas, died 5 April 1883, Washington County, Arkansas.
#4-3-2-5-9.	Mary Evaline Leach, born 28 April 1883, Washington County, Arkansas.
#4-3-2-5-10.	Clara Leach, born 5 June 1885, Washington County, Arkansas, died 14 November 1914, Washington County, Arkansas.
#4-3-2-5-11.	Tersie E. Leach, born 10 June 1889, Washington County, Arkanses.

Ambrose Decatur Leach, born 8 September 1858, Washington County, Arkansas, married Martha Carter Tharp 23 September 1879, Benton County, Arkansas. Martha was born 29 December 1860, in Seldana, Missouri and died 16 June 1949, Oklahoma County, Oklahoma. Ambrose participated in the Oklahoma Land Run and Homesteaded property in what is now Oklahoma County. Ambrose was a Farmer. He died 26 February 1916, Oklahoma County, Oklahoma. Both Ambrose and Martha are buried in the Kolb Cemetery, Spencer, Oklahoma.

Children of Ambrose Decatur Leach and Martha Carter Tharp

#4-3-2-7-1.	Ethel Leach, Born 29 September 1880, Benton County, Arkansas.
#4-3-2-7-2.	Elmond Leach, born 8 August 1883, Colorado.
#4-3-2-7-3.	Eldora Leach, Born 15 July 1886, Benton County, Arkansas.
#4-3-2-7-4.	Clarissa "Essie" Leach, born 19 June 1889, Benton County, Arkansas.
#4-3-2-7-5.	James Ambrose Leach, born 19 October 1892, Oklahoma Territory.
#4-3-2-7-6.	Bernice Clementine Leach, born 16 October 1896, Oklohoma Territory.
#4-3-2-7-7.	Ella Mae Leach, born 9 April 1901, Oklahoma Territory.

#3-3-3-1   MELVINA LEACH

Melvina "Mallie" Leach born, 1849, Washington County, Arkansas, first married Thomas Alexander Edmiston 1 July 1866, Washington County, Arkansas. Thomas was born 25 September 1845, Washington County, Arkansas and died 20 may 1875. Thomas was a farmer. In May 1875 Melvina went to Ft Smith, Arkansas to pursue a claim for goods taken by the Union Army during the Civil War. Thomas could not pursue the claim because he had fought for the confederacy. While she was gone Thomas was working in the rain, got Pneumonia and died. After the death of Thomas, Melvina married William Fudge. William was born in Tennessee in 1826 and died in Tulare County, California before 1900. Melvina died in Tulare County, California 19 August 1935.

Children of Melvina Leach and Thomas Alexander Edmiston

#4-3-3-1-1.	Montgomery I. Edmiston, born 1871, Washington County, Arkansas.
#4-3-3-1-2.	Infant son buried Edminston Cemetery at 5 days age born 5 April 1871, Washington County, Arkansas, died 11 May 1871.
#4-3-3-1-3.	Thomas A. Edmiston, born 23 December1872, Washington County, Arkansas.

Children of Melvina Leach and William Fudge

#4-3-3-1-4.	Iola E. Fudge, born 1880, Tulare County, California.
#4-3-3-1-5.	Alice Lenora Fudge, born 29 August1885, Tulare County, California.
#4-3-3-1-6.	Annie Gertrude Fudge, born 13 January 1890, Tulare County, California.

#3-3-4-2   MARY CLEMENTINE LEACH

Mary Clementine Leach, born 27 August 1849, Washington County, Arkansas, married George W. Murray 15 August 1875, Washington County, Arkansas. George was born in Arkansas in 1855 and died in Los Angeles, California before 1900 census. While in Arkansas George farmed. Mary died 18 May 1926, Morrow, Arkansas. Mary was in Los Angeles, California in 1900 with her two younger children. The census shows her to be the mother of 3 children all living. This is confusing because the 1880 census show two children born prior to 1880 census. The 1900 census shows two children born after the 1880 census. It would appear that she had four children, not three.

Children of Mary Clementine Leach and George W. Murray

#4-3-4-2-1.	Randolph Edgar Murray, born 1876, Washington County, Arkansas.
#4-3-4-2-2.	Edward M. Murray, born April 1880, Washington County, Arkansas.
#4-3-4-2-3.	Verona Murray, born December 1884, Washington County, Arkansas.
#4-3-4-2-4.	Adrain Murray, born November 1888, Los Angeles, California.

#3-3-4-3   CORNELIA JANE LEACH

Cornelia Jane Leach, born 24 August 1851, Washington County, Arkansas, married David Ashley Edmiston 3 February 1871, Washington County, Arkansas. David was born, 20 February 1850, Washington County, Arkansas and died 3 February 1924. David and Cornelia Farmed and raised their family In Washington County, Arkansas. Cornelia died 10 May 1893, Benton County, Arkansas. Both Cornelia and David are buried in the Edmiston Cemetery, Morrow, Arkansas.

Children of Cornelia Jane Leach and David Ashley Edmiston

#4-3-4-3-1.	Kenneth A. Edmiston, born July 1871, Washington County, Arkansas.
#4-3-4-3-2.	Olga Belle Edmiston, born 9 July 1873, Washington County, Arkansas.
#4-3-4-3-3.	Doria A. Edmiston, born 1875, Washington County, Arkansas.
#4-3-4-3-4.	Thomas C. Edmiston, born July 1878, Washington County, Arkansas.
#4-3-4-3-5.	Frank Edmiston, born 31 January 1883, Washington County, Arkansas.
#4-3-4-3-6.	Hugh Edmiston, born 19 December 1884, Washington County, Arkansas.

#4-3-4-3-7.	Raburn Edmiston, born 2 July 1887, Washington County, Arkansas.
#4-3-4-3-8.	Laura Eunice Edmiston, born 7 August 1890, Washington County, Arkansas.
#4-3-4-3-9.	Vera Edmiston, born April 1893, Washington County, Arkansas.

#3-3-4-9   NORRIS F. LEACH

Norris F. Leach, born 9 December 1859, Washington County, Arkansas, married Annie Lillian Yates, 13 August 1882, Washington County, Arkansas. Annie was born 7 May 1860, and died 25 October 1943, Los Angeles, California. The 1900 census reflects that Norris was a day laborer. The 1930 census shows that he was a grocery clerk. Norris died in Los Angeles, California, 18 May 1941.

Children of Norris F. Leach and Annie Lillian Yates

#4-3-4-9-1.	Connie Leach, born 27 March 1884, Washington County, Arkansas, died 31 July 1885, Washington County, Arkansas, buried Cane Hill Cemetery.
#4-3-4-9-2.	Bert Eugene Leach, born 11 December 1885, Washington County, Arkansas.

#3-3-4-10   ALBERT ERNEST LEACH

Albert Ernest Leach, born 27 September 1861, Washington County, Arkansas, first married Ruth Etta Johnson 7 November 1882, Boonsboro, Washington County, Arkansas. Ruth was born in 1862, at Cane Hill, Washington County, Arkansas and died in 1899, in Altus, Jackson County, Oklahoma Territory. After Ruth's death Albert married Jennie Mitchell 12 October 1901, Washington County, Arkansas. Albert farmed in Greer county, Oklahoma, until his death just prior to 1920. The 1920 census shows Jennie living with her Brother in Law and two children in Greer County, Oklahoma. Jennie was born 1 August

1866, Cane Hill, Arkansas and died 11 April 1953, Orange County, California.

Children of Albert Ernest Leach and Ruth Etta Johnson

#4-3-4-10-1.	Ina Leach, born 24 June1884, Washington County, Arkansas.
#4-3-4-10-2.	Laura Iva Leach, born June 1886, Washington County, Arkansas.
#4-3-4-10-3.	Oliver Randolph Leach, born September 1889, Washington County, Arkansas.
#4-3-4-10-4.	Edna Greer Leach, born 11 December 1891, Greer County, Oklahoma.
#4-3-4-10-5.	T. Grey Leach, born February 1894, Altus, Oklahoma.
#4-3-4-10-6.	Renna E. Leach, born 4 August 1896, Altus, Oklahoma.
#4-3-4-10-7.	Ernest Franklin Leach, born February 1898, Altus, Oklahoma.

Children of Albert Ernest Leach and Jennie Mitchell

#4-3-4-10-8.	Geneva "Little Lady" Leach, born 10 May 1903, Altus, Oklahoma.
#4-3-4-10-9.	Claude E. Leach, born 1907, Altus, Oklahoma.

#3-3-5-1   GEORGE THOMAS MORROW

George Thomas Morrow, born 4 August 1844, Washington County, Arkansas, married Cynthia J. Grimsley in 1866. Cynthia was born August, 1852, Fall Branch, Tennessee. George farmed in Washington County, Arkansas until about 1891, when they moved to California. While in California George worked as a Farm Laborer. He died 4 April 1916, Dinuba, California.

#4-3-5-1-1.	John Evan Morrow, born September 1866, Washington County, Arkansas.
#4-3-5-1-2.	Lillie Elma Morrow, born 10 September 1869, Washington County, Arkansas.
#4-3-5-1-3.	William Gage Morrow, born 4 July 1871, Washington County, Arkansas.
#4-3-5-1-4.	Hattie Tula Morrow, born 23 April 1873, Washington County, Arkansas.
#4-3-5-1-5.	Dove Pauline Morrow, born 1875, Washington County, Arkansas.
#4-3-5-1-6.	Richard Morrow, born 1877, Washington County, Arkansas.
#4-3-5-1-7.	Charles Dick Morrow, born September 1879, Washington County, Arkansas.
#4-3-5-1-8.	Mary Pet Morrow, born February 1884, Washington County, Arkansas.
#4-3-5-1-9.	Fannie Morrow, born May 1886, Washington County, Arkansas.
#4-3-5-1-10.	Oswald T. Morrow, born May 1887, Washington County, Arkansas.
#4-3-5-1-11.	Lettie Morrow, Born November 1889, Washington County, Arkansas.

#3-3-5-2   SEMANTHA ANN "ANNIE" WALKER

Semantha Ann "Annie" Walker, born 25 June 1849, Washington County, Arkansas, married Bailey Johnston Butler 14 December 1871, Hays County, Texas. Bailey was born in December 1849, in Virginia. Bailey and Annie farmed in Guadalupe County, Texas. Annie died 22 November 1892, Sequin County, Texas. After Annie's death Bailey married her sister in law in 1896.

Children of Semantha Ann "Annie" Walker and Bailey Johnston Butler

#4-3-5-2-1.   Mary Butler, born November 1872, Guadalupe County, Texas.

#4-3-5-2-2.   Fred Walker Butler, born 10 October 1881, Guadalupe County, Texas.

#3-3-5-4   RICHARD LEACH "DICK" WALKER

Richard Leach "Dick" Walker, born 28 April 1854, Washington County, Arkansas, married Ophelia Shiflette 6 December 1883, Williamson County, Texas. Ophelia was born February 25, 1855, in Texas. Dick farmed and was a Carpenter in Williamson County, Texas. Dick died 8 June 1922, in Williamson County, Texas.

Children of Richard Leach "Dick" Walker and Ophelia Shiflette

#4-3-5-4-1.   Lilburn Winston Walker, born 25 November 1884, Williamson County, Texas.

#4-3-5-4-2.   Wilburn Wilson Walker, born 25 November 1884, Williamson County, Texas.

#4-3-5-4-3.   Cloris Virginia Walker, born 22. September 1888, Williamson County, Texas.

#3-3-5-5   EVAN JONES WALKER

Evan Jones Walker, born 4 December 1856, Washington County, Arkansas, married Nancy Caroline "Carrie" Harris, 6 September1894. Nancy was born August 1875, at Oak Island, 15 miles South of San Antonio, Texas. Evan worked as a Grocery Clerk and later as a Grocery Store Operator. Evan died 23 November 1948, Uvalde, Uvalde County, Texas.

#4-3-5-5-1.	Marcus Walker, born March 1895, Uvalde County, Texas.
#4-3-5-5-2.	Harold Walker, born 13 April 1898, Uvalde County, Texas.
#4-3-5-5-3.	John Walker, born 1907, Uvalde County, Texas.

#3-3-5-6   NETTA "NETTIE" WALKER

Netta "Nettie" Walker, born 1 August 1858, Washington County, Arkansas, married Allen Box Dockery, 7 May 1879, Lavaca County, Texas. Allen was born 26 April 1857, in Texas. Allen was a Farmer, Butcher and Cattle Breeder. Nettie died 4 April 1884, Guadalupe County, Texas. After Nettie's death Allen married Ada. Allen died 7 February 1904, Guadalupe County, Texas.

Child of Netta "Nettie" Walker and Allen Box Dockery

| #4-3-5-6-1. | James Dockery, born May 1880, Lavaca County, Texas. |

#3-3-6-2   GEORGE NIMROD LEACH

George Nimrod Leach, born 18 January 1858, Washington County, Arkansas, married Harriet Frances "Hattie" Linebaugh 14 March 1885, Mississippi County, Missouri. Hattie was born 31 December 1867, Green County, Ohio and died 20 May 1944, Washington County, Arkansas. George was named after his Grandfather Nimrod Scott and his Uncle George Scott. George and Hattie first homesteaded in Crawford County Arkansas, then made their home in Washington County on a ridge between Blue mountain and Sky Light Mountain, with Cove creek to the East and Fly Creek to the West. George farmed apple orchards in the summer and peddled apples in the winter. He died 11 May 1934, Washington County, Arkansas. Both George and Hattie are buried in Scott Cemetery. One of the few memories George had of the Civil Was were when Union Calvary rode through their chicken yard cutting the heads off chickens. Another was the neighbors hiding food in Leach Cave back of his father's house between Clyde and Morrow, Arkansas.

Children of George Nimrod Leach and Harriet Frances
  "Hattie" Linebaugh

#4-3-6-2-1.	Roy Valentine Leach, born 14 February 1886, Mississippi County, Missouri, married Gertrude Scott, 1 December 1912, Washington County, Arkansas. Gertrude was born 2 April 1888, Washington County, Arkansas and died 25 October 1937, Washington County, Arkansas. Both Roy and Gertrude are buried in the Scott Cemetery.
#4-3-6-2-2.	Lee Onester Leach, born about 1887 and died in 1888, both in Washington County, Arkansas. He is believed to be buried in Bethesda Cemetery.
#4-3-6-2-3.	Murah Ellen Leach, born 31 March 1889, Crawford County, Arkansas.
#4-3-6-2-4.	John Ralph Leach, born November 1890, Crawford County, Arkansas, died 19 August 1914, Washington County, Arkansas, buried Scott Cemetery.
#4-3-6-2-5.	Grover Cleveland Leach, born November 1892 Crawford County, Arkansas, died 1910, Washington County, Arkansas, buried Scott Cemetery.
#4-3-5-2-6.	Lulu Frances Leach, born 30 June 1894 Crawford County, Arkansas, Married Arthur M. Shalley. She died, 21 June 1959, Washington County, Arkansas, buried at Scott Cemetery.
#4-3-6-2-7.	Henry Clarence Leach, born 23 December 1895, Crawford County, Arkansas.
#4-3-6-2-8.	Sarah Edna Leach, born 12 September 1897, Crawford County, Arkansas.

#4-3-6-2-9.	Mary Elizabeth "Lizzie" Leach", born 24 September 1899, Crawford County, Arkansas.
#4-3-6-2-10.	Hattie Emma Leach, born 14 July 1901, Washington County, Arkansas.
#4-3-6-2-11.	George Harrison Leach, born April 13, 1903, Washington County. Arkansas.
#4-3-6-2-12.	Alice Myrtle Leach, born 7 January 1905, Washington County, Arkansas, married Chester Lincoln Remington 21 September 1932, Washington County, Arkansas. Chester was born 12 February 1909, and died 3 February 1975, West Plains, Missouri. Alice died, 6 May 1984, Gassville, Baxter County, Arkansas. Both Alice and Chester are buried in Prairie Grove Cemetery, Prairie Grove, Arkansas.
#4-3-6-2-13.	Mina Mae Leach, born 9 November 1906, Washington County, Arkansas.

#3-3-6-4   SAMUEL R. LEACH

Samuel R. Leach, born June 1862, Washington County, Arkansas, married Julia Beady 16 February 1894, Washington County, Arkansas. Julia was born October 1877, in Arkansas. Samuel farmed in Washington County and later moved to Crawford County where he worked for the Railroad. Sam died about 1916, in Springfield, Missouri, from Pneumonia. Samuel was buried in the Railroad Cemetery, Springfield, Missouri.

Children of Samuel R. Leach and Julia A Beady

#4-3-6-4-1.	Liza Leach, born December 1895, Washington County, Arkansas.
#4-3-6-4-2.	James Alvin Leach, born December 1897, Washington County, Arkansas.
#4-3-6-4-3.	William Renfroe Leach, born 1903, Crawford County, Arkansas, died about 1920 escaping from a Juvenile institution in Arkansas.

#3-3-7-1   BULA WEST LEACH

Bula West Leach, born 7 December 1874, Benton County, Arkansas, married Ruth Ambercrombie 15 October1899, Benton County, Arkansas. Ruth was born May 1877, Arkansas and died 1940, Benton County, Arkansas. Bula was a prosperous grain farmer in Benton County, Arkansas. Bula died 28 December 1946, Washington County, Arkansas. Both Bela and Ruth are buried in the Robinson or Yell Cemetery, Benton County, Arkansas.

Children of Bula West Leach and Ruth Ambercrombie

#4-3-7-1-1.	Mary Margie Leach, born 21 July 1900, Benton County, Arkansas.
#4-3-7-1-2.	Hubert Bela Leach, born 1 December 1901, Weatherford, Oklahoma.
#4-3-7-1-3.	Robert LaFayette Leach, born 20 April 1904, Benton County, Arkansas.
#4-3-7-1-4.	Samuel Harrison Leach, born 24 July 1906, Benton County, Arkansas
#4-3-7-1-5.	Ira Leach, born 8 January 1914, Benton County, Arkansas.

#3-3-7-2   JOHN ALVIN LEACH

John Alvin Leach, born 4 March 1876, Benton County, Arkansas, married Dona B. Collins 12 June 1892, Benton County, Arkansas. Dona was born July 1874, in Arkansas and died 22 March 1924, Siloam Springs, Arkansas. John was a farmer who moved from Arkansas to Texas then Oklahoma then finally back to Arkansas where he settled after 1908. John died 18 July 1931, Siloam Springs, Arkansas. Both John and Dona are buried in Yell Cemetery, Benton County, Arkansas.

Children of John Alvin Leach and Dona B. Collins

#4-3-7-2-1.	Elmer Monroe Leach, born 24 march 1894, Benton County, Arkansas.

#4-3-7-2-2.	Rosetta E. Leach, born July 1895, Benton County, Arkansas.
#4-3-7-2-3.	Nathan Jesse Leach, born 19 November 1899, Texas.
#4-3-7-2-4.	Foy W. Leach, born 24 June 1905, Oklahoma.
#4-3-7-2-5.	Leonard Leach, born 1908, Benton County, Arkansas.
#4-3-7-2-6.	Wayne Leach, born 1910, Benton County, Arkansas.
#4-3-7-2-7.	Dona B. Leach, born August 1912, Benton County, Arkansas.
#4-3-7-2-8.	Laura Lila Marie Leach, born June 1915, Benton County, Arkansas.

#3-3-7-3   ORELLA LEACH

Orella "Arley" Leach, born 2 January 1879, Benton County, Arkansas, married Lilly Gregory, 4 November 1897, Benton County, Arkansas. Lilly was born November 1880, in Arkansas. Arley was a Farmer. The 1900 census showed that they had one child living but did not list the child. It was probably not living at home. Arley died in 1904 and is buried in the Robinson or Yell Cemetery.

#3-3-7-4   ARTHUR JAMES LEACH

Arthur James Leach, born 9 January 1881, Benton County, Arkansas, married Nora Bell Wilson, 7 January 1904, Benton County Arkansas. Nora was born 3 March 1884, Arkansas and died April 1975, Benton County, Arkansas. Arthur was a lifetime resident and prosperous grain farmer in Benton County. He died March of 1965, Benton County, Arkansas

Children of Arthur James Leach and Nora Bell Wilson

#4-3-7-4-1.	Lena Mae Leach, born 27 April 1903, Benton County, Arkansas.
#4-3-7-4-2.	Clifford L. Leach, born 12 February 1906, Benton County, Arkansas.
#4-3-7-4-3.	James Barnett Leach, born 1911, Benton County, Arkansas.
#4-3-7-4-4.	Ina Angel Leach, born July 1915, Benton County, Arkansas.
#4-3-7-4-5.	Laura Lorene Leach, born September 1919, Benton County, Arkansas.
#4-3-7-4-6.	Billy Richard Leach, born in 1924, Benton County, Arkansas.

#3-3-7-5   LEAVEY BELLE LEACH

Leavey Belle Leach, born 5 May 1887, Benton County, Arkansas, married Edward Emer Carter 16 December 1906, Benton County, Arkansas. Edward was born 26 June, 1881, Fairfield, Wayne County, Illinois and died 5 March 1870, at Tulare, Tulare County, California and is buried in the Woodville Cemetery. Edward and Leavey moved several times during their years on marriage, to-wit: 1906-1909 Benton County, Arkansas, 1910 Orange County, California, 1911-1920, Park Hill, Cherokee County, Oklahoma and after 1820, Wauhillau, Cherokee County, Oklahoma. Edward farmed at all these places. Leavey died 22 January 1924, and is buried in the Stilwell Cemetery, Stilwell, Adair County, Oklahoma.

Children of Leavey Belle Carter and Edward Emer Carter

#4-3-7-5-1.	Lela Mae Carter, born 15 October 1907, Benton County, Arkansas, married C. C. "Connolle" Butler 1832. (in Cherokee Connolle means good associate you run around with).
#4-3-7-5-2.	Eva Viola Carter, born 5 January 1909, Benton County, Arkansas.

#4-3-7-5-3.	Joy Ruth Carter, born 13 November 1911, Benton County, Arkansas.
#4-3-7-5-4.	Amzie Nathan Carter, born 5 February 1914, Benton County, Arkansas.
#4-3-7-5-5.	Orin William Carter, born 5 March 1916, Cherokee County, Oklahoma
#4-3-7-5-6.	John Wesley Carter, born 19 February 1918, Cherokee County, Oklahoma.
#4-3-7-5-7.	Leatha Naomi Carter, born 22 July 1920, Cherokee County, Oklahoma.
#4-3-7-5-8.	Galeta Luniel Carter, born 2 January 1922, Cherokee County, Oklahoma, Married Clarence Breshears 20 July 1942, Muskogee, Oklahoma. Galeta died 12 February 1978, Muskogee, Oklahoma. Clarence died 16 July 1882, Muskogee, Oklahoma.

#4-3-8-2   LAURA LEACH

Laura Leach, born 1877, Benton County, Arkansas, married first Harris. According to the 1910 census she was a widow. In the 1820 census she was marries to Issac Warren Downer and living in Lamar Prowers County, Colorado. Issac was born about in 1865, Iowa or Illinois, depending on which census is correct. Laura was living in Lamar, Colorado, when her father died in 1924. The 1920 census shows neither Laura or Issac being employed.

Child of Laura Leach and Harris

#4-3-8-2-1.	Cuthbert Harris, born 1900, Arkansas.

#3-3-8-4   EMMA LEACH

Emma Leach, born April 1881, Benton County, Arkansas, married William P. Grimes, in 1903. William was born 6 June 1882, in Georgia and died 20 May 1963, Los Angeles, California. In 1910, William owned a farm in Roger Mills County, Oklahoma.

In 1920, he clerked in a service station in Lamar, Colorado. In 1930, he had moved to Los Angeles, California, where he remained the remainder of his years. William died 20 May 1963, Los Angeles, California. Emma died before, 1940.

Children of Emma Leach and William P. Grimes

#4-3-8-4-1.	Norma Grimes, born 1911, Roger Mills County, Oklahoma.
#4-3-8-4-2.	Thelma Grimes, born 1914, Roger Mills County, Oklahoma.

#3-3-8-5   LOULA LEACH

Loula Leach, born March 1883, Benton County, Arkansas, married Thomas L. Postlewaite, 1914. Thomas was born in Illinois, in 1882. He owned and operated a gas station in Lamar, Colorado and was prosperous. Loula died 13 January 1940, Los Angeles, California. Thomas died, 15 May 1966, in Laporte, Latimer County, Colorado.

#3-3-8-6   MYRTLE V. LEACH

Myrtle V. Leach, born December 1886, Benton County, Arkansas, married Frank J. Spear 1909. Frank was born in 1872, Iowa. He was a carpenter and operater a building construction company. Frank was a widower when he married Myrtle. Myrtle died, 6 February 1971, Los Angeles, California.

Child of Myrtle V. Leach and Frank J. Spear

#4-3-8-6-1.	Daryl J. Spear, born 17 July 1909, Norton County, Kansas.

Thomas Benjamin Leach, born September 1881, Benton County, Arkansas, married Florence Alice Elam, 30 May 1904. Thomas was called Tom and Florence was called Alice. Based on the birthplace of their children, Tom and Alice moved a number of timed in their early years of their marriage. In 1906, they were in Benton County, Arkansas. In 1908, Kansas. In 1909 and 1911, they were in Idaho. Then back to Benton County in 1913 and finally on to San Springs, Oklahoma where they lived their remaining years. Tom worked as a Stilman at an Oil Refinery.

Children of Thomas Benjamin Leach and Florence Alice Elam

#4-3-9-1-1.	Oather Leach, born 1906, Benton County, Arkansas.
#4-3-9-1-2.	Marvin Leach, born 1908, Kansas, married Edna.
#4-3-9-1-3.	Myrtle Leach, born 1909, Idaho.
#4-3-9-1-4.	Howard Leach, born 1911, Idaho.
#4-3-9-1-5.	Glen Leach, born 1913, Benton County, Arkansas.

#3-3-9-2   FLORA ALICE LEACH

Flora Alice Leach, born 12 September 1883, Benton County, Arkansas, married Elijah Other Gray, 22 November1905. Elijah was born 28 September 1883, Benton County, Arkansas and died 4 December 1948, Oakland, Alameda, California. Elijah farmed in Benton County until after 1930. Flora died 9 February 1959, Stockton, San Joaquin, California. Both Flora and Elijah are buried in Oakland, California.

Children of Flora Alice Leach and Elijah Other Gray

#4-3-9-2-1.	Dorothy May Gray, born 21 September 1907, Benton County, Arkansaas.

#4-3-9-2-2.	William Glen Gray, born 19 January 1910, Wallace Idaho.
#4-3-9-2-3.	Elmer Boyd Gray, born 1 January 1913, Benton County, Arkansas.
#4-3-9-2-4.	Leonard Ray Gray, born 19 October 1914, Benton County, Arkansas.
#4-3-9-2-5.	Sarah Ester Gray, born 19 October 1917, Benton County, Arkansas.
#4-3-9-2-6.	Jason Roy Gray, born 25 January 1922, Benton County, Arkansas.

#3-3-9-3   MALEY ESTER LEACH

Maley Ester Leach, born August 1888, Benton County, Arkansas, married, Richard Bert Marrs, 16 February 1910. Richard was born 16 February 1883, Arkansas and died 18 August 1955, Imperial, California. Maley apparently died before 1940. In 1920, Richard was a Junk Dealer, In 1930 a Stockman.

Children of Maley Ester Leach and Richard Bert Marrs

#4-3-9-3-1.	Olive Marrs, born 4 January 1911, Benton County, Arkansas.
#4-3-9-3-2.	Wanda Marrs, born 1916, Benton County, Arkansas.
#4-3-9-3-3.	Ralph Berton Marrs, born 17 May 1921, Ontario, San Bernardino, California.

#3-3-9-5   FLORENCE ANGELINE LEACH

Florence Angeline Leach, born 3 March 1899, Benton County, Arkansas, married Ray Jennings Brandon 27 October 1917, Benton County, Roy, was_born 13October 1898, Centerton, Benton County, Arkansas and died, January 1966. Ray was a farmer in Benton County. Florence died, 31 October 1959.

Children of Florence Angeline Leach and Ray Jennings Brandon

#4-3-9-5-1.   Raymond Howard Brandon, born 1919, Benton County, Arkansas.

#4-3-9-5-2.   Josephine Brandon, born 1920, Benton County, Arkansas.

#4-3-9-5-3.   Robert Lee Brandon, born 1925, Benton County, Arkasnsas.

#4-3-9-5-4.   Evelene Brandon, born 1927, Benton County, Arkansas.

#3-3-10-1   N. A. "NETTIE" LEACH

N. A. "Nettie" Leach, born about 1882, Benton county, Arkansas, first married Samuel Longshore Miller, April 7, 1902, Gentry, Benton County, Arkansas. Samuel was born about 1883. Nettie next married Warden Lee Coffman, July 20, 1916, at Carthridge, Jasper County, Missouri. Warden died in 1944. Nettie next married Martin Pearl Ward, July 3, 1923. Martin died in 1952. Nettie died in Bartlesville, Washington County, Oklahoma, in 1947.

Children of N. A. "Nettie" Leach ans Samuel Longshore Miller

#4-3-10-1-1.   Letta "Grace" Miller, born 1905.
#4-3-10-1-2.   Perry Leroy "Roy" Miller, born 1909

Child of N. A. "Nettie" Leach and Warden Lee Coffman

#4-3-10-1-3.   Will H. "Billy" Coffman, born 1917, died 1925.

#4-3-10-2   WILLIAM L. LEACH

William L. Leach, born November 23, 1883, Benton County, Arkansas, married Ella Guoge, 29 July1903. Ella was born 21 December 1885, Missouri. William worked in Orchards and the Fruit business. In 1920 he and Ella were living in McDonald County, Missouri.

Children of William L. Leach and Ella Gouge

#4-3-10-2-1.	Florence Leach, born 1905, Benton County, Arkansas
#4-3-10-2-2.	Jessie Leach, born 1908, Benton County, Arkansas.
#4-3-10-2-3.	Merl Leach, born 1912, Benton County, Arkansas.
#4-3-10-2-4.	Earl Leach, born 1918, Benton County, Arkansas.

#3-3-10-3   MELVIN FRANKLIN LEACH

Melvin Franklin Leach, born November 23, 1883, Benton County, Arkansas, married Cora B. Gough, 11 April, 1909 Benton County, Arkansas. Cora was born 1881 in Missouri. Melvin was a foreman of a Railroad Section Crew. Melvin died April 21, 1948, Gentry, Benton County, Arkansas. Cora died in 1970.

Children of Frank M. Leach and Cora B. Gough

#4-3-10-3-1.	Everett H. Leach, born 1912, Benton County, Arkansas, died 29 May 1923, Benton County, Arkansas.
#4-3-10-3-2.	Lawrence A. Leach, born 1917, Benton County, Arkansas.
#4-3-10-3-3.	Beryl F. Leach, born 1921, Benton County, Arkansas, died 1948, Liberal, Kansas.

#3-3-10-4   DELILA J. "LILA" LEACH

Delila J. Leach, born January 6, 1886, Benton County, Arkansas, married Alexander William Miller, May 23, 1902, Benton County, Arlansas. Alexander was born May 26, 1869, Henry County, Illinois, and died October 4, 1961, Topeka, Shawnee County, Kansas. Delila died August 8, 1961, Topeka, Shawnee County, Kansas.

#4-3-10-4-1.	Mable Miller, born june 24, 1905, Arkansas.
#4-3-10-4-2.	Frances Irene Miller, born January 4, 1907, Arkansas.
#4-3-10-4-3.	Alfred Miller, born 1909, Arkansas.
#4-3-10-4-4.	Arthur Miller, born 1911. Died 1912.
#4-3-10-4-5.	Irvin Edward Miller, born September 20, 1912 Kansas.
#4-3-10-4-6.	Sadie Miller, born August 28, 1915. Died August 29, 1915.
#4-3-10-4-7.	Lyda Agnes Miller, born February 22, 1921, Grantsville, Shawnee County, Kansas.
#4-3-10-4-8.	Carrie "Marie" Miller, born September 2, 1924, and died May 20 1996, Kansas.

#3-3-10-5   THOMAS CLIFFORD LEACH

Thomas Clifford Leach, born December 25, 1888, Benton County, Arkansas, married Florence Eula Eloue May 30, 1904. Florence was born in Missouri October 15, 1895. Thomas was a laborer with a Railroad Section Crew. Thomas died September 10, 1973, Temple, Bell County, Texas. Florence died May 10, 1988, Vernon, Wilbarger County, Texas.

Child of Thomas Clifford Leach and Florence Eula Eloue

#4-3-10-5-1.	Leta E. Leach, born 1913, Benton County, Arkansas.

#3-3-11-1   MAUDE LEE HOGAN

Maude Lee Hogan, born October 1882, Benton County, Arkansas, married William Chamberland Woods, 1896, Killere, Oklahoma, Indian Territory. William was born July 1874, in Tennessee. In a brief ten years of marriage Maude and William moved from Carter County,

Oklahoma, to Custer County, Oklahoma, then on to Caddo County, Oklahoma, then to Potter County, Texas, where Maude died in 1907.

Children of Maude Lee Hogan and William Chamberland Woods

#4-3-11-1-1.	Owen S. Woods, born 27 April 1898, Carter County, Oklahoma.
#4-3-11-1-2.	Roy Woods, born 1900, Custer County, Oklahoma.
#4-3-11-1-3.	J. B. Woods, born 1903, Caddo County, Oklahoma.

#3-3-11-4   FRANK J. HOGAN

Frank J. Hogan, born July 1885, (according to 1920 and 1930 census) Texas, married Georgia Baly, March 3, 1910, Custer county, Oklahoma. Georgia was born in Texas, 1893. Frank was a farmer in Custer County, Oklahoma.

Children of Frank J. Hogan and Georgia Bald

#4-3-11-4-1.	Alvin Hogan, born 1911, Custer County, Oklahoma.
#4-3-11-4-2	Ethel Hogan, born 1913, Custer County, Oklahoma.
#4-3-11-4-3.	J. B. Hogan, born 1915, Custer County, Oklahoma.
#4-3-11-4-4.	Winona Hogan, born May 1917, Custer County, Oklahoma.
#4-3-11-4-5.	Margueritt Hogan, born September 1919, Custer County, Oklahoma.
#4-3-11-4-6.	Gerald Hogan, born 1924, Custer County, Oklahoma.
#4-3-11-4-7.	Harold Hogan, born 1924, Custer County, Oklahoma.
#4-3-11-4-8.	Harley Hogan, born 1928, Custer County, Oklahoma.

#3-3-11-5   ALONZO A. HOGAN

Alonzo A. Hogan, born 17 November 1890, Ardmore, Oklahoma, married Lana R. Walker, about 1917. Lana was born in Missouri. Alonzo Died 6 March 1967, Sacramento, California. In 1920, he was farming in Custer County, Oklahoma.

Children of Alonzo A. Hogan and Lana C. Walker

| #4-3-11-5-1. | Ruth G. Hogan, born 1919, Missouri. |
| #4-3-11-5-2. | Flora Hogan, born 1921, Caddo County, Oklahoma. |

#3-3-11-6   COMMODORE HOGAN

Commodore Hogan, born 17 November 1891, Carter County, Oklahoma, married Lula Belle Riley, 1918. In 1920, Commodore was living in Hughes County, Oklahoma, with Commodore working as a Grocery Clerk. Commodore and Lula moved to Los Angeles about 1903. In 1930, Commodore was working as a Motorman for a Railway and Lula was working as a Automobile driver for a School Board. Lula was born 16 October 1894, and died 24 June 1981, Los Angeles, California.

Children of Commodore Hogon and Lula Belle Riley

#4-3-11-6-1.	Commodore Hogan, Jr., born July 1919, Hughes County, Oklahoma.
#4-3-11-6-2.	Orien Hogan, born 1921, Hughes County, Oklahoma.
#4-3-11-6-3.	Virginia V. Hogan, born 1922, Hughes County, Oklahoma.
#4-3-11-6-4.	John A. Hogan, born 1924, Hughes County, Oklahoma.

#3-3-11-7   BLANCH ETHEL HOGAN

Blanch Ethel Hogan, born October 1894 Oklahoma Territory, first married J. W. Moss June 12, 1812. J.W. Moss was 23 at the time of the marriage. All the records show about J. W. Moss is that he was born in Oklahoma. About 1918, Blanch next married Ray D. Smith. He was born in Iowa, 1889 and operated a Photograph Studio. In 1920, Blanch and Ray were living in Caddo County, Oklahoma, in 1830, they had moved to Blaine County, Oklahoma.

Children of Blanch Ethil Hogan and Moss

#4-3-11-7-1.   Katharine E. Moss, born 1915, Caddo County, Oklahoma.
#4-3-11-7-2.   Justiana Moss, born 1917, Caddo County, Oklahoma.

Children of Blanche Ethil Hogan and Ray D. Smith

#4-3-11-7-3.   Bertie Lon Smith, born 1922, Oklahoma.
#4-3-11-7-4.   Stella Mae Smith, born 1924, Oklahoma.

#3-3-12-1   COUNCIL B. SITTON

Council B. Sitton, born 18 June 1881, Benton County, Arkansas, married Effie Jenkins, 1904. Effie was born in Arkansas, 6 February 1883 and died 23 March 1978, Benton County, Arkansas. Council Farmed in Benton and Boone County, Arkansas. Council died in Benton County, Arkansas 4 December1959.

Children of Council B. Sitton and Effie Jenkins

#4-3-12-1-1.   R. Mc Coy Sitton, born 14 February 1905, Benton County, Arkansas.
#4-3-12-1-2.   Ray Sitton, born 1907, Benton County, Arkansas.

#4-3-12-1-3.	Jackson Sitton, born 1909, Benton County, Arkansas.
#4-3-12-1-4.	Floyd Sitton, born 1910, Benton County, Arkansas.
#4-3-12-1-5.	Frank A. Sitton, born 1914, Benton County, Arkansas.
#4-3-12-1-6.	Iva M. Sitton, born May 1918, Benton County, Arkansas.
#4-3-12-1-7.	Ida F. Sitton, born May 1918, Benton County, Arkansas.
#4-3-12-1-8.	Herman E. Sitton, born 1921, Benton County, Arkansas.

#3-3-12-2   ADOLPHUS J. SITTON

Adolphus J. Sitton, born September 1882, Benton County, Arkansas, married, Georgia Carter in 1909. Georgia was born in Arkansas on 2 September 1890, and died in Washington County, Arkansas, July 1986. Adolphus Farmed in Benton County, Arkansas. Adolphus died in 1959.

Children of Adolphus J. Sitton and Georgia Carter

#4-3-12-2-1.	Audria F. Sitton, born 1918, Benton County, Arkansas.
#4-3-12-2-2.	Loyd E. Sitton, born 1925, Benton County, Arkansas.

#3-3-12-3   GROVER A SITTON

Grover A. Sitton, born 15 November 1885, Benton County, Arkansas, married Ila A. in 1913. Ila was born 7 September 1884, in Missouri and died 17 September 1998, Dallas, Texas. Grover was a Farmer. He died in June 12, 1955, Benton County, Arkansas.

Children of Grover A. Sitton and Ila A.

#4-3-12-3-1.   Irene A. Sitton, born 1916, Benton County, Arkansas.

#4-3-12-3-2.   Russell H. Sitton, born April 1930, Benton County, Arkansas.

#3-3-12-5   GEORGE CONNER SITTON

George Conner Sitton, born January1891, Benton County, Arkansas. He first married Velma Hardcastle. Velma was born in Missouri in 1894, and died in Benton County, Arkansas, 1921. After the death of Velma, George married Gladys Nola about 1921. Gladys was born, 1895 in Missouri. In 1930, George was Farming in Joplin County, Missouri. He died in Benton County, Arkansas, 1942.

Children of George Conner Sitton and Velma Hardcastle

#4-3-12-5-1.   Garland Sitton, born 1915, Benton County, Arkansas.

#4-3-12-5-2.   Inetta Sitton, born aboet 1917, Benton County, Arkansas.

Children of George Conner Sitton and Gladys

#4-3-12-5-3.   Anna Belle Sitton, born 1926, Joplin County, Missouri.

#4-3-12-5-4.   Gerald Sitton, born 1927, Joplin County, Missouri.

#4-3-12-5-5.   David Sitton, born October 1928, Joplin County, Missouri.

#3-3-12-7   WALTER BOOKER SITTON

Walter Booker Sitton, born 15 March 1897, Benton County, Arkansas, married Maudie "Maudean" Long, 5 December 1915. Maudie was born in Missouri, 16 November, 1898 and died Benton County, Arkansas, 4 March, 1964. Walter was a farmer. Walter died 9 November 1961, Benton County, Arkansas. After 15 years of marriage there were no children in 1930.

#3-4-1-1   AMANDA A. LIERLE

Amanda A. Lierle, born 2 May 1845, Adams County, Illinois, married James Allen October 7, 1869, Adams County, Illinois. James Allen was born July, 1845, in Ohio. On the 1900 census James is listed as a Day Laborer. According to census reports Amanda was the mother of six children with four of them living in 1900.

Children of Amanda A. Lierle and James Allen

#4-4-1-1-1.	Stella A. Allen, born 1870, Adams County, Illinois.
#4-4-1-1-2.	William A. Allen, born 1873, Adams County, Illinois.
#4-4-1-1-3.	Lawrence E. Allen, born 1875, Adams County, Illinois.
#4-4-1-1-4.	Walter E. Allen, born 1877, Adams County, Illinois.
#4-4-1-1-5.	Willard M. Allen, born 1879, Adams County, Illinois.
#4-4-1-1-6.	Mabel E. Allen, born December 1885, Adams County, Illinois

#3-4-1-3   WILLIAM B. LIERLE, JR.

William B. Lierle, Jr, born March, 1847, Adams County, Illinois, Married, Eliza A. "Elmira" Schwartz, March 3, 1876, Adams County, Illinois. Eliza was born in 1854, in Illinois and died before the 1900 census. William was a Farmer.

Children of William B. Lierle, Jr. and Eliza A. "Elmira" Schwartz

#4-4-1-3-1.	Jessie Lierle, born 1876, Adams County, Illinois.
#4-4-1-3-2.	George A. Lierle, born 1878, Adams County, Illinois.
#4-4-1-3-3.	Mattie J. Lierle, born January 1880, Adams County, Illinois.
#4-4-1-3-4.	William R. Lierle, born November 1886, Adams County, Illinois.

#3-3-1-6   RICHARD LIERLE

Richard Lierle, born January 1, 1852, Adams County, Illinois, married Jerusha Willis Seirs, October 20, 1874, Adams County, Illinois. Jerusha was born January, 1853, Illinois. Richard was a Farmer. He and Jerusha moved from Adams County, Illinois to Clifford, Butler County, Kansas after 1886. After 56 years of marriage Richard and Jerusha were still living in 1930.

Children of Richard Lierle and Jerusha Willis Siers

#4-4-1-6-1.	Iona Lierle, born 1876, Adams County, Illinois.
#4-4-1-6-2.	Albert William Lierle, born 1877, Adams County, Illinois.
#4-4-1-6-3.	Emma Lierle, born September 1882, Adams County, Illinois.
#4-4-1-6-4.	Charles "Babe" Lierle, born December 1885, Adams County, Illinois.

#3-4-1-7   JAMES WILLIS LIERLE

James Willis Lierle, born December 27, 1853, Adams County, Illinois, married Melissa Jane Swartz, February 3, 1876, Adams County, Illinois. Melissa was born May 13, 1856, Adams County, Illinous. James was a Farm Laborer. The 1900 census reported that Melissa was the mother of 13 children with 10 of them living. After 53 years of marriage James and Melissa were still living in 1930.

Children of James Willis Lierle and Malissa Jane Swartz

#4-4-1-7-1.	William Oliver Lierle, born July, 1875, Adams County, Illinois.
#4-4-1-7-2.	Maude Lierle, born 1881, Adams County, Illinois.
#4-4-1-7-3.	Stella Lierle, born December, 1881, Adams County, Illinois.
#4-4-1-7-4.	Clifford Lierle, born March, 1883, Adams County, Illinois.
#4-4-1-7-5.	Pearl Lierle, born April, 1884, Adams County, Illinois.
#4-4-1-7-6.	Quendo Lierle, born September, 1886, Adams County, Illinois.
#4-4-1-7-7.	Emma Lierle, born October, 1888, Adams County, Illinois.
#4-4-1-7-8.	Roxie Lierle, born June, 1890, Adams County, Illinois.
#4-4-1-7-9.	Chloe Lierle, born January, 1895, Adams County, Illinois.
#4-4-1-7-10.	Alva Lierle, born July, 1897, Adams County, Illinois.

#4-4-2-1   DIANA LEACH

Diana Leach, born 1839, Gasconade County, Missouri, married Daniel Miller June 4, 1857, Gasconade County, Missouri. Daniel was born September, 1839 in Tennessee. In 1880 and 1900 Daniel was a black smith in Montgomery and Hickory County, Missouri. Diana died before 1900 and Daniel was married to Estia A.

Children of Diana Leach and Daniel S. Miller

#4-4-2-1-1.	Mary S. Miller, born 1858, Missouri.

#4-4-2-1-2.	James M. Miller, born 1860, Missouri.
#4-4-2-1-3.	Hilda C. Miller, Born 1862, Missouri.
#4-4-2-1-4.	William R. Miller, born 1866, Missouri.
#4-4-2-1-5.	Eli R. Miller, born 1867, Missouri.
#4-4-2-1-6.	Mary Jane Miller, born 1870, Missouri.
#4-4-2-1-7.	B. F. Miller, born 1877, Missouri.
#4-4-2-1-8.	Martha A. Miller, born February, 1884, Hickory County, Missouri.
#4-4-2-1-9.	Laura E. Miller, born September, 1887, Hickory County, Missouri.

#3-4-2-2   JOHN T. LEACH

John T. Leach, born 1841, Gasconade Missouri, first married Harriet S. Mattlock. Harriet who was born in Missouri, died shortly after the 1880 census. John Farmed at Jefferson, Osage County, Missouri. On August 9, 1883, John married Melissa Pimter in Osage County, Missouri. John apparently died before the 1900 census.

Children of John T. Leach and Harriet Mattlock

| #4-4-2-2-1. | Mary C. Leach, born 1864, Missouri. |
| #4-4-2-2-2. | Martha L. Leach, born 1867, Missouri. |

#3-4-2-3   MALINDA LEACH

Malinda Leach, born May, 1842, Gasconade County, Missouri, married Perry D. Cooper in 1876. Perry was born in Missouri, April, 1841. Perry was a carpenter in Crawford County, Missouri, where he and Malinda lived most of their married lives. They were both living in 1900. According to 1900 census Malinda had three children with two of them living.

Children of Malinda Leach And Perry D. Cooper

| #4-4-2-3-1. | Mary D. Cooper, born 1868, Missouri. |

| #4-4-2-3-2. | Edward D. Cooper, born September, 1874, Missouri |
| #4-4-2-3-3. | Logan Cooper, born 1877, Missouri. |

#3-4-2-4   HULDA LEACH

Hulda Leach, born February 28, 1844, Gasconade County, Missouri, married William Russey Holt, March 24, 1864, Gasconade County, Missouri. William was born in 1840, Missouri and died December 24, 1920. William was a Farmer. Hulda died February 5, 1875, Topaz, Douglas County, Missouri. After the Death of Hulda William married Martha J.

Children of Hulda Leach and William Russey Holt

#4-4-2-4-1.	Silas Monroe Holt, born February 28, 1865, Missouri.
#4-4-2-4-2.	Cordelia A. Holt, born November 23, 1866, Missouri.
#4-4-2-4-3.	Mary E. Holt, born February 23, 1868, Missouri.
#4-4-2-4-4.	Almira Diana Holt, born April 25, 1870, Missouri.
#4-4-2-4-5.	Eliza L. J. Holt, born December 25, 1872, Missouri.
#4-4-2-4-6.	Hulda Norsissas Holt, born January 19, 1874, Missouri.

#3-4-2-5   MARY "POLLY" LEACH

Mary "Polly" Leach, born March 19, 1846, Gascanade County, Missouri, married David Hubbard Stites about 1881. David was born in Missouri December 10, 1832, and died March 4, 1913. David was a Farmer. Mary died August 23, 1911, Maries County, Missouri. Both Mary and David are buried in the Higate Cemrtery, Maries County, Missouri.

Child of Mary "Polly" Leach and David Hubbard Stites

#4-4-2-5-1.   Addie L. Stites, born 1886, Missouri.

#3-4-2-9   JAMES M. LEACH

James M. Leach, born May, 1855, Gasconade County, Missouri, married Dora L. about 1888. Dora was born in June of 1869, and died December 30, 1945, St Clair County, Illinois. James was a Farmer. James died in 1910, Gasconade County, Illinois.

Children of James M. Leach and Dora L.

#4-3-2-9-1.   William Robert Leach, born August 6, 1896, Gascanada County, Missouri.
#4-3-2-9-2.   Flora M. Leach, born 1901, Gascanada County, Missouri.

#3-4-3-1   RICHARD LEACH

Richard Leach, born 1843, St Clair County, Illinois, married Lucy Bayless October 26, 1868 Crawford County, Missouri. Lucy was born March 15, 1848 in Missouri and died November 30, 1927, Springfield, Greene County, Missouri. Richard was a Farmer. Both Richard and Lucy are buried at Cuba, Crawford County, Missouri.

Children of Richard Leach and Lucy Bayless

#4-4-3-1-1.   John R. Leach, born November 26, 1869, Franklin County, Missouri.
#4-4-3-1-2.   Alice M. Leach, born 1885, Missouri.

#3-4-3-2   ROBERT T. LEACH

Robert T. Leach, born 1845, Gasconade County, Missouri, married Nancy L. Holt January 11, 1866 Gasconade County, Missouri. Nancy was born 1847, Missouri. In the 1870 census Robert was a Farm Laborer. No records found after that date.

Child of Robert T. Leach and Nancy L. Holt

#4-4-3-2-1.   Franzis Leach, born 1866, Missouri.

#3-4-3-5   MARIAN LEMUEL LEACH

Marian Lemuel Leach, born January 20, 1852 Gasconade County, Missouri, married Mary E. in 1872. Mary was born May 14, 1852 in Indiana. Marian was a Farmer according to the1880 census and a Minister in all later census reports. He and Mary moved from Hickman County, Missouri to Grady County, Oklahoma about 1905. Mary died August 15, 1942. Marion died February 29, 1929. Both are buried in the Evergreen Cemetery, Grady County, Oklahoma.

Children of Marian Lemeul Leach and Mary E.

#4-4-3-5-1.	Benjamin Andrew Leach, born Novemver 9, 1873 Missouri.
#4-4-3-5-2.	Levi Henry Leach, born January 30, 1876, Missouri.
#4-4-3-5-3.	Francis Leach, born 1877, Missouri.
#4-4-3-5-4.	Myrtle Louise Leach, born January, 1878, Missouri.
#4-4-3-5-5.	Gilbert Leach, born October, 1879, Missouri.
#4-4-3-5-6.	Mary Leach, March, 1880, Crawford County, Missouri.
#4-4-3-5-7.	Sarah B. Leach, born November, 1882, Missouri.
#4-4-3-5-8.	Margaret Anne Leach, born January 5, 1885 Missouri.

#4-4-3-5-9.   John Marian Leach, born February 16, 1887, Weaubleau, Missouri.

#3-4-3-7   LOUIS LEACH

Louis Leach born, 1857, Missouri, married Mary Friend approximately 1877. Mary was born in Missouri in 1856. According to 1880 census report Louis was a Farmer.

Child of Louis Leach and Mary Friend

#4-4-3-7-1.   William E. Leach, born 1878, Missouri.

#3-5-1-3   WILLIAM F. GREEN

William F. Green, born January, 1849, Holmes County, Mississippi, married Martha B. 1882. Martha was born in Mississippi. Both William and Martha were living in 1930. According to 1900 census Martha was the mother of five children, all living. William had an earlier wife that died before the 1880 census. Her name is unknown. Older sister Mary E. Green, single and living with William in the 1880, 1900, 1910 and 1920 census.

Children of William F. Green and Martha B.

#4-5-1-3-1.   Malinda B. Green born 1875 Holmes County, Mississippi. (child of first marriage)
#4-5-1-3-2.   Alice Green, born January 1884, Holmes County, Mississippi.
#4-5-1-3-3.   Mary Ethel Green, born May 1885, Holmes County, Mississippi.
#4-5-1-3-4.   Fannie Green, Born August 1886, Holmes County, Mississippi.
#4-5-1-3-5.   Hattie Green, born December 1887, Holmes County, Mississippi.

#4-5-1-3-6.   John Wesley Green, born March 1889, Holmes County, Mississippi.

#3-5-3-2   FRANCIS W. RENSHAW

Francis W. "Frank" Renshaw, born July 1849, Jackson County, Alabama, Married Mary J. in 1881. Mary was born August 1862 in Texas and died before 1920. Francis was a Farmer. He died after 1930.

Children of Francis W. Renshaw and Mary J.

#4-5-3-2-1.   Leonades C. "Lee" Renshaw, born June 1882, Texas.
#4-5-3-2-2.   John F. Renshaw, born August 1883, Texas.

#3-5-3-13   NANCY T. RENSHAW

Nancy T. Renshaw, born January 12, 1874, Wood County, Texas, married Benjamin A. Browning, September 10, 1884, Wood County, Texas. Benjamin was born, 1868, Texas. Benjamin Was a Farmer, both he and Nancy were still living in 1930. Nancy's older brother, John E. Renshaw, was single and living with Benjamin and Nancy in the 1910, 1920 and 1930 census.

Children of Nancy T. Renshaw and Benjamin A. Browning

#4-5-3-13-1.   Katie Browning, born 1895, Wood County, Texas.
#4-5-3-13-2.   Minnie L. Browning, born 1897, Wood County, Texas.
#4-5-3-13-3.   Odis Browning, born 1899, Wood County, Texas.
#4-5-3-13-4.   Trudy Browning, born 1903, Wood County, Texas.
#4-5-3-13-5.   Gladys Browning, born 1905, Wood County, Texas.

#4-5-3-13-6.	Corine Browning, born 1905, Wood County, Texas.
#4-5-3-13-7.	Benjamin Marvin Browning, born 1908, Wood County, Texas.
#4-5-3-13-8.	Thomas Ambrose Browning, born 1910, Wood County, Texas.
#4-5-3-13-9.	Barto Adell Browning, born 1912, Wood County, Texas.
#4-5-3-13-10.	Paul P. Browning, born 1914, Wood County, Texas.
#4-5-3-13-11.	Perry Browning, born 1916, Wood County, Texas.

#3-6-2-1 MARTHA J. LEACH

Martha J. Leach, born 1849, St Clair County, Illinois, married Miles F. Kehoe April 29, 1864, St Louis, St Louis County, Missouri. Miles was born, 1849, New York. Miles worked as a Stable Hand. Martha was a Dressmaker.

Children of Martha J. Leach and Miles F. Kehoe

| #4-6-2-1-1. | Emma Kehoe, born 1864, Illinois. |
| #4-6-2-1-2. | Robert Kehoe, born 1865, Missouri. (Adopted) |

#3-6-4-1 ELIZABETH D. PULLIAM

Elizabeth D. Pulliam, born November, 1850, St Clair County, Illinois, married Emory H. Maddox May 27, 1880, Jefferson County, Illinois. Emory was born January, 1858 in Illinois. Emory was a House Painter. The 1900, Jefferson County, Illinois census reported that Elizabeth was the mother of six children with five of them living.

Children of Elizabeth D. Pulliam and Emory D. Maddox

#4-6-4-1-1.	Addie P. Maddox, born August, 1881, Jefferson County, Illinois.
#4-6-4-1-2.	Herbert Carl Maddox, born February 28, 1884, Jefferson County, Illinois.
#4-6-4-1-3.	Geneva Maddox, born May, 1886 Jefferson County, Illinois.
#4-6-4-1-4.	Earnest Maddox, born June 21, 1888, Jefferson County, Illinois.
#4-6-4-1-5.	Richard Maddox, born January, 1884 Jefferson County, Illinois.

#3-6-4-2   OSCAR J. PULLIAM

Oscar J. Pulliam, born June, 1855, St Clair County, Illinois, married Mary Sprouse November 26, 1885, Jefferson County, Illinois. Mary was born in Illinois, July, 1864. Oscar was a Farmer. According to 1900 census Oscar and Mary were the parents of two children with both of them living.

Children of Oscar J. Pulliam and Mary Sprouse

#4-6-4-2-1.	Rena Pulliam, born May, 1894, Jefferson County, Illinois.
#4-6-4-2-2.	Ray Pulliam, born June, 1898, Jefferson County, Illinois.

#3-6-4-4   LAURA M. PULLIAM

Laura M. Pulliam, born September 1859, St Clair County, Illinois, married Joseph J. Chambliss, November 24, 1886 Jefferson County, Illinois. Joseph was born in May, 1845 in Tennessee. He was a Farmer. According to 1900, Jefferson County, Illinois Laura was the mother of eight children with seven living.

Children of Laura M. Pulliam and Joseph J. Chambliss

#4-6-4-4-1.	Walter Chambliss, born September 13, 1887, Jefferson County, Illinois.
#4-6-4-4-2.	Ray Chambliss, born April, 1890, Jefferson County, Illinois.
#4-6-4-4-3.	Susie Chambliss, born May, 1891, Jefferson County, Illinois.
#4-6-4-4-4.	Harry Chambliss, born November 24, 1892, Jefferson County, Illinois.
#4-6-4-4-5.	Oscar Chambliss, born July 30, 1894, Jefferson County, Illinois.
#4-6-4-4-6.	Charles Chambliss, born January, 1900, Jefferson County, Illinois.

#3-6-4-5   ALBERT R. PULLIAM

Albert R. Pulliam, born April, 1864, St Clair Count, Illinois, married Mary A. Davis, October 7, 1886, Jefferson County, Illinois. Mary was born in October, 1867, Illinois. Albert was a farmer. The 1900 Jefferson County, Illionis reports that Albert and Mary were the parents of five children with four of them living.

Children of Albert R. Pulliam and Mary A. Davis

#4-6-4-5-1.	Arthur A. Pulliam, born July 9, 1887, Jefferson County, Illinois.
#4-6-4-5-2.	George Elmer Pulliam, born July 23, 1889, Jefferson County, Illinois.
#4-6-4-5-3.	Ethel G. Pulliam, born April 1892, Jefferson County, Illinois.
#4-6-4-5-4.	Curtis Edward Pulliam, born November 21, 1895, Jefferson County, Illinois.

Harry L. Simmons, born February, 1864, Illinois, married Anna B. Anna B. was born in Ohio, 1870. Harry moved with his parents from Illionis to Cowley County, Kansas and then on to Kansas City, Missouri where he lived next door to his mother in 1910. He worked as a clerk in a drug store from 1910-1930, in Kansas City. The 1910 census reported Harry and Anna as being the parents of three children with two living.

Children of Harry L. Simmons and Anna B.

#4-6-9-1-1.	Oliver B. Simmons, born October 19, 1896, Arkansas City, Kansas.
#4-4-9-1-2.	Dorothy Simmons, born 1900, Kansas.
#4-4-9-1-3.	Donald W. Simmons, born 1906, Missouri.

FIFTH GENERATION

#4-1-1-1-2   JOHN H. EARNEST

John H. Earnest, born May, 1867, Linn County, Kansas, married Ella. Ella was born in Kansas, March, 1872. Ella was still alive for the 1920 census. John was a Farmer. The 1900 census show that John and Ella were the parents of three children with two of then living. John died between the 1910 and 1920 census.

Children of John H. Earnest and Ella

#5-1-1-1-2-1.	Raymond Earnest, born September, 1895, Linn County, Kansas.
#5-1-1-1-2-2.	Rena Earnest, born September, 1899, Linn County, Kansas.

#4-2-1-1-3   WILLIAM D. HENDRICHS

William D. Hendricks, born December 1, 1872, Kaufman County, Texas, married Annie Reynolds, 1895, Robert Lee, Coke County, Texas. Annie was born July 6, 1873, Louisiana and died January 23, 1946. William, as a young man, Farmed in Kaufman County, Texas, then Coke County, Texas. In the 1820 and 1830 census he was Farming in Marshall County, Oklahoma. William died October 25, 1948. In 1820 William's 72 year old mother was living with him and Annie.

Children of William D Hendricks and Annie Reynolds

#5-2-1-1-3-1.	Valera Hendricks, born 1897, Oklahoma.
#5-2-1-1-3-2.	Frank Hendricks, born 1900, Texas.
#5-2-1-1-3-3.	Virgie Hendricks, born 1903, Texas.
#5-2-1-1-3-4.	Grace Hendricks, born 1907, Sterling County, Texas.

#4-2-1-3-1   MILDRED ELIZABETH HENDRICKS

Mildred Elizabeth Hendricks, born November, 1871, Kaufman County, Texas, married John T. Reeves, 1887. John was born in Arkansas, June, 1863. John was a Blacksmith. The family was in Kaufman County, Texas in 1900. In Choctaw County, Oklahoma in 1910 and 1920 census. John died before 1930 and Mildred had moved to Ardmore, Carter County, Oklahoma.

Children of Mildred Elizabeth Hendricks and John T. Reeves

#5-2-1-3-1-1.	Rondia Reeves, born December, 1887, Kaufman County, Texas.
#5-2-1-3-1-2.	Letcher B. Reeves, born September, 1892, Kaufman County, Texas.
#5-2-1-3-1-3.	John S. Reeves, born October, 1895, Kaufman County, Texas.
#5-2-1-3-1-4.	Annie Reeves, born 1903, Texas (Adopted).
#5-2-1-3-1-5.	Sherley Louise Reeves, born 1917, Choctaw County, Oklahoma.

#4-2-1-3-2   ROY NEELY HENDRICKS

Roy Neely Hendricks, born October 1, 1878, Kaufman County, Texas, married Grace, 1910. Grace was born in Missouri, 1893. In 1910 Roy and Grace were living in Choctaw County, Oklahoma. In 1930 they were Farming in Harmon County, Oklahoma.

Children of Roy Neely Hendricks and Grace

#5-2-1-3-2-1.	Louis Hendricks, born 1912, Oklahoma.
#5-2-1-3-2-2.	Lala B. Hendricks, born 1913, Oklahoma.
#5-2-1-3-2-3.	Lillie B. Hendricks, born 1916, Oklahoma.
#5-2-1-3-2-4.	R. C. Hendricks, born 1919, Oklahoma.
#5-2-1-3-2-5.	Earl E. Hendricks, born 1922, Oklahoma.
#5-2-1-3-2-6.	Dona Hendricks, born 1928, Oklahoma.

#4-2-2-1-4   WILLIAM A. RENSHAW

William A. Renshaw, born 1870, Texas, married Ceorge C. George. She was born in Texas, 1881. William was a Farmer. He and George made their home in Johnson County, Oklahoma.

Children of William A. Renshaw And George C.

#5-2-2-1-4-1.	Laura B. Renshaw, born 1888, Johnson County, Oklahoma.
#5-2-2-1-4-2.	Sidney Renshaw, born 1904, Johnson County, Oklahoma.
#5-2-2-1-4-3.	William Renshaw, born 1907, Johnson County, Oklahoma.
#5-2-2-1-4-4.	James W. Renshaw, born 1909, Johnson County, Oklahoma.
#5-2-2-1-4-5.	Jane Renshaw, born 1910, Johnson County, Oklahoma.
#5-2-2-1-4-6.	Maud Renshaw, born 1912, Johnson County, Oklahoma.
#5-2-2-1-4-7.	Keith Renshaw, born 1918, Johnson County, Oklahoma.

#4-2-2-1-6   JAMES F. RENSHAW

James F. Renshaw, born 1875, Texas, married Alvaria P. Presley, 1893. Alvaria was born 1875, Arkansas. James was a farmer. He and Alvira made their home in Oklahoma, Indian Territory in what later became Garvin County until 1920 when they moved to Midland, Pontotoc County, Oklahoma.

Children of James F. Renshaw and Alvaria P. Presley

| #5-2-2-1-6-1. | Vela L. Renshaw, born August, 1894, Oklahoma, Indian Territory. |
| #5-2-2-1-6-2. | John F. Renshaw, born February, 1896, Oklahoma, Indian Territory. |

#5-2-2-1-6-3.	Vivien L. Renshaw, born October, 1899, Oklahoma, Indian Territory.
#5-2-2-1-6-4.	Marion S. Renshaw, born 1901, Garvin County, Oklahoma.
#5-2-2-1-6-5.	Orvialle Renshaw, born 1904, Garvin County, Oklahoma.
#5-2-2-1-6-6.	Irene Renshaw, born 1906, Garvin County, Oklahoma.
#5-2-2-1-6-7.	Effie M. Renshaw, born 1908, Garvin County, Oklahoma.
#5-2-2-1-6-8.	Sherman F. Renshaw, born 1909, Garvin County, Oklahoma.
#5-2-2-1-6-9.	Taft Renshaw, born 1912, Garvin County, Oklahoma.

#4-2-2-2-1   JESSE A. RENSHAW

Jesse A. Renshaw, born January, 1873, Kaufman County, Texas, married Syble about 1902. Syble was born 1883, Texas. In 1910 Jesse and Syble were living in Van Zandt, County, Texas. In 1920 and 1930 they were living in Quinlan, Hunt County, Texas. Jesse was a Blacksmith by trade. In 1930 he was Farming.

Children of Jesse A. Renshaw and Syble

#5-2-2-2-1-1.	Mable M. Renshaw, born 1905, Van Zandt County, Texas.
#5-2-2-2-1-2.	Jesse Renshaw, born 1908, Van Sandt County, Texas.
#5-2-2-2-1-3.	Earl Renshaw, born 1916, Texas.
#5-2-2-2-1-4.	Paul Renshaw, born 1917, Texas.

#4-2-2-2-2   MAGGIE F. RENSHAW

Maggie F. Renshaw, born 1875, Kaufman County, Texas, married T. A. Brown April 3, 1895, Hunt County, Texas. No information can be found on T. A. Brown. Both T. A. and Maggie died before the 1910 census. In the 1910 census their child was living with her grandparents.

Child of Maggie F. Renshaw and T. A. Brown

#5-2-2-2-2-1.   Maggie Brown, born 1897, Texas.

#4-2-3-1-1   RA JAMES DENTON HENDREN

Ra James Denton Hendren, born July, 1858, Davie County, North Carolina, married Sarah J. Bishop December22, 1879. Sarah was born in May, 1859, Tennessee. James was a Farmer. He and Sarah were both still living in Dyer County, Tennessee, in 1930.

Children of Ra James Denton Hendren and Sarah J.

#5-2-3-1-1-1.	Anna B. Hendren, born September, 1880, Dyer County, Tennessee.
#5-2-3-1-1-2.	George N. Hendren, born January, 1883, Dyer County, Tennessee.
#5-2-3-1-1-3.	Winnie D. Hendren, born November, 1885, Dyer County, Tennessee.
#5-2-3-1-1-4.	Robert Taylor Hendren, born August, 1888, Dyer County, Tennessee.
#5-2-3-1-1-5.	Beulah Ellis Hendren, born June, 1891, Dyer County, Tennessee.

#4-2-3-1-3   JOHN GARLAND HENDREN

John Garland, born November, 1864, Davie County, North Carolina, married Nin, 1891. Nin was born in Tennessee, October, 1874. John farmed in Dyer County, Tennessee. The 1900 census reported that Nin was the mother of three children with two of then living.

Children of John Garland Hendren and Nin

#5-2-3-1-3-1.	Everet Hendren, born October, 1892, Dyer County, Tennessee.
#5-2-3-1-3-2.	Rosa Hendren, born July, 1897, Dyer County, Tennessee.

#4-2-3-1-4   WILLIAM L. HENDREN

William L. Hendren, born May, 1869, Davie County, North Carolina, married Georgia A. in 1888. Georgia was born in May, 1868, Tennessee. William was a farmer. according to 1910 census. William and Georgia were the parents of nine children with eight of them living. Both William and Georgia were living in 1930.

Children of William Lee Hendren and Georgia A.

#5-2-3-1-4-1.	Chester Hendren, born December, 1889, Dyer County, Tennessee.
#5-2-3-1-4-2.	Hassell Hendren, born August, 1891, Dyer County, Tennessee.
#5-2-3-1-4-3.	Oscie Hendren, born May, 1893, Dyer County, Tennessee.
#5-2-3-1-4-4.	Ida K. Hendren, born May, 1895, Dyer County, Tennessee.
#5-2-3-1-4-5.	Bedford W. Hendren, born December, 1896, Dyer County, Tennessee.
#5-2-3-1-4-6.	A. Bristol Hendren, born 1900, Dyer County, Tennessee.
#5-2-3-1-4-7.	P. Martin Hendren, born 1907, Dyer County, Tennessee.
#5-2-3-1-4-8.	Ezell B. Hendren, born 1908, Dyer County, Tennessee.
#5-2-3-1-4-9.	Harry Hendren, born 1911, Dyer County, Tennessee.

#4-2-3-1-5   SIDNEY J. HENDREN

Sidney J. Hendren, born February, 1871, Davie County, North Carolina, married Fanny in 1904. Fannie was born 1876, Tennessee. Sidney was a farmer. Both Sidney and Fanny were still living according to the 1930 census.

Children of Sidney J. Hendren and Fanny

#5-2-3-1-5-1.	Howard Hendren, born 1905, Dyer County, Tennessee.
#5-2-3-1-5-2.	Curry Hendren, born 1908, Dyer County, Tennessee.
#5-2-3-1-5-3.	Guy Hendren, born 1910, Dyer County, Tennessee.
#5-2-3-1-5-4.	Margaret Hendren, born 1912, Dyer County, Tennessee.
#5-2-3-1-5-5.	Florette Hendren, born 1916, Dyer County, Tennessee.

#4-2-3-5-1   AUSTIN N. HENDREN

Austin N. Hendrin born November, 1871, Davie County, North Carolina, first married Carrie L in 1898. Carrie L. was born in North Carolina, 1876 and died before the 1920 Census. After the death of Carrie, Austin moved to Charlotte County, Virginia and married Mildred D. in 1924. Mildred was born in Virginia. Austin was a farmer. Both he and Mildred were living in 1930.

Children of Austin N. Hendren and Carrie L.

#5-2-3-5-1-1.	Richard Paul or Paul Richard Hendren, born 1900, Davie County, North Carolina.
#5-2-3-5-1-2.	Albert Hendren, born 1901, Davie County, North Carolina.
#5-2-3-5-1-3.	Amie Hendren, born 1904, Davie County, North Carolina.

#5-2-3-5-1-4.	Mary Hendren, born 1906, Davie County, North Carolina.
#5-2-3-5-1-5.	Maggie Ruth or Ruth Maggie Hendren, born 1909, Davie County, North Carolina.
#5-2-3-5-1-6.	Clarence Hendren, born 1915, Davie County, North Carolina

Children of Austin N. Hendren and Mildred D.

#5-2-3-5-1-7.	Austin D. Hendren, born 1925, Charlotte County, Virginia.
#5-2-3-5-1-8.	Cecil L. Hendren, born 1926, Charlotte County, Virginia.
#5-2-3-5-1-9.	Edith L. Hendren, born 1927, Charlotte County, Virginia.
#5-2-3-5-1-10.	Helen L. Hendren, born 1928, Charlotte County, Virginia.

#4-2-3-5-2   HALL D. HENDREN

Hall D. Hendren, born May, 1873, Davie County, North Carolina, married Josephine in 1895. Josephine was born in North Carolina, November, 1873. Hall was a farmer. The 1910 census reported that they had six children, all living. Neither Hall or Josephine could be found in the 1930 census.

Children of Hall D. Hendren and Josephine

#5-2-3-5-2-1.	Charlie Clifford Hendren, born October, 1896, Davie County, North Carolina.
#5-2-3-5-2-2.	Ether E. Hendren, born May, 1898, Davie County, North Carolina.
#5-2-3-5-2-3.	Ethel S. Hendren, born 1901, Davie County, North Carolina.
#5-2-3-5-2-4.	Mary L. Hendren, born 1902, Davie County, North Carolina.

#5-2-3-5-2-5.	Bulah E. Hendren, born 1905, Davie County, North Carolina.
#5-2-3-5-2-6.	Wiliy L. Hendren, born 1907, Davie County, North Carolina.
#5-2-3-5-2-7.	Pearl E. Hendren, born 1910, Davie County, North Carolina.

#4-2-3-5-4   WILLIE LINVILLE HENDREN

Willie Linville Hendren, born June 1, 1878, Davie County, North Carolina, married Jessie G. in 1902. Jessie was born in 1883, North Carolina. Willie was a farmer. Willie and Jessie were both living in 1930. Willie died January 10, 1949, Irdell County, North Carolina.

Children of Willie Linville Hendren and Jessie G.

#5-2-3-5-4-1.	Walter L. Hendren, born 1905, Davie County, North Carolina.
#5-2-3-5-4-2.	Ina D. Hendren, born 1908, Davie County, North Carolina.
#5-2-3-5-4-3.	John Hendren, born 1911, Davie County, North Carolina.
#5-2-3-5-4-4.	Mary E. Hendren, born 1919, Davie County, North Carolina.
#5-2-3-5-4-5.	Annie L. Hendren, born 1923, Davie County, North Carolina.

#4-2-4-3-1   CLAUDIA M. CAPELL

Claudia M. Capell, born 1872, Dyer County, Tennessee, married James W. Gentry in 1900. James was a farmer. He was born in Tennessee in 1861. James and Claudia made their home in Crocket County, Tennessee.

Child of Claudia M. Chapell and James W. Gentry

#5-2-4-3-1-1.   Raymond E. Gentry, born 1901, Crocket County, Tennessee.

#4-2-4-3-3   LESTER SYLVERTER CAPELL

Lester Sylvester Capell, born September 12, 1877, Dyer County, Tennessee, married Lela Connell in 1904. Lela was born in Tennessee, 1887. In 1910 Lester was farming in Dyer County, Tennessee. Lester and Lela were the parents of two children with one of them deceased. In 1918 when Lester registered for draft he was living in Hickman, Fulton County, Kentucky and listed his next of kin as his sister, Claudia Gentry. In the 1920 census Lester listed his marital status as divorced. Lester died in Fulton County, Kentucky, July 5, 1948.

Child of Lester Sylvester Capell and Lela Connell

#5-2-4-3-3-1.   Mary R. Capell, born 1908, Dyer County, Tennessee.

#4-2-4-4-4   CECIL H. E. BESSENT

Cecil H. E. Bessent, born 1895, Dyer County, Tennessee, married Lula in 1914. Lula was born in Tennessee in 1898. Cecil was a farmer. Both Cecil and Lula were still living in 1930.

Children of Cecil H. E. Bessent and Lula

#5-2-4-4-4-1.   James H. Bessent, born 1922, Dyer County, Tennessee.

#5-2-4-4-4-2.   Herbert E. Bessent, born January, 1926, Dyer County, Tennessee.

#5-2-4-4-4-3.   Kitty Lou Bessent, born January, 1930, Dyer County, Tennessee.

#4-3-1-1-2   JOHN CREED PERKINS

John Creed Perkins, born January 6, 1873, Benton County, Arkansas, married Olive Mary Brigman, December 17, 1905 Washington County, Arkansas. Olive was born in Arkansas, February 7, 1881. Both John and Olive were living at the time the 1930 census was taken. John was a farmer. John died October 20, 1930. Olive died April 7, 1952. Both John and Olive are buried in Bethesda Cemetery, Washington County, Arkansas.

Children of John Creed Perkins and Olive Mary Brigman

#5-3-1-1-2-1.	James Perkins, born 1907, Washington County, Arkansas.
#5-3-1-1-2-2.	Liston B. Perkins, born March 6, 1916, Washington County, Arkansas.

#4-3-1-2-2   LEE FRANCISCO LEACH

Lee Francisco Leach, born May 3, 1865, Indian Territory, Oklahoma, married Mary Elizabeth Chapham, October 21, 1888, Crawford County, Arkansas. Mary was born November 18, 1871, Hardin County, Ada, Ohio. The 1900 census lists Lee's occupation as a capitilist. Mary died January 14, 1926 and Lee July 24, 1936, both in Vacaville, California.

Children of Lee Francisco Leach and Mary Elizabeth Chapham

#5-3-1-2-2-1.	Elzie Gilbert Leach, born May, 1891, Indian Territory, Oklahoma.
#5-3-1-2-2-2.	Bertha F. Leach, born March 1893, Indian Territory, Oklahoma.
#5-3-1-2-2-3.	Pearl A. Leach, born August, 1895, Indian Territory, Oklahoma.
#5-3-1-2-2-4.	Roy H. Leach, born February, 1899, Indian Territory, Oklahoma.
#5-3-1-2-2-5.	Carl West Leach, born April 4, 1900, Siloam Springs, Benton County, Arkansas.

#5-3-1-2-2-6.   William Lee Leach, born May5, 1907, Oklahoma.

#4-3-1-2-3   ALICE LOUISE LEACH

Alice Louise Leach, born January 15, 1868, Crawford County, Arkansas, married John James Garrison March 3, 1887, Crawford County, Arkansas. John was born July, 26 1862, Smith County, Tennessee and died December 26, 1936, Fanning County, Texas. John was a farmer. Alice and John first lived in Crawford County, Arkansas, then in 1895 they lived in Maysville, Indian Territory, Oklahoma. In 1896 they were in Pitsburg County, Texas, in 1902, Delta County, Texas. Finally in 1907 they were in Fanning County, Texas, where they settled for their remaining years. Alice died March 31, 1946 in Parker County, Texas. Both Alice and John are buried in Porter Cemetery, Orangeville, Fanning County, Texas.

Children of Alice Louise Leach and John James Garrison

#5-3-1-2-3-1.   Allen W. Garrison, born February 22, 1888, Crawford County, Arkansas.
#5-3-1-2-3-2.   Ransom E. Garrison, born March 4, 1890, Crawford County, Arkansas.
#5-3-1-2-3-3.   Leland Gilbert Garrison, born July 6, 1892, Crawford County, Arkansas.
#5-3-1-2-3-4.   Edgar Garrison, born June 14, 1895, Marsville, Indian Territory, Oklahoma. Died 14 July 1896 and buried along fence row near Pittsburg, Texas.
#5-3-1-2-3-5.   Leo Garrison, born October 16, 1899, Texas. Died November 7, 1900.
#5-3-1-2-3-6.   Marvin Garrison, born May 14, 1902, Delta County, Texas.
#5-3-1-2-3-7.   Raymond Jack Garrison, born August 16, 1907, Orangeville, Fanning County, Texas.
#5-3-1-2-3-8.   John Calvin Garrison, born June 4, 1910, Orangeville Fanning County, Texas.

#4-3-1-2-4   TONY GILBERT LEACH

Tony Gilbert Leach, born June 3, 1874, Union Town, Crawford County, Arkansas, married Sarah Isabelle Rigsby, May 16, 1895, Ft Smith, Arkansas. Sarah was born February 4, 1869, Jerseyville, Jersey County, New Jersey. Sarah died March 11, 1964, Britton, Oklahoma. Tony was a day laborer and a farm laborer. Tony died October 9, 1911, Sallisaw, Sequoyah County, Oklahoma. Both Tony and Sarah were buried in the Sallisaw Cemetery, Sequoyah County, Oklahoma.

Children of Tony Gilbert Leach and Sarah Isabelle Rigsby

#5-3-1-2-4-1.	Faye Ona Leach, born September 15, 1896, Sequoyah County, Oklahoma.
#5-3-1-2-4-2.	Raymond Cisco Leach, born July 5, 1898, Sequoyah County, Oklahoma.
#5-3-1-2-4-3.	Caroline "Carrie" Leach, born February 5, 1900, Sequoyah County, Oklahoma.
#5-3-1-2-4-4.	Tony L. "Little T" Leach, born April 30, 1902, Sequoyah County, Oklahoma.
#5-3-1-2-4-5.	May Marie Leach, born August 29, 1904, Sequoyah County, Oklahoma.
#5-3-1-2-4-6.	Verna Margaret Leach, born July 10, 1907, Sequoyah County, Oklahoma.
#5-3-1-2-4-7.	Carnell Leach, born March 25, 1909 Sequoyah County, Oklahoma.

#4-3-1-3-1   CAMERON "CAMMA" CISCO LEACH

Cameron "Camma" Cisco Leach, born October 15, 1866, Van Buren, Arkansas, married Adah C. Thompson. Adah was born in 1866, Ohio and died after 1920 and before 1930. Camma and Adah made their home near Holdenville, Oklahoma. Camma was a Cotton Broker and later a Commissioner. He and Adah made their home near Holdenville, Oklahoma. Camma died March 17, 1949.

Children of Cameron "Camma" Cicero Leach and Adah C. Thompson

#5-3-1-3-1-1.　　　Grace Emily Leach, born October 23, 1896, Sequoyah County, Oklahoma and died February 20, 1897.

#5-3-1-3-1-2.　　　Mary Adah Leach, born March 17, 1907, Wetumka, Oklahoma.

#5-3-1-3-1-3.　　　Albert Comma Leach, born December 25, 1908, Holdenville, Oklahoma.

#4-3-1-3-3　　RAYMOND FREDERICK LEACH

Raymond Frederick Leach, born May 15, 1900, Muldrow, Cherokee Nation, Oklahoma, married Essie Hester Hale, July 7, 1926, Sequoyah County, Oklahoma. Essie was born October 7, 1905, Muldrow, Cherokee Nation, Oklahoma, and died January 9, 1993. According to 1930 census Raymond was an Irrigator on a Hay Ranch. Raymond died June 21, 1972 in Shasta County, California. Both Raymond and Essie are buried in Redding, Shasta County, California.

Children of Raymond Frederick Leach and Essie Hester Hale

#5-3-1-3-3-1.　　　Fred R. Leach, born June 27, 1927, Sallisaw, Sequoyah County, Oklahoma.

#5-3-1-3-3-2.　　　Dick Hale Leach, born, July 31, 1931, Imperial County, California.

#5-3-1-3-3-3.　　　Gerald Wayne Leach, born August 29, 1938, California.

#4-3-1-3-4　　JAMES RICHARD LEACH

James Richard Leach, born January 25, 1901, Muldrow, Cherokee Nation, Oklahoma, married Iva Lonera Garner, December 15, 1933, Sequoyah County, Oklahoma. Iva was born October 23, 1907, Clarksville, Johnson County, Arkansas, and died September 8, 1997, Midwest City, Oklahoma. James and Iva moved about their first few years of marriage, first living in Ft Smith, Arkansas, Then finally to Coffyville, Kansas where they lived out their married lives. James died in Coffeville, Kansas, September 14, 1967. Iva died in Midwest City, Oklahoma, September 8, 1997.

Children of James Richard Leach and Iva Lenora Garner

#5-3-1-3-4-1.	Norma Jean Leach, born March 10, 1935, Ft Smith, Sebastain County, Arkansas.
#5-3-1-3-4-2.	Peggy Joyce Leach, born December 11, 1936, Ft Smith, Sebastain County, Arkansas.
#5-3-1-3-4-3.	Donald Boyce Leach, born December 11, 1936, Ft Smith, Sebestain County, Arkansas.

#4-3-1-3-5 JOHN WESLEY LEACH

John Wesley Leach, born December 30, 1904, Muldrow, Cherokee Nation, Oklahoma, married, Velma Owens July 5, 1928, Sequoyah County, Oklahoma. Velma was born December 21, 1908, Muldrow, Sequoyah County, Oklahoma. According to 1930 census John was a Farmer. John died January 10, 1991, El Centro, Imperial County, California.

Children of John Wesley Leach and Velma Owens

#5-3-1-3-5-1.	Bob G. Leach, born December 21, 1934, Muldrow, Sequoyah County, Oklahoma.
#5-3-1-3-5-2.	Betty Ann Leach, born August 19, 1932 Muldrow, Sequoyah County, Oklahoma.

#4-3-1-3-6 WILBUR JULIAN LEACH

Wilbur Julian Leach, born February 6, 1907, Muldrow, Sequoyah County, Oklahoma, married Rosalene Battle, February 22, 1941 Oakland, California. Rosalene was born April 19, 1911, San Francisco County, California.

Children of Wilbur Julian Leach and Rosalene Battle

#5-3-1-3-6-1.   Robert Michel Leach, born February 24, 1942,
                       Los Angeles County, California.
#5-3-1-3-6-2.   William Richard Leach, born February 10,
                       1947, Alameda County, California.

#4-3-1-5-1   JAMES RICHARD STOUT

James Richard Stout, born October 25, 1867, Washington County,
Arkansas, James was apparently married three times. The name of his
first wife if unknown. She was born in Oklahoma, Indian Territory. She
and James married about 1885. She died about 1895. James's second
marriage was to Martha in 1897. Martha was born in Oklahoma, 1870
and died in Tulsa, Oklahoma, about 1914. After the death of Martha
James married Clara M. about 1915. Clara was born in Kansas, 1894.
James was a Carpenter, Farmer and later a Dairy Farmer. He died in
Owassa, Oklahoma, April 25, 1951.

Children of James Richard Stout and First Wife

#5-3-1-5-1-1.   Edna Stout, born May, 1885, Oklahoma, Indian
                       Territory.
#5-3-1-5-1-2.   Lee Stout, born October, 1890, Oklahoma,
                       Indian Territory.

Child of James Richard Stout and Martha

#5-3-1-5-1-3.   Russel Stout, born December, 1897, Tulsa
                       County, Oklahoma, Indian Territory.

Children of James Richard Stout and Clara M.

#5-3-1-5-1-4.   James S. Stout, born September, 1918, Tulsa
                       County, Oklahoma.
#5-3-1-5-1-5.   Sally M. Stout, born 1922, Tulsa County,
                       Oklahoma.

#5-3-1-5-1-6.	Jack W. Stout, born 1925, Tulsa County, Oklahoma.
#5-3-1-5-1-7.	Mary L. Stout, born November, 1929, Tulsa County, Oklahoma.

#4-3-1-5-3　　MARY JANE STOUT

Mary Jane Stout born October 21, 1871, Baxter Springs, Kansas, married Joseph Robinson Griffith, October 31, 1887, Shawnee Mission, Kansas. Joseph was born September 27, 1854, Edgar County, Illinois and died April 30, 1935, Bristow, Oklahoma.

Joseph was a Farmer and ran a Nursery. Mary and Joseph moved several times during the early years of their marriage, first living in Kansas, then Missouri, then Logan County, Oklahoma and finally in Bristow, Oklahoma, where they remained the remainder of their lives. Mary died April 27, 1935, Bristow, Oklahoma.

Children of Mary Jane Stout and Joseph Robinson Griffith

#5-3-1-5-3-1.	Leslie Harrison Griffith, born November 1, 1888, Seneca, Missouri.
#5-3-1-5-3-2.	Mary Jane Griffith, born April 27, 1892, Logan County, Oklahoma Territory.
#5-3-1-5-3-3.	Joseph R. Griffith, Jr., born April, 1897, Logan County, Oklahoma Territory.
#5-3-1-5-3-4.	Elsee Fay Griffith, born December, 1898, Logan County, Oklahoma Territory.
#5-3-1-5-3-5.	Martha Ellen Griffith, born January 3, 1904, Logan County, Oklahoma Territory.
#5-3-1-5-4-6.	Orville Charles Griffith, born March 10, 1907, Logan County, Oklahoma Territory.
#5-3-1-5-4-7.	Juan R. Stout, born 1911, Oklahoma. (boy raised by the Griffiths).

#4-3-1-5-7   ELMER BETRAM STOUT

Elmer Betram Stout, born April 25, 1878, Cherokee County, Kansas, married Stella Robinson in 1903. Stella was born in 1881, Kansas and died about 1925, Logan County, Oklahoma. Elmer and Stella lived their entire married lives in Logan County, Oklahoma. He was a Farmer. Elmer died December 30, 1941, Cowlitz, Washington.

Children of Elmer Bertram Stout and Stella Robinson

#5-3-1-5-7-1.	Ruby D. Stout, born 1904, Logan County, Oklahoma.
#5-3-1-5-7-2.	Otis S. Stout, born 1906, Logan County, Oklahoma.
#5-3-1-5-7-3.	Cecil E. Stout, born 1908, Logan County, Oklahoma.
#5-3-1-5-7-4.	Jame Stout, born 1911, Logan County, Oklahoma.
#5-3-1-5-7-5.	Eva Stout, born 1915, Logan County, Oklahoma.

#4-3-1-6-1   JULIUS ALEXANDER MORRIS

Julius Alexander Morris, born January 14, 1879, Benton County, Arkansas, married Vinnie Crone in 1903. Vinnie was born April 3, 1881, Arkansas and died March 29, 1962, Benton County, Arkansas. Julius and Vinnie were lifetime residents of Benton County, Arkansas. Julius's occupation was farming. Julius died May 14, 1963, Benton County, Arkansas. Both Julius and Vinnie are buried in the Fairmont Cemetery, Benton County, Arkansas.

Children of Julius Alexander Morris and Vinnie Chrone

#5-3-1-6-1-1.	Audmon Morris, born 1907, Benton County, Arkansas.
#5-3-1-6-1-2.	Lasson Morris, born 1908, Benton County, Arkansas.

#5-3-1-6-1-3.	Berl Morris, born 1909, Benton County, Arkansas.
#5-3-1-6-1-4.	Zona Morris, born 1911, Benton County, Arkansas.
#5-3-1-6-1-5.	Fay Morris, born 1913, Benton County, Arkansas.
#5-3-1-6-1-6.	Carl Morris, born June, 1916, Benton County, Arkansas.

#4-3-1-6-4   LAURA JANE MORRIS

Laura Jane Morris, born November 14, 1886, Benton County, Arkansas, first married Singleton about 1905. Since no census was taken during the marriage, information on Singleton is not available other than, he was born in Arkansas. On March 19, 1912, Laura married Gus Angelius Chulufus in Carney, Kansas. Gus was born May 21, 1887, Corinth, Greece and died November 3, 1964, Benton County, Arkansas. Gus ran a Cleaners. Laura died October 19, 1970, Benton County, Arkansas.

Child of Laura Jane Morris and Singleton

#5-3-1-6-4-1.	Luther Singleton, born 1907, Benton County, Arkansas.

Children of Laura Jane Singleton and Gus Angelus Chulufus

#5-3-1-6-4-2.	Eulia Ann Chulufus, born December 14, 1916, Franklin County, Kansas.
#5-3-1-6-4-3.	Dorothy Ellen Chulufus, born January 19, 1919, Franklin County, Kansas
#5-3-1-6-4-4.	James Morris Chulufus, born February 2, 1922, Franklin County, Kansas.
#5-3-1-6-4-5.	Catherine Jane Chulufus, born October 14, 1923, Franklin County, Kansas.
#5-3-1-6-4-6.	Genevive Lorraine Chulufus, born July 14, 1927, Franklin County, Kansas.

#5-3-1-6-4-7.	Richard Franklin Chulufus, born January 9, 1927, Franklin County, Kansas.
#5-3-1-6-4-8.	Donald Chulufus, born August 23, 1929, Franklin County, Kansas.
#5-3-1-6-4-9.	Robert Lee Chulufus, born June 6, 1931, Franklin County, Kansas.
#5-3-1-6-4-10.	Audrey Chulufus, born June 6, 1931, Franklin County, Kansas.

#4-3-1-7-1 ALONZO THEADORE CHESNEY

Alonzo Theadore Chesney, born July 9, 1874, Illinois, married Della Chew in 1898. Della was born in Illinois February 25, 1874. Alonzo was a Miner. He started working in mines and progressed up into management. In the 1930 census Alonzo had moved to Washington, District of Columbia and was employed as a Reps. Minder.

Children of Alonzo Theadore Chesney and Della Chew

#5-3-1-7-1-1.	Ester J. Chesney, born June 22, 1899, Illinois.
#5-3-1-7-1-2.	Isom Chesney, born 1901, Illinois.
#5-3-1-7-1-3.	Faye Ckesney, born 1902, Illinois.
#5-3-1-7-1-4.	Claude Chesney, born 1903, Illinois.
#5-3-1-7-1-5.	Alonzo Chesney, born 1906, Illinois.
#5-3-1-7-1-6.	Cecil Chesney, born 1910, Illinois.
#5-3-1-7-1-7.	James Chesney, born 1912, Illinois.
#5-3-1-7-1-8.	Johnnie Chesney, born 1915, Illinois.
#5-3-1-7-1-9.	Robert Chesney, born 1919, Illinois.

#4-3-1-9-1 DONNA ALICE LEACH

Donna Alice Leach, born June, 1885, Washington County, Arkansas, married Elonzo C. McCaleb in 1906. Elinzo was born in September, 1880, Arkansas. In 1910 Donna and Elonzo were living in Stilwell, Adair County, Oklahoma, where Elonzo was Farming. In the 1920 and

1930 census Donna was divorced and living in Santa Rosa, California, where Donna was working as a Telephone Operator.

Children of Donna Alice Leach and Elonzo C. McCaleb

#5-3-1-9-1-1.   Arley K. McCaleb, born 1907, Washington County, Arkansas.
#5-3-1-9-1-2.   Melvin Linus McCaleb, born May 29, 1908 Washington County, Arkansas. Linus was a maritime sailor who became a ships captain and transported war materials to U S Soldiers during WW ll. He was living in Santa Rosa, California, in 1999.
#5-3-1-9-1-3.   Verbie A. McCaleb, born 1912, Adair County, Oklahoma,

#4-3-1-9-4   ROWENA LEACH

Rowena Leach, born February, 1892, Washington County, Arkansas, married Thomas Fletcher Hicks, November 11, 1914, Washington County, Arkansas. Thomas was born November 19, 1885, Nicholas County, West Virginia. In the 1920, Washington County, Arkansas census Thomas's occupation is listed as Farming.

Child of Rowena Leach and Thomas Fletcher Hicks

#5-3-1-9-4-1.   Marie Hicks, born December, 1915, Washington County, Arkansas.

#4-3-1-10-2   BESSIE LEACH

Bessie Leach, born April, 1890, Creek Nation, Oklahoma Indian Territoty, married William Thogdon in 1907. William was born in Tennessee, 1861 and died around 1918. William was a Building Carpenter in St Louis, Missouri. In 1920 and 1930 Bessie was living in St Louis, St Louis County, Missouri. In 1920 she was working as a Seamstress from her home. In 1930 she was working for a Fuel Company.

Children of Bessie Leach and Trogden

#5-3-1-10-2-1.   Fannie   Mae   Trogdon,   born   May,   1908, Missouri.
#5-3-1-10-2-2.   Ruby Trogdon, born December, 1909, Missouri.
#5-3-1-10-2-3.   William Trogdon, born 1913, Missouri.
#5-3-1-10-2-4.   Marie Trogdon, born 1915, Missouri.
#5-3-1-10-2-5.   Dorothy Trogdon, born 1918, Missouri.

#4-3-1-10-4   RUFUS ELSWORTH LEACH

Rufus Elsworth Leach, born September 5, 1892, Creek Nation, Oklahoma Indian Territory, married Susie L. in 1917. Susie was born in Oklahoma in 1897 and died May 4, 1959. In 1920 and 1930 Rufus and Susie were living in Wagoner County, Oklahoma. In 1920 Rufus was working as a Grocery Clerk. In 1930 he was employed as a Butcher in a Meat Market. In 1917 when Rufus registered for draft he reported that he had a wife and child. That child apparently died before the 1920 census. Rufus died March 11, 1977 in Tulsa, Osage County, Oklahoma.

Child of Rufus Elsworth Leach and Susie L.

#5-3-1-10-4-1.   Emma M. Leach, born 1921, Wagoner, Wagoner County, Oklahoma.

#4-3-1-10-6   SUSIE J. LEACH

Susie J. Leach, born December, 1897, Creek Nation, Oklahoma Indian Territory, married Grover C. Stockton, February 1, 1917, Wagoner, Oklahoma. Grover was born in the Creek Nation, Oklahoma Indian Territory. In 1920 Grover was a Grocery Clerk in Wagoner, Oklahoma. In 1930 he was the foreman of a Garage in Coeta, Wagoner County,

Oklahoma. Grover's son operated a Tomato Cannery in Lincoln, Arkansas until about 1955.

Children of Susie J. Leach and Grover C. Stockton

#5-3-1-10-6-1.   Mary Ann Stockton, born 1919, Wagoner County, Oklahoma.

#5-3-1-10-6-2.   Grover Stockton, Jr., born 1922, Wagoner County, Oklahoma.

#4-3-1-10-7   JAMES C. LEACH

James C. Leach, born December, 1897, Creek Nation, Oklahomas Indian Territory, married Ada about 1922. Ada was born in Oklahoma, 1898. James was a Fireman for the City of Tulsa in 1930.

Child of James C. Leach and Ada

#5-3-1-10-7-1.   James A. Leach, born 1924, Oklahoma.

#4-3-1-10-8   ANNA LEACH

Anna Leach, born April 3, 1899, Creek Nation, Oklahoma Indian Territory, married Waldo Durr Shockley, 1920. Waldo was born in Kansas, August 25, 1900 and died June, 1972, Lincoln, Washington County, Arkansas. Anna and Waldo moved about over the years. She obtained a Social Security card in Indiana. He obtained his card in Nebraska. Waldo managed and operated a laundry and cleaners. Anna was a beautician who operated her own beauty shop.

Child of Anna Leach and Waldo Durr Shockley

#5-3-1-10-8.   Roger Patrick Shockley, (adopted after 1930).

#4-3-1-11-1   RAYMOND LUTHER LEACH

Raymond Luther Leach, born June 14, 1891, Washington County, Arkansas, married Ruth Elsie McCarty, December 8, 1915, Washington County, Arkansas. Ruth was born March 17, 1895, Arkansas and died December 8, 1973, Muskogee, Oklahoma. In his early life Raymond was a Farmer. In later life he Operated a General Store in Dutch Mills, Washington County, Arkansas. Raymond died January 4, 1959, Washington County, Arkansas. Both Raymond and Ruth are buried in the Cemetery at Dutch Mills, Arkansas.

Children of Raymond Luther Leach and Ruth Elsie McCarty

#5-3-1-11-1-1.	Bonita R. Leach, born April 23, 1917, Washington County, Arkansas.
#5-3-1-11-1-2.	Dortha Ann Leach, born April 20, 1925, Washington County, Arkansas.
#5-3-1-11-1-3.	Raymond McCarty Leach, born dead February 12, 1929, Washington County, Arkansas.
#5-3-1-11-1-4.	Jerry Allen Leach, born October 12, 1935, Washington County, Arkansas.

#4-3-1-11-3   CHARLES ALEX LEACH

Charles Alex Leach, born March 17, 1894, Washington County, Arkansas, married Hazel M. Yarty, December 23, 1923, Washington County, Arkansas. Hazel was born 1903, West Virginia. Charles was a lifetime Farmer in Washington County, Arkansas. Charles died October 30, 1962, Washington County, Arkansas.

Children of Charles Alex Leach and Hazel M. YARTY

#5-3-1-11-3-1.	Charles Harold Leach, born October 24, 1924, Washington County, Arkansas.
#5-3-1-11-3-2.	Howard Lee Leach, born February 21, 1932, Washington County, Arkansas.

#5-3-1-11-3-3.	George Arthur Leach, born September 23, 1934 Washington County, Arkansas.
#5-3-1-11-3-4.	James Leach, born September 27, 1943, Washington County, Arkansas.

#4-3-2-1-1   REUBEN A. SMITH

Reuben A. Smith, born October, 1859, Benton County, Arkansas, married Elizabeth M., May 29, 1884, Sedan, Chautauqua, Kansas. Elizabeth was born in March, 1867, Iowa. In 1885, Kansas State census Reuben and Elizabeth were living in Sedan, Kansas. In 1900 Reuben and Elizabeth were living in King County, Washington, where Reuben was a Blacksmith. In 1910 they were still in King County, Washington, and Reuben was working as a Carpenter. In 1920 Reuben was working as foreman for County Roads. Reuben died in 1936.

Children of Reuben A. Smith and Elizabeth M.

#5-3-2-1-1-1.	Tracy G. Smith, born February, 1885, Sedan, Chautauqua, Kansas
#5-3-2-1-1-2.	Harry E. Smith, born November, 1886, Sedan, Chautauqua, Kansas.
#5-3-2-1-1-3.	Christine L. Smith, born January, 1889, Sedan, Chautauqua, Kansas.
#5-3-2-1-1-4.	Winifred M. Smith, born March, 1891, King County, Washington.
#5-3-2-1-1-5.	Bert C. Smith, born April, 1893, King County, Washington.
#5-3-2-1-1-6.	Dewey E. Smith, born February, 1898, King County, Washington.
#5-3-2-1-1-7.	Scotty M. Smith, born 1902, King County, Washington.

Violet C. Smith, born November, 1864, Kansas, first married Henderson about 1883. Henderson was born in Tennessee. Violet next married William Orin Baxter in 1890. William was born in Illinois, June, 1868. William was a Farmer. He and Violet first lived in Oregon and then King County, Washington. Violet died in King County, Washington, May 19, 1946.

Children of Violet C. Smith and Henderson

#5-3-2-1-2-1.   Laura Henderson, born December, 1884, Kansas.
#5-3-2-1-2-2.   Lenora F. Henderson, born October, 1886, Kansas.
#5-3-2-1-2-3.   Evalena M. Henderson, born October, 1888, Kansas.

Children of Violet C. Smith and William Orin Baxter

#5-3-2-1-2-4.   Bessie A. Baxter, born October, 1891, Oregon.
#5-3-2-1-2-5.   Hugh W. Baxter, born July, 1894, King County, Washington.
#5-3-2-1-2-6.   Margaret S. Baxter, born 1903, King County, Washington.

#4-3-2-1-4   WALTER TRAVIS SMITH

Walter Travis Smith, born October, 1869, Sedan, Chatauqua County, Kansas married Mary Eleanor Parker, December 4 1894. Mary was born February 12, 1878, Caldwell, Summers County, Kansas, and died September 26, 1953, King County, Washington. Walter and Mary were living in Washington in October, 1895, where Walter was listed as a farmer. Walter died February 16, 1953, King County, Washington.

Children of Walter Travis Smith and Mary Eleanore Parker

#5-3-2-1-4-1.	Percy C. Smith, born October, 1895, King County, Washington.
#5-3-2-1-4-2.	Herbert M. Smith, born June, 1898, King County, Washington.

#4-3-2-1-6   DANIEL E. SMITH

Daniel E. Smith, born May, 1873, Washington County, Arkansas, married Clara June Hume, November 5, 1892, Elberton, Whitman County, Washington. Clara was born December 2, 1872, Iowa and died May 30, 1961 at Longview, Cowlitz County, Washington. Daniel worked as a Farm Laborer in the early years of his marriage but later owned and Operated a Dairy Farm. Daniel died March 4, 1950, Seattle, King County, Washington.

Children of Daniel E. Smith and Clara June Hume

#5-3-2-1-6-1.	Wilbur M. Smith, born 1894, Washington.
#5-3-2-1-6-2.	Vergie P. Smith, born 1896, Washington.
#5-3-2-1-6-3.	Fred W. Smith, born 1898, Washington.
#5-3-2-1-6-4.	Hazel K. Smith, born 1900, Washington.
#5-3-2-1-6-5.	Edna M. Smith, born 1902, Washington.
#5-3-2-1-6-6.	Daniel O. Smith, born 1906, Washington.
#5-3-2-1-6-7.	Nellie C. Smith, born 1908, Washington.
#5-3-2-1-6-8.	Georgia R. Smith, born 1910, Washington.
#5-3-2-1-6-9.	Richard Smith, born 1914, Washington.

#4-3-2-1-7   EMMA ALICE SMITH

Emma Alice Smith, born February 15, 1875, Washington County, Arkansas, married Thomas E. Mowris in 1901. Thomas was born November 28, 1872, Warren, Warren County, Pennsylvania and died March 28, 1958 Seattle King County, Washington. Thomas was a Farmer. Emma died February 6, 1911, King County, Washington.

Children of Emma Alice Smith and Thomas E. Mowris

#5-3-2-1-7-1.	Gladys J. Mowris, born 1901, King County, Washington.
#5-3-2-1-7-2.	Llora L. Mowris, born 1908, King County, Washington.
#5-3-2-1-7-3.	Margaret C. Mowris, born 1910, King County, Washington.

#4-3-2-2-1   MONROE LEACH

Monroe Leach, born July 1, 1869, Washington County, Arkansas, married Nora A. in 1895. Nora was born in Texas, November, 1875. In the 1900 census Monroe was a Salesman living in Oklahoma City, Indian Territory. In 1910 he was in King County, Washington. Monroe died July 8, 1926, Snohomish County, Washington.

Children of Monrow Leach and Nora A.

#5-3-2-2-1-1.	Nellie E. Leach, born June, 1896, Oklahoma City, Indian Territory.
#5-3-2-2-1-2.	Glen W. Leach, born September, 1898, Oklahoma City, Indian Territory.
#5-3-2-2-1-3.	Paul S. Leach, born 1901, Oklahoma City, Indian Territory.

#4-3-2-2-9   ELMINA LEACH

Elmina Leach, born January 1, 1883, Washington County, Arkansas, first married William Pierce Blasier, November, 1899, Stillwater, Payne County, Oklahoma. William was born in October, 1869, Kewaunee, Kewaunee County, Wisconsin and died February 22, 1907, Marena, Payne County, Oklahoma. William was a farmer. After the death of William, Elmina married Fred Varner August 25, 1910. Elmina died October 19, 1966, Lawton, Comache County, Oklahoma.

Children of Elmina Leach and William Pierce Blasier

#5-3-2-2-9-1.   Alta Blasier, born 1901, Payne County, Oklahoma.
#5-3-2-2-9-2.   Ralph Waldo Blasier, born March 5, 1902 Mulhall, Logan County, Oklahoma.

#4-3-2-5-1   ALICE ANN LEACH

Alice Ann Leach, born June, 1870, Washington County, Arkansas, first married Daniel Henry Glidewell, January 23, 1890, Washington County, Arkansas. Daniel was born in Tennessee, March 5, 1833 and died in Washington County, Arkansas, September 17, 190 3. After the death of Daniel Alice married Giles Henderson Glidewell. Giles was born in Tennessee, July 28, 1874. Daniel and Giles may have been related but were not brothers. Both Daniel and Giles were farmers.

Children of Alice Ann Leach and Daniel Henry Glidewell

#5-3-2-5-1-1.   James Elza Glidewell, born October 18, 1890, Washington County, Arkansas.
#5-3-2-5-1-2.   Murta M. Glidewell, born 1892, Washington County, Arkansas.
#5-3-2-5-1-3.   Olva Earls Glidewell, born October 21, 1894, Washington County, Arkansas.

Child of Alice Ann Glidewell and Giles Henderson Glidewell

#5-3-2-5-1-4.   Pearl C. Glidewell, born 1903, Washington County, Arkansas.

#4-3-2-5-4   SAMUEL HENRY LEACH

Samuel Henry Leach, born August, 1875, Washington County, Arkansas, married Amanda America Reed, September 6, 1894, Washington County, Arkansas. Amanda was born February 20, 1873,

Arkansas and died in 1965. Samuel was a farmer. He died February 3, 1945, Washington County, Arkansas. Both Henry and Amanda are buried in the Cox Cemetery, Washington County, Arkansas.

Children of Samuel Henry Leach and Amanda America Reed

#5-3-2-5-4-1.   Virginia Elizabeth Leach, born January, 1895, Washington County, Arkansas, died before 1900 census.

#5-3-2-5-4-2.   Bennett Henry Leach, born June 11, 1897, Washington County, Arkansas.

#5-3-2-5-4-3.   Luther Dale Leach, born September 3, 1899, Washington County, Arkansas.

#5-3-2-5-4-4.   Audo Ray Leach, born June 22, 1901, Washington County, Arkansas.

#5-3-2-5-4-5.   Winnie Leach, born June 13, 1903, Washington County, Arkansas.

#4-3-2-5-5   ETTA N. LEACH

Etta N. Leach born, May, 1876, Washington County, Arkansas, married John W. Burgess January 29, 1900, Washington County, Arkansas. John was born in 1874, Arkansas. In 1910 census John was working at odd Jobs in Washington County, Arkansas. In 1920 he was farming in Washington County, Arkansas. In 1930 census he was operating a retail grocery store in Reagan County, Texas. Etta died in Reagan County, Texas April 16, 1943.

Children of Etta N. Leach and John W. Burgess

#5-3-2-5-5-1.   Mary E. Burgess, born 1901, Washington County, Arkansas.

#5-3-2-5-5-2.   Jessie Jewel Burgess, born 1903, Washington County, Arkansas.

#5-3-2-5-5-3.   Sarah Levena Burgess, born 1907, Washington County, Arkansas.

#5-3-2-5-5-4.	Malcom Lee Burgess, born 1910, Washington County, Arkansas.
#5-3-2-5-5-5.	Tersie Burgess, born November 11, 1914, Washington County, Arkansas, died before 1920.
#5-3-2-5-5-6.	James Burgess, born July 14, 1921, Washington County, Arkansas, died September 20, 1924, Washington County, Arkansas. He is Buried in Cox Cemetery, Washington County, Arkansas.

#4-3-2-5-6   EARL LEACH

Earl "Doc" Leach born May 13, 1879, Washington County, Arkansas, married Isabelle I. Reed, May 13, 1901, Washington County, Arkansas. Isabelle was born October 18, 1880, Washington County, Arkansas and died February 25, 1938, Washington County, Arkansas. Earl farmed until after 1920. The 1930, Washington County, Arkansas, census shows him as a wholesale oil and gas dealer. The 1900, Washington County, Arkansas census show that Isabelle had given birth to four children with only one living. These three deceased children have not been identified. Earl died in 1965. Both Earl and Elizabeth are buried in the Cox Cemetery, Washington County, Arkansas.

Children of Earl Leach and Isabelle I. Reed

#5-3-2-5-6-1.	Ethel Ophelia Leach, born September 15, 1902, Washington County, Arkansas, died December 20, 1925, Washington County, Arkansas.
#5-3-2-5-6-2.	Ernest J. Leach, born May 15, 1910, Washington County, Arkansas.
#5-3-2-5-6-3.	Mary Leta Leach, born March 14, 1919, Washington County, Arkansas, died March 6, 1920 Washington County, Arkansas.
#5-3-2-5-6-4.	Lillian Leach, born December 28, 1923, Washington County, Arkansas, died August 21, 1924, Washington County, Arkansas.

#4-3-2-5-7   EMMA LEACH

Emma Leach, born May 24, 1882, Washington County, Arkansas, married Cyrus Henry Rinehart December 24, 1899, Washington County, Arkansas. Henry was born February 20, 1879, in Arkansas and died September 10, 1956, Stilwell, Adair County, Oklahoma. Henry was a lifetime farmer in Washington County, Arkansas. Emma died December 23, 1930, Washington County, Arkansas. Both Henry and Emma are buried in Cox Cemetery, Washington County, Arkansas.

Children of Emma Leach and Cyrus Henry Rinehart

#5-3-2-5-7-1. Opal Rinehart, born December 18, 1900, Washington County, Arkansas.

#5-3-2-5-7-2. Harley Rinehart, born December 19, 1902, Washington County, Arkansas.

#5-3-2-5-7-3. James Rinehart, born October 19, 1904, Washington County, Arkansas.

#5-3-2-5-7-4. Orvil Lee Rinehart, born November 14, 1906, Washington County, Arkansas.

#5-3-2-5-7-5. Lillus Rinehart, born June 6, 1909, Washington County, Arkansas.

#4-3-2-5-9   MARY EVALINE LEACH

Mary Evaline Leach, born April 28, 1883, Washington County, Arkansas, first married Walter Reed April 19, 1900, Washington County, Arkansas. Walter was born in Arkansas, January 20, 1881, and died May 2, 1901, Washington County, Arkansas. After the death of Walter, Mary married Joseph Roland Abshire, December 25, 1910. Joseph was born in Arkansas, March 28, 1878, and died April 28, 1966, Washington County, Arkansas. Joseph was a Farmer. Mary died 27 March 1980 Washington County, Arkansas.

Child of Mary Evaline Leach and Walter Reed

#5-3-2-5-9-1.   John Walter Reed, born April 25, 1901, Washington County, Arkansas.

Children of Mary Evaline Leach and Joseph Roland Abshire

#5-3-2-5-9-2.   Roscoe King Abshire, born October 2, 1912, Washington County, Arkansas.
#5-3-2-5-9-3.   Dow Leach Abshire, born March 24, 1914, Washington County, Arkansas.
#5-3-2-5-9-4.   Elizabeth Dorcas Abshire, born February 22, 1920, Washington County, Arkansas.
#5-3-2-5-9-5.   Dorothy Ellen Abshire, born July 29, 1924, Washington County, Arkansas.
#5-3-2-5-9-6.   Connie Laverne Abshire, born January 8, 1928, Washington County, Arkansas.

#4-3-2-7-1   ETHEL LEACH

Ethel Leach, born September 29, 1880, Benton County, Arkansas, married William Randolph Shelton, December 16, 1899, Munger, Oklahoma Territory. William was born in Texas, March 5, 1978, and died January 31, 1964. William is buried at the Tecumseh Mission Cemetery, Tecumseh, Oklahoma. According to 1920 census William was a farm operator. Ethel died January 31, 1964, Oklahoma City, Oklahoma and is buried in the Kolb Cemetery, Oklahoma City, Oklahoma.

Children of Ethel Leach and William Randolph Shelton

#5-3-2-7-1-1.   Albert Glen Shelton, born October 29, 1900, Munger, Oklahoma Territory.
#5-3-2-7-1-2.   Gilbert Gerald Shelton, born October 20, 1902, Oklahoma City, Oklahoma Territory.
#5-3-2-7-1-3.   Lillian Ina Shelton, born February 11, 1905, Oklahoma City, Oklahoma Territory.

#5-3-2-7-1-4.	Thelma (NMI) Shelton, born January 21, 1908, Oklahoma City, Oklahoma.
#5-3-2-7-1-5.	Clara Bernice Shelton, born June 15, 1915, Oklahoma City, Oklahoma.
#5-3-2-7-1-6.	Lavita Marie Shelton, born January 18, 1918, Oklahoma City, Oklahoma.
#5-3-2-7-1-7.	Mary Catherine Shelton, born December 20, 1920, Chandler, Oklahoma, died 20 December 1920, buried Chandler, Oklahoma.

#4-3-2-7-2 ELMOND LEACH

Elmond Leach, born August 8, 1883, Colorado, married Maggie Bell Scoggins About 1906. Maggie was born in Missouri, August 4, 1885 and died August 27, 1965. Elmond moved to Canada after 1907, back to Oklahoma County, Oklahoma before 1911, where he remained for over ten years before returning to Canada. Elmond was a farmer. He died October 18, 1951, Edmond, Alberta, Canada. He is buried in the Fairview Cemetery.

Children of Elmond Leach and Maggie Bell Scoggins

#5-3-2-7-2-1.	Edward Donovan Leach, born 1907, Oklahoma.
#5-3-2-7-2-2.	Jerry Leach, born 1909, Canada.
#5-3-2-7-2-3.	Ester Palmer Leach, born 1911, Oklahoma.

#4-3-2-7-3 ELDORA LEACH

Eldora Leach, born July 15, 1886, Benton County, Arkansas, married Thomas Jefferson Allen, 1905. Thomas was born in Missouri August 1, 1876, and died in 1952.

Thomas was a Teamster and truck driver for a Wholesale Drug Company. Eldora died April 5, 1963 in Oklahoma City, Oklahoma, and is buried in the Kolb Cemetery.

Children of Eldora Leach and Thomas Jefferson Allen

#5-3-2-7-3-1.	Johnnie Elmond Allen, born 1908, Oklahoma County, Oklahoma.
#5-3-2-7-3-2.	Thomas Everett Allen, born 1909, Oklahoma City, Oklahoma.
#5-3-2-7-3-3.	Archie Decator Allen, born 1912, Oklahoma City, Oklahoma.

#4-3-2-7-4   CLARISSA "ESSIE" LEACH

Clarissa "Essie" Leach, born June 19, 1889, Benton County, Arkansas, married Homer Richardson, May 29, 1912, Oklahoma City, Oklahoma. Homer was born 1988, Indiana and died April 29, 1968, Missouri. Homer was a Railroad Postal Clerk. Clarissa died October 8, 1981, Missouri. Both Clarissa and Homer are buried in the Ozark Memorial Garden, Rolla, Missouri.

Children of Clarissa "Essie" Leach and Homer Richardson

#5-3-2-7-4-1.	Ruth Tillott Richardson, born 1918, St Louis County, Missouri.
#5-3-2-7-4-2.	Edwin L. Richardson, born 1923, St Louis County, Missouri.
#5-3-2-7-4-3.	Reba Waters Richardson, born 1925, St Louis County, Missouri.

#4-3-2-7-6   BERNICE CLEMENTINE LEACH

Bernice Clementine Leach, born July 16, 1896, Oklahoma Territory, married Ray Longwith, December 8, 1916 Oklahoma City, Oklahoma. Ray was born in Oklahoma Territory, December 4, 1895 and died March 5, 1968, Oklahoma. Ray was a farmer. Bernice died February 27, 1996, Moore, Oklahoma County, Oklahoma.

#5-3-2-7-6-1.	Rose Yvonne Longwith, born July 12, 1917, Oklahoma City, Oklahoma.
#5-3-2-7-6-2.	Ralph Longwith, born November 22, 1919, Bluejacket, Oklahoma, died November 22, 1919, Bluejacket, Oklahoma.
#5-3-2-7-6-3.	Kathleen Aseneth Longwith, born October 30, 1920, Bluejacket, OK.
#5-3-2-7-6-4.	Evelyn Wilda Longwith, born November 6, 1922, Bluejacket, Oklahoma.
#5-3-2-7-6-5.	Joseph Decatur Longwith, born March 24, 1925, Bluejacket, Oklahoma.
#5-3-2-7-6-6.	Harold Wilton Longwith, born December 15, 1928, Bluejacket, Oklahoma.
#5-3-2-7-6-7.	Virginia Marguerite Longwith, born January 16, 1931, Bluejacket, Oklahoma.
#5-3-2-7-6-8.	James Eugene Longwith, born June 3, 1931, Blue Jacket, Oklahoma.

#4-3-2-7-7   ELLA MAE LEACH

Ella Mae Leach, born April 9, 1901, Oklahoma Territory, married Lucien E. Lansden, October, 1922, Oklahoma County, Oklahoma. Lucien was born 1899, Alabama and died in Oklahoma, 1965. Lucien worked for an Advertising Company. Ella died December 12, 1945, Oklahoma City, Oklahoma. She is buried in the Kolb Cemetery.

Children of Ella Mae Leach and Lucien E. Lansden

#5-3-2-7-7-1.	Lucien E. Lansden, Jr., born May, 1926, Oklahoma County, Oklahoma.
#5-3-2-7-7-2.	Catherine Lansden, born Oklahoma County, Oklahoma.

#4-3-3-1-1   MONTGOMERY I. EDMISTON

Montgomery I. "Gummie" Edminson, born February, 1869, Washington County, Arkansas, married Donna Lillian Burum, 1906. Donna was born in California, November 16, 1886 and died June 17, 1941, Tulare County, California. Gummie was a Fruit farmer. He died before 1920. After Gummies' death Donna married Warren E. Ragle.

Children of Montgomery I. Edmiston and Donna L. Burum

#5-3-3-1-1-1.	Velma Lenore Edmiston, born June 3, 1907, Tulare County, California.
#5-3-3-1-1-2.	Hugh Edmiston, born July, 1908 Tulare County, California,
#5-3-3-1-1-3.	Earl Edmiston, born 1910, Tulare County, California.

#4-3-3-1-3   THOMAS A. EDMISTON

Thomas Alexander Edmiston born December 23, 1872, Washington County, Arkansas, married Erma R. Ricker, February 24, 1909. Erma was born in Iowa, October 4, 1880 and died in Fresno, California, January 4, 1954. Thomas was a Fruit Farmer. Thomas died November 6, 1945, Tulare County, California.

Children of Thomas Alexander Edmiston and Erma R. Riker

#5-3-3-1-3-1.	Frank Riker Edmiston, born December 23, 1909, Tulare County, California.
#5-3-3-1-3-2.	Frederick Delzell Edmiston, born April 19, 1911, Tulare County, California.
#5-3-3-1-3-3.	Marian Elizabeth Edmiston, born July 14, 1912, Tulare County, California.
#5-3-3-1-3-4.	Richard Thomas Edmiston, born December 9, 1923, Tulare County, California.

#4-3-3-1-4   IOLA EMILY FUDGE

Iola Emily Fudge, born March 24, 1880, Tulare County, California, first married Wilmot L. Chatten, 1903. Wilmot was born in California, 1878. Wilmot was a Fruit Farmer in Tulare County, California. Iola later married a Miller.

Children of Iola Emily Fudge and Wilmot L. Chatten

| #5-3-3-1-4-1. | Meredith William Chatten, born December 26, 1903, Tulare County, California. |
| #5-3-3-1-4-2. | Dallas Chatten, born 1908, Tulare County, California. |

#4-3-3-1-5   ALICE LENORA FUDGE

Alice Lenora Fudge, born January 29, 1885, Tulare County, California, married Marion Forrest Woodard about 1908. Marion was born June 30, 1884, California and died July 30, 1949, Tulare County, California. Marion was a Tree Man for a Fruit Packing Shed. Alice died September 16, 1958, Tulare County, California.

Children of Alice Lenora Fudge and Marion Forrest Woodard

#5-3-3-1-5-1.	Homer Woodard, born June 19, 1908, Tulare County, California.
#5-3-3-1-5-2.	Howard Woodard, born March 31, 1915, Tulare County, California.
#5-3-3-1-5-3.	Virginia Woodard, born 1917, Tulare County, California.

#4-3-3-1-6   ANNIE GERTRUDE FUDGE

Annie Gertrude Fudge, born July 2, 1890, Tulare County, California, married Leslie Everett Runyon, 1913. Leslie was bornJune 26, 1898,

California and died November 4, 1978, Tulare County, California. Leslie was a Farmer. Annie died January 13, 1980, Tulare County, California.

Children of Annie Gertrude Fudge and Leslie Everett Runyon

#5-3-3-1-6-1.   Alvin M. Runyon, born May 25, 1913, Tulare County, California.
#5-3-3-1-6-2.   Malva Zaidee Runyon, born December 23, 1914, Tulare County, California.
#5-3-3-1-6-3.   Helen E. Runyon, born March 12, 1918, Tulare County, California.

#4-3-4-2-1   RANDOLPH EDGAR MURRAY

Randolph Edgar Murray, born May, 1876, Washington County, Arkansas, married Fannie May Anderson about 1897. Mary was born in Missouri, May, 1878. Randolph and Fannie moved often, from 1899 to 1907 they were in California, from 1907 to 1910 Randolph had his own Butcher Shop in Washington County, Arkansas, in 1920 Randolph was a Pipe Fitter for an Oil Company in Muskogee, Oklahoma.

Children of Randolph Edgar Murray and Fannie May

#5-3-4-2-1-1.   Ruby E. Murray, born February, 1899, Las Angeles County, California.
#5-3-4-2-1-2.   Frank E. Murray, born 1901, Los Angeles County, California.
#5-3-4-2-1-3.   Harold Murray, born 1905, Los Angeles County, California.
#5-3-4-2-1-4.   Edna Murray, born 1907, Los Angeles County, California.
#5-3-4-2-1-5.   Joyce Murray, born 1909, Washington County, Arkansas.

VERONA S. MURRAY

Verona S. Murray, born March 9, 1880, Washington County, Arkansas, married Marton Lacy Patterson, 1903. Marton was born in North Carolina, 1879. Marton was a Shipping Clerk for a Citrus Packing House. Verona died February 6, 1953, Los Angelus County, California.

Child of Verona S. Murray and Marton Lacy Patterson

#5-3-4-2-3-1.   Owen L Patterson, born April, 1917, San Bernardino County, California.

#4-3-4-3-4   **ADRIAN C. MURRAY**

Adrian C. Murray, born November, 1888, Los Angeles County, California, married Estelle Marie Finn in 1912. Estelle was born August 21, 1890, Missouri and died July 12, 1952, Los Angeles County, California. Adrian was a repairman for a Can Company.

Children of Adrian C. Murray and Estelle Marie Finn

#5-3-4-2-4-1.   Mildred Alma Murray, born 1913, Los Angeles County, California.
#5-3-4-2-4-2.   Roy A. Murray, born 1915, Los Angeles County, California.
#5-3-4-2-4-3.   Mary Jean Murray, born 1916, Los Angeles County, California.

#4-3-4-3-1   **KENNETH A. EDMISTON**

Kenneth A. Edmiston, born July, 1871, Washington County, Arkansas, married three times but the names of his first two wives are unknown. Kenneth's third wife was Rosa. Rosa was born in Arkansas about 1892. Kenneth was a farmer according to the 1900 and 1920 census. In 1830 he was living in Westville, Oklahoma and working as a Sales Clerk for a Lumber Company.

Children of First Marriage of Kenneth A. Edmiston

#5-3-4-3-1-1.	Lee Edmiston, born July, 1892, Washington County, Arkansas.
#5-3-4-3-1-2.	Clifford Edmiston, born May, 1894, Washington County, Arkansas.
#5-3-4-3-1-3.	Bryan Edmiston, born October, 1896, Washington County, Arkansas.
#5-3-4-3-1-4.	Lena Edmiston, born September, 1898, Washington County, Arkansas.

Child of Second Marriage of Kenneth A. Edmiston

#5-3-4-3-1-5.	Bessie L. Edmiston, born 1906, Washington County, Arkansas.

Children of Marriage of Kenneth A. Edmiston and Rosa

#5-3-4-3-1-6.	Gregory Edmiston, born 1914, Oklahoma.
#5-3-4-3-1-7.	Leta Mary Edmiston, born 1915, Oklahoma.
#5-3-4-3-1-8.	Mabel L. Edmiston, born 1918, Oklahoma.
#5-3-4-3-1-9.	Thornton D. Edmiston, born 1919, Oklahoma.
#5-3-4-3-1-10.	Grady B. Edmiston, born 1921, Crawford County, Arkansas.
#5-3-4-3-1-11.	J. D. Edmiston, born 1924, Crawford County, Arkansas.
#5-3-4-3-1-12.	Duain L. Edmiston, born 1926, Adair County, Oklahoma.
#5-3-4-3-1-13.	Harley D. Edmiston, born 1929, Adair County, Oklahoma.

#4-3-4-3-2   OLGA BELLE EDMISTON

Olga Belle Edmiston, born July 9, 1873, Washington County, Arkansas, married John Evan Morrow March 15, 1891, Washington County, Arkansas. John was born September 11, 1867, Washington County, Arkansas. Shortly after their marriage Olga and John migrated to Tulare

County, California. In 1900 he was working odd jobs in Tulare County. In 1910 He was doing day labor in Los Angeles County, California. In 1920 He was a School Janitor in Los Angeles County, California. In 1930 he lists himself as a retired Farmer in Los Angeles County, California.

Children of Olga Belle Edmiston and John Evin Morrow

#5-3-4-3-2-1.	Calvin R. Morrow, born December 4, 1891, Tulare County, California.
#5-3-4-3-2-2.	Reta E. Morrow, born April 20, 1894, Tulare County, California.
#5-3-4-3-2-3.	Charles Edgar Morrow, born April 16, 1896, Tulare County, California.
#5-3-4-3-2-4.	Herman Earl Morrow, born January 3, 1906, Los Angeles County, California.
#5-3-4-3-2-5.	Elbert L. Morrow, born February 28, 1908, Los Angeles County, California.
#5-3-4-3-2-6.	Iola Morrow, born May 21, 1910, Los Angeles County, California.
#5-3-4-3-2-7.	George Lee Morrow, born November 11, 1912, Los Angeles County, California.

#4-3-4-3-4   THOMAS C. EDMISTON

Thomas C. Edmiston, born July, 1878, Washington County, Arkansas, married Mary Ellen Seay, February 16, 1899, Washington County, Arkansas. Mary was born May, 1880, Washington County, Arkansas. Thomas was a farmer. No record found after 1920 census.

Children of Thomas C. Edmiston and Mary Ellen Seay

#5-3-4-3-4-1.	Gail E. Edmiston, born 1904, Washington County, Arkansas.
#5-3-4-3-4-2.	Mary A. Edmiston, born 1918, Washington County, Arkansas.

#4-3-4-3-5   DAVID FRANK EDMISTON

David Frank Edmiston, born January 31, 1883, Washington County, Arkansas, married Bertha O. Freeman in 1904. Bertha was born March 30, 1886, Washington County, Arkansas and died April 21, 1971, Los Angeles County, California. In 1910 David was a Meat Cutter in a Meat Market. In 1920 he was a Farmer. David died September 11, 1957, Los Angeles County, California.

Children of David Frank Edmiston and Bertha O. Freeman

#5-3-4-3-5-1.	William L. Edmiston, born 1906, Los Angeles County, California.
#5-3-4-3-5-2.	William D. Edmiston, born 1908, Los Angeles County, California.
#5-3-4-3-5-3.	Alvin R. Edmiston, born 1913, Los Angeles County, California.

#4-3-4-3-6   HUGH CLEVLAND EDMISTON

Hugh Cleveland Edmiston, born December 19, 1884, Washington County, Arkansas, married Flora F. Glidewell in 1905. Flora was born February 8, 1886, Washington County, Arkansas and died November 9, 1972, San Bernardino County, California. In 1010, Hugh was a Farmer in Washington County, Arkansas. In 1920 he was a Railroad Section Hand in Iron County, Utah. In 1930 he was a Laborer in Street Construction in Los Angelus County, California. Hugh died November 22, 1967, Los Angeles County, California.

Children of Hugh Cleveland Edmiston and Flora F. Glidewell

#5-3-4-3-6-1.	Orval Edmiston, born 1908, Washington County, Arkansas.
#5-3-4-3-6-2.	Noah T. Edmiston, born January 13, 1909 Washington County, Arkansas.
#5-3-4-3-6-3.	David E. Edmiston, born 1913, Washington County, Arkansas.

#5-3-4-3-6-4.	Hugh C. Edmiston, born 1920, Iron County, Utah.
#5-3-4-3-6-5.	Vera L. Edmiston, born 1927, Iowa.

#4-3-4-3-7   RABURN EDMISTON

Raburn Edmiston, born July 2, 1887, Washington County, Arkansas, married Luvena K. Reed in 1906. Luvena was born January 27, 1883, Washington County, Arkansas and died April 11, 1971, Orange County, California. Raburn was a farmer in Washington County, Arkansas in1910 and 1920. In 1930 he was working in a Warehouse in Orange County, California. Raburn died September 11, 1961, Orange County, California.

Children of Raburn Edmiston and Luvena K. Reed

#5-3-4-3-7-1.	Adron J. Edmiston, born April 6, 1908, Washington County, Arkansas.
#5-3-4-3-7-2.	Verna Rae Edmiston, born June 2, 1910, Washington County, Arkansas.
#5-3-4-3-7-3.	Ola . E. Edmiston, born 1913, Washington County, Arkansas.
#5-3-4-3-7-4.	David S. Edmiston, born July 13, 1913, Washington County, Arkansas.

#4-3-4-9-2   BERT EUGENE LEACH

Bert Eugene Leach, born December 11, 1885, Washington County, Arkansas, married Anna Edmiston, 1907, Washington County, Arkansas. Anna was born, 1892, Washington County, Arkansas. Bert and Anna moved several times. In 1900 they were living in Los Angeles County, California. In 1910 they were in Washington County, Arkansas. In 1930 Bert was Grocery Merchant in Los Angeles County, California. Bert died July 26, 1944, Los Angeles County, California.

Children of Bert Eugene Leach and Anna Edmiston

#5-3-4-9-2-1.	Norris Edmund Leach, born August 4, 1913, Los Angeles County, California.
#5-3-4-9-2-2.	Cecil G. Leach, born, December 31, 1920, Los Angeles County, California.

#4-3-4-10-1   INA E. LEACH

Ina E. Leach, born June 24, 1884, Washington County, Arkansas, married John Floyd Carter, October 22, 1902. John was born March 22, 1877, Missouri and died July 12, 1957, Orange County, California. In 1920 census John was listed as Manager of a Grocery Store in Altus, Oklahoma. In 1930 census he was a Carpenter, Building Houses, in Orange County, California. Ina died August 2, 1971, Los Angeles County, California.

Children of Ina E. Leach and John Floyd Carter

#5-3-4-10-1-1.	John Cecil Carter, born October 4, 1903, Jackson County, Oklahoma.
#5-3-4-10-1-2.	Hansel E. Carter, born January 3, 1907, Jackson County, Oklahoma.

#4-3-4-10-2   LAURA IVA LEACH

Laura Iva Leach, born June, 1886, Washington County, Arkansas, married William Z. Mitchell January 24, 1905, Altus, Oklahoma. William was born in Arkansas in 1872. He was a Real Estate Broker. After marriage Laura and William moved to Louisiana, then back to Jackson County, Oklahoma, and finally on to Garfield County, Oklahoma.

Children of Laura Iva Leach and William Z. Mitchell

#5-3-4-10-2-1.	Ina L. Mitchell, born 1905, Louisiana.

#5-3-4-10-2-2.	William A. Mitchell, born 1907, Jackson County, Oklahoma.
#5-3-4-10-2-3.	James E. Mitchell, born 1909, Jackson County, Oklahoma.

#4-3-4-10-3   OLIVER RANDOLPH LEACH

Oliver Randolph Leach, born September, 1889, Washington County, Arkansas, married Ola M. in 1922. Ola was born in Arkansas, 1903. Oliver moved from Jackson County. Oklahoma, on to Oklahoma County. Then in 1830 he listed himself as a Grocery Merchant in Greene County, Missouri. He died in Grants Pass, Oregon.

Children of Oliver Randolph Leach and Ola M.

#5-3-4-10-3-1.	Desta Leach, born 1923, Oklahoma County, Oklahoma.
#5-3-4-10-3-2.	Helen R. Leach, born 1924, Oklahoma County, Oklahoma.
#5-3-4-10-3-3.	Margaret Leach, born 1926, Oklahoma County, Oklahoma.
#5-3-4-10-3-4.	Wanda M. Leach, born 1927, Oklahoma County, Oklahoma.

#4-3-4-10-4   EDNA GREER LEACH

Edna Greer Leach, born December 11, 1891, Ledger, Greer County, Oklahoma, married Bertram William Kisbey, 1927. Bertram was born February 22, 1890, Arizona and died May 14, 1959, Kern County, California. In the 1930 census, Bertram lists his employment as the Yardman for a Steam Railroad. Edna was the first white female child born in Greer County, Oklahoma. Edna died September 7, 1974, Fresno, California.

Child of Edna Greer Leach and Bertram William Kisbey

#5-3-4-10-4-1.   Richard C. Kisbey, born June, 1928, Kern
                        County, California.

#4-3-4-10-5   T. GREY LEACH

T. Grey Leach, born February, 1894 Altus, Jackson County, Oklahoma, married Bessie Vandella Sanders about 1916. Bessie was born October 26, 1898, Texas. According to 1920 census T. Grey was a Farmer. No record found of this family after 1920.

Child of T. Grey Leach and Bessie

#5-3-4-10-5-1.   Len Leach, born 1917, Jackson County,
                        Oklahoma.

#4-3-4-10-6   RENNA E. LEACH

Renna E. Leach, born August 4, 1896, Altus, Jackson County, Oklahoma, married Donald W. Webster, July 30, 1917, Michigan. Donald was born October 30, 1888, Wisconsin and died April 20, 1966, Oscoda, Michigan. Donald was an Independent Electrical Contractor. Renna died February 3, 1979, Ft Worth, Texas, and is buried in the Pinecrest Cemetery, Oscoda, Michigan.

Children of Renna E. Leach and Donald W. Webster

#5-3-4-10-6-1.   Stanley W. Webster, born 1918, Washtenaw
                        County, Michigan
#5-3-4-10-6-2.   Richard L. Webster, born 1920, Washtenaw
                        County, Michigan.
#5-3-4-10-6-3.   Patricia I. Webster, born 1922, Washtenaw
                        County, Michigan.
#5-3-4-10-6-4.   Barbara Jean Webster, born 1928, Washtenaw
                        County, Michigan.

#5-3-4-10-6-5.	Calvin A. Webster, born 1930, Washtenaw County, Michigan.
#5-3-4-10-6-6.	Robert Webster, born 1933, Washtenaw County, Michigan.
#5-3-4-10-6-7.	Nancy Webster, born 1934, Washtenaw County, Michigan.
#5-3-4-10-6-8.	Sue Marie Webster, born 1936, Washtenaw County, Michigan.

#4-3-4-10-7   ERNEST FRANKLIN LEACH

Ernest Franklin Leach, born January 14, 1898, Altus, Jackson County, Oklahoma, married Sadie Burns, 1920. Sadie was born in Missouri, December 21, 1898, and died in Los Angeles County, California, February 5, 1989. Ernest lists himself in the 1930 census as a Grocery and Meat Merchant. Earnest died November 1, 1993, Los Angeles County, California.

Children of Ernest Franklin Leach and Sadie Burns

| #5-3-4-10-7-1. | Ella L. Leach, born 1922, Jackson County, Oklahoma. |
| #5-3-4-10-7-2. | Catherine E. Leach, born Los Angeles County, California. |

#4-3-5-1-1   JOHN EVAN MORROW

John Evan Morrow, born September 11, 1867, Washington County, Arkansas, married Olga Belle Edmiston, #4-3-4-3-2. (Information on children on this marriage can be found under the following number, above #4-3-4-3-2).

#4-3-5-1-2   LILLIE ELMA MORROW

Lillie Elma Morrow, born September 10, 1869, Washington County, Arkansas, married Philip L. Erwin about 1900. Philip was born September 25, 1868, Missouri. Philip was a Contract Carpenter. Lillie died March 3, 1943, Los Angeles, California. Philip died June 15, 1944, Los Angeles, California.

Children of Lillie Elma Morrow and Phillip L. Erwin

#5-3-5-1-2-1.	Edith R. Erwin, born 1902, Arizona.
#5-3-5-1-2-2.	Howard M. Erwin, born March 19, 1906, Oregon.
#5-3-5-1-2-3.	Charlotte E. Erwin, born 1911, California.

#4-3-5-1-4   HATTIE TULA MORROW

Hattie Tule Morrow, born July 4, 1871, Washington County, Arkansas, married Robert E. Halstead about 1895. Robert was born January, 1874, California. Robert was employed as a General Carpenter. Hattie died June 14, 1942, Fresno County, California.

Children of Hattie Tule Morrow and Robert E. Halstead

#5-3-5-1-4-1.	Grant R. Halstead, born December 5, 1896, Fresno County, California.
#5-3-5-1-4-2.	Violet Halstead, born 1901, California.
#5-3-5-1-4-3.	Ruth Halstead, born April 25, 1907, Los Angeles County, California.

#4-3-5-1-8   PET MORROW

Pet Morrow, born February, 1884, Washington County, Arkansas, married Eichstaedt. Eichstaedt was born in Arkansas. The 1910, Los Angeles County, California, census lists Pet as a widow, no employment, own income.

Child of Pet Morrow and Eichstaedt

#5-3-5-1-8-1.   Hellen C. Eichstaedt, born 1905, Los Angeles County, California.

#4-3-5-2-1   MARY TEMPERANCE BUTLER

Mary Temperance Butler, born November, 1872, Guadalupe County, Texas, married Edward Emory Rogers in 1895. Edward was born April, 1874 in Texas and died March 6, 1947, Medina County, Texas. According census reports Edward was a lifetime farmer.

Children of Mary Temperance Butler and Edward Emory Rogers

#5-3-5-2-1-1.   Bailey G. Rogers, born September, 1896, Guadalupe County, Texas
#5-3-5-2-1-2.   Emory Grayford Rogers, born 1906, Medina County, Texas.

#4-3-5-2-2   FRED WALKER BUTLER

Fred Walker Butler, born October 10, 1881, Guadalupe County, Texas, married Delia. Delia was born August 13, 1886, Texas and died March 9, 1890, Hays County, Texas. According to 1920 Medina County, Texas census Fred was a farmer.

Children of Fred Walker Butler and Delia

#5-3-5-2-2-1.   Annie Florence Butler, born 1907, Medina County, Texas.
#5-3-5-2-2-2.   Lois Butler, born 1910, Medina County, Texas.
#5-3-5-2-2-3.   Fred Walker Butler, Jr., born April 1, 1914, Hays County, Texas.

#4-3-5-4-1   LILBURN WINSTON WALKER

Lilburn Winston Walker, born April 28, 1884, Liberty Hill, Williamson County, Texas, married Willie Aline Gibbson, February 26, 1923, Ft. Stockton, Texas. Willie was born February 26, 1904, Arkansas and died January 3, 1991 Reno, Nevada. Lilburn died August 29, 1946, Austin, Travis County, Texas.

Children of Lilburn Winston Walker and Willie Aline Gibbson

#5-3-5-4-1-1.	Bleakley Ashley Walker, born June 3, 1924, Texas.
#5-3-5-4-1-2.	Willie Lilburn Walker, born August 27, 1925, Texas.
#5-3-5-4-1-3.	Verena Valerie Walker, born September 9, 1926, Jones County, Texas.
#5-3-5-4-1-4.	Horace Glen Walker, born July 23, 1928, Lubbock, Texas.

#4-3-5-4-2   WILBURN WILSON WALKER

Wilburn Wilson Walker, born November 25, 1884, Williamson County, Texas married Beatrice Lenora Smith July 21, 1913, Williamson County, Texas. Beatrice was born March 13, 1887, Williamson County, Texas and died February 7, 1951, Travis County, Texas. According to 1920 Williamson County, Texas census, Wilburn was a carpenter. Wilburn died June 17, 1952, Travis County, Texas.

Children of Wilburn Wilson Walker and Beatrice Lenora Smith

#5-3-5-4-2-1.	Mildred Cloris Walker, born June 15, 1915, Williamson County, Texas. Mildred died May 12, 1918, Williamson County, Texas.
#5-3-5-4-2-2.	Edward Wilburn Walker, born July 24, 1916, Williamson County, Texas.
#5-3-5-4-2-3.	Mary Ophilia Walker, born January 6, 1919, Williamson County, Texas.

#5-3-5-4-2-4.	Vivian Lucille Walker, born July 22, 1920, Williamson County, Texas.
#5-3-5-4-2-5.	Verna Gene Walker, born October 1, 1925, Texas.

#4-3-5-4-3 CLORIS VIRGINIA WALKER

Cloris Virginia Walker, born September 22, 1888, Williamson County, Texas, married Wiley Jackson Williams, March 20, 1920, Liberty Hill, Williamson County, Texas. Wiley was born March 12, 1892, Franklin, Robertson County, Texas and died September 12, 1968, Austin, Travis County, Texas. Cloris died August 10, 1970, Lampasas County, Texas.

Children of Cloris Virginia Walker and Wiley Jackson Williams

#5-3-5-4-3-1.	Ophelia Virginia Williams, born August 10, 1921, Williamson County, Texas. Ophelia died August 21, 1921, Williamson County, Texas.
#5-3-5-4-3-2.	James Walter Williams, born July 21, 1922, Williamson County, Texas.

#4-3-5-5-1 MARCUS E. WALKER

Marcus E. Walker, born March 23, 1895, Uvalde County, Texas, married Tempie Carter, 1923. Tempe was born May 2, 1907, Zavala County, Texas and died December 11, 1968, Uvalde County, Texas. Marcus was a clerk for the U. S. Post Office. Marcus died May 19, 1968, Uvalde County, Texas.

Children of Marcus E. Walker and Tempie Carter

#5-3-5-5-1-1.	Edward J. Walker, born 1925, Uvalde County, Texas.
#5-3-5-5-1-2.	Elizabeth N. Walker, born 1926, Uvalde County, Texas.

#5-3-5-5-1-3.	Sam Allen Walker, born November 3, 1928, Uvalde County, Texas
#5-3-5-5-1-4.	Jack Paul Walker, born January 7, 1932, Uvalde County, Texas.
#5-3-5-5-1-5.	Joe Ann Walker, born December 27, 1932, Uvalde County, Texas.

#4-3-5-5-2   HAROLD EVERETT WALKER

Harold Everett Walker, born March, 1895, Uvalde County, Texas, married Louise Marie Clark. Harold served in the United Stated Army as a Lieutenant from 1918 until 1935. He died in August 1979 and is buried in the National Cemetery at San Antonio, Texas. His Children came late in life.

Children of Harold Everett Walker and Louise Marie Clark

#5-3-5-5-2-1.	Carolyn Marie Walker, born December 11, 1948, Grayson County, Texas.
#5-3-5-5-2-2.	Harold Neal Walker, born January 1, 1951, Dallas County, Texas.
#5-3-5-5-2-3.	Katherine Jean Walker, born January 10, 1952, Dallas County, Texas.
#5-3-5-5-2-4.	Ronald Lynn Walker, born January 22, 1957, Dallas County, Texas.

#4-3-5-6-1   JAMES EDWIN DOCKERY

James Edwin Dockery, born May, 1980, Lavaca County, Texas, married Maude L. Parsons, 1903. Maude was born 1882 in Texas and died April 11, 1963, Lamar County, Texas. James and Maude moved from Uvalde county to Bexar County after 1911 and remained there the rest of their lives. James was a Carpenter by Profession. James died April 10, 1962, Bexar County, Texas.

#5-3-5-6-1-1.	James Willis Dockery, born 1904, Uvalde County, Texas.
#5-3-5-6-1-2.	Bernece L. Dockery, born 1906, Uvalde County, Texas, died before the 1920 census.
#5-3-5-6-1-3.	Alice L. Dockery, born 1908, Uvalde County, Texas.
#5-3-5-6-1-4.	Alvin Dockery, born 1911, Uvalde County, Texas.

#4-3-6-2-3   MURAH ELLEN LEACH

Murah Ellen Leach, born March 31, 1889, Crawford County, Arkansas, married Tom Sands November 29, 1911, Charleston, Mississippi County, Missouri. Tom was born in Tennessee March 7, 1885, and died in 1962, Charleston, Mississippi County, Missouri. Tom was a farmer. Murah died April 15, 1976, Charleston, Mississippi County, Missouri. Both Tom and Murah are buried in the Oak Grove Cemetery.

Children of Murah Ellen Leach and Tom Sands

#5-3-6-2-3-1.	George H. Sands, born December 21, 1912, Charleston, Mississippi County, Missouri.
#5-3-6-2-3-2.	Robert L. Sands, born May 26, 1914, Charleston, Mississippi County, Missouri, died February 27, 1925, Scott County, Missouri.
#5-3-6-2-3-3.	Roy Sands, born October 18, 1915, Charleston, Mississippi County, Missouri, died December 7, 1971, (never married).
#5-3-6-2-3-4.	Paul W. Sands, born January 16, 1917, Charleston, Mississippi County, Missouri, died December 7, 1932, Scott County, Missouri.
#5-3-6-2-3-5.	Alberta Sands, born April, 1918, Charleston, Mississippi County, Missouri.

#5-3-6-2-3-6.	Hattie Sands, born December 7, 1918, Charleston, Mississippi County, Missouri, died December 17, 1930, Scott County, Missouri.
#5-3-6-2-3-7.	Herbert Marshal "Jake" Sands, born January 8, 1922, Charleston, Mississippi County, Missouri.
#5-3-6-2-3-8.	Minnie Pearl Sands, born May 8, 1927, Charleston, Mississippi County, Missouri.
#5-3-6-2-3-9.	Regena Ellen Sands, June 30, 1930, Scott County, Missouri.

#5-3-6-2-7 HENRY CLARENCE LEACH

Henry Clarence Leach, born December 23, 1895, Crawford County, Arkansas, married Ola Katherine Kirk, May 15, 1921, Washington County, Arkansas. Ola was born September 7, 1896, Washington County, Arkansas and died January 8, 1984, Washington County, Arkansas. Clarence was a Farmer and highly intelligent man, who really never put his intelligence to work for what most would call the right purposes. He had a powerful punch with his right hand, of which many could and many have testified. He was a good provider to his family and father to his children. For my part, a better uncle could not have been found. Clarence died in Washington County, Arkansas December 10, 1965, both he and Ola are buried in the Ganderville Cemetery, Washington County, Arkansas.

Children of Henry Clarence Leach and Ola Katherine Kirk

#5-3-6-2-7-1.	Helen Maxine Leach, born September 26, 1922, Washington County, Arkansas.
#5-3-6-2-7-2.	William Paul "Bill" Leach, born February 14, 1925, Washington County, Arkansas.
#5-3-6-2-7-3.	Anna Phyllis Leach, born February 6, 1927, Washington County, Arkansas.
#5-3-6-2-7-4.	Hattie Lillus Leach, born February 6, 1927, Washington County, Arkansas.
#5-3-6-2-7-5.	Henry Harrison "Jack" Leach, born April 19, 1928, Washington County, Arkansas.

#5-3-6-2-7-6.	John Ralph Leach, born December 5, 1933, Washington County, Arkansas.
#5-3-6-2-7-7.	George Preston Leach, born June 27, 1935, Washington County, Arkansas.

#4-3-6-2-8   SARAH EDNA LEACH

Sarah Edna Leach, born June, 1862 Washington County, Arkansas, married Charles Webb Hanes March 16, 1921, Mississippi County, Missouri. Charles was born August 7, 1889, in Tennessee and died December 8, 1961, Mississippi County, Missouri. In the 1930 Mississippi County, Missouri census, Charles was a WW 1 Pensioner. Edna died January 15, 1983, Charleston, Mississippi County, Missouri. Both Edna and Charles are buried in the Oak Grove Cemetery, Mississippi County, Missouri.

Children of Sarah Edna Leach and Charles Webb Hanes

#5-3-6-2-8-1.	Charles Webb Hanes, Jr., born January 20, 1923, Charleston, Mississippi County, Missouri.
#5-3-6-2-8-2.	Maxine Hanes, born August 5, 1924, Charleston, Mississippi County, Missouri.
#5-3-6-2-8-3.	Lula Mae Hanes, born August 26, 1926, Charleston, Mississippi County, Missouri.

#4-3-6-2-9   MARY ELIZABETH "LIZZIE" LEACH

Mary Elizabeth "Lizzie" Leach born September 24, 1899, Crawford County, Arkansas, married Robert Edward Biggs February 13, 1921, Washington County, Arkansas. Robert was born July 11, 1900, Washington County, Arkansas. Robert farmed and worked at various jobs. During WW11 he moved his wife and two younger children to California and worked in Defense Manufacturing Plants. Robert was a diabetic and went into a diabetic coma and died December 13, 1946, Prairie Grove, Washington County, Arkansas. Lizzie died May 23, 1992,

Washington County, Arkansas. Both Robert and Lizzie are buried in the Prairie Grove Cemetery, Prairie Grove, Arkansas.

Children of Mary Elizabeth "Lizzie" Leach and Robert Edward Biggs

#5-3-6-2-9-1.	Ethel E. Biggs, born January 11, 1922, Washington County, Arkansas.
#5-3-6-2-9-2.	James Albert "Buster" Biggs, born February 24, 1924, Washington County, Arkansas.
#5-3-6-2-9-3.	Louise Biggs, born December 9, 1932, Washington County, Arkansas.
#5-3-6-2-9-4.	George Ray Biggs, born December 31, 1934, Washington County, Arkansas.

#4-3-6-2-10   HATTIE EMMA LEACH

Hattie Emma Leach Born July 14, 1901, Washington County, Arkansas, married Izzie C. Nelson. Little is known about Izzie, he was a ranking official in the union in Galveston, Texas, in the 1920's. Emma was a Telephone Operator in Galveston, Texas, and later in San Francisco, California, where she remained employed until her retirement. Emma died August 5, 1982, Burlingame, San Mateo, California. She is buried in the Scott Cemetery, Washington County, Arkansas.

Child of Hattie Emma Leach

#5-3-6-2-10-1.	Marshall Webb Leach, born April1, 1924, Memphis, Shelby County, Tennessee.

#4-3-6-2-11   GEORGE HARRISON LEACH

George Harrison Leach, born April 13, 1903, Washington County, Arkansas, married Bertha Belle Allen, January 29, 1933, Washington County, Arkansas. Bertha was born November 9, 1914, Odell, Crawford County, Arkansas and died April 25, 1986, Stilwell, Oklahoma. Harrison was educated much like his siblings at the Fly Creek School,

Washington County, Arkansas. He ran away from home at 16 years and joined the army, was a WW1 Veteran and a charter member of the Boiler Makers Union in Galveston, Texas. One of Harrison's most infamous acts was a gun fight he had with Craig Fulkerson a/k/a, Banjo Billy, Craig had previously had a fight with Harrison's older brother, Clarence. Clarence had won the fight but Craig later shot at him. On the night of August 9, 1928, Harrison rode his horse to Cane Hill, Arkansas, to obtain information about Cumberland Law School in Tennessee. On the way there Craig's dogs barked at him and he fired shots at them. On the way home later that night he was warned by Harley Rinehart, who had earlier traveled the road he was about to take, that Craig was waiting behind a big white oak tree to ambush him, this was near where Craig lived. It was a bright moon light night. When Harrison approached Craig jumped out in front of him and yelled "now G-D—I have you, you SOB. Craig had a pistol in his right hand. Harrison shot first, someone shot back and kept shooting. Harison kept shooting as Craig approached him with the pistol in his right hand yelling don't shoot G-D—it you have killed me. Harrison thought Craig had been shooting at him all this time but instead it had been a second gunman on the hill. Harrison's first shot had shot Craig's thumb off and Craig had been unable to pull the hammer back on his pistol after the first shot. Craig was shot five times in the stomach. Harrison was shot from the side under his horse through his left leg, with the bullet lodging in his right knee. William Arnold "Arn" Walker, who is thought to have been the shooter on the hill, committed suicide early the next morning. Both Harrison and Craig recovered. Criminal charges were filed against both Craig and Harrison. Charges were dismissed against Craig if he would leave the State of Arkansas and never return. He moved to his sisters in Oregon, where he died February 1, 1937, Umatilla County, Oregon. The charges against Harrison were dismissed. In later years Harrison was highly respected. He was a farmer, Operated canning plants in Washington County, Arkansas, Stilwell, Oklahoma and Plainview Texas. Harrison died May 27, 1994, at Stilwell, Oklahoma. Both he and Bertha are buried in the Stilwell Cemetery, Stilwell, Oklahoma.

#5-3-6-2-11-1.	Reva Mae Leach, born January 1, 1934, Washington County, Arkansas.
#5-3-6-2-11-2.	Frances Leach, born January 30, 1936, Washington County, Arkansas.
#5-3-6-2-11-3.	George Harrison Leach ll, born October 10, 1938, Washington County, Arkansas.

#4-3-6-2-13   MINA MAE LEACH

Mina Mae Leach, born November 9, 1906, Washington County, Arkansas, married Walter Johnson Spratt December 24, 1927 Washington County, Arkansas. Walter was born at Rosebud, Washington County, Arkansas and died February 8, 1995, Gassville, Baxter County, Arkansas. Walter worked for Standard Oil and retired after many years. He was the best fisherman I ever knew. After retirement he operated a Motel and Boat Dock near Mountain Home, Arkansas. Mina died August 4, 1991, at Gassville, Baxter County, Arkansas. Both she and Walter are buried at Mountain Home, Arkansas.

Children of Mina Mae Leach and Walter Johnson Spratt

#5-3-6-2-13-1.	Alfred Andrew Spratt, born October 30, 1928, Washington County, Arkansas.
#5-3-6-2-13-2.	Gene Derald Spratt, born August 4, 1930, Drumright, Oklahoma
#5-3-6-2-13-3.	Eugene Jerald Spratt, born August 4, 1930, Drumright, Oklahoma.
#5-3-6-2-13-4.	William Walter Spratt, born January 4, 1933, Washington County, Arkansas.

#4-3-6-4-1   ELIZA JOSEPHINE LEACH

Eliza Josephine Leach, born December 31, 1883, Crawford County, Arkamsas, married John T. Cavin July 22, 1912, Washington County,

Arkansas. John was born October 10, 1883, Washington County, Arkansas. Eliza died about April 10, 1976, Muskogee County, Oklahoma.

Children of Eliza Josephine Leach and John T. Cavin

#5-3-6-4-1-1.   Verna Bell Cavin, born October 9, 1914, Cherokee County, Oklahoma.
#5-3-6-4-1-2.   Hazel Mae Cavin, born November 13, 1919, Tulsa County, Oklahoma.
#5-3-6-4-1-3.   Richard E. Cavin, born May 20, 1921, Tulsa County, Oklahoma.

#4-3-7-1-1   MARY MARGIE LEACH

Mary Margie Leach, born July 21, 1900, Logan, Benton County, Arkansas, married Andrew Mc Clinton Guthrey June 3, 1925, Benton County, Arkansas. Andy was born November 5, 1887, Logan, Benton County, Arkansas and died October 15, 1955, Siloam Springs, Arkansas. Both Mary and Andrew were School Teachers. Mary died December 9, 1996, Siloam Springs, Benton County, Arkansas.

Children of Mary Margie Leach and Andrew Mc Clinton Guthrey

#5-3-7-1-1-1.   Betty Sue Guthrey, born May 24, 1926, Benton County, Arkansas, died May 24, 1926, Benton County, Arkansas.
#5-3-7-1-1-2.   Bobby Gene Guthrey, born November 13, 1927, Benton County, Arkansas.
#5-3-7-1-1-3.   Patricia Louise Guthrey, born December 3, 1932, Benton County, Arkansas.
#5-3-7-1-1-4.   Mary Ruth Guthrey, born March 29, 1941 Benton County, Arkansas.

#4-3-7-1-2   HUBERT BELLA LEACH

Hubert Bella Leach, born December 1, 1901, Weatherford, Oklahoma, married Mildred Koranck. In the 1930 Chicago, Cook County census Hubert was a Loborer working in a Warehouse. Hubert died in Madisonville, Monroe County, Tennessee.

Child of Hubert Bela Leach and Mildred Koranck

#5-3-7-1-2-1.   Paul Bela Leach, born April 28, 1954, Oak Park, Illinois.

#4-3-7-1-3   ROBERT LAFAYETTE LEACH

Robert LaFayette Leach, born April 20, 1904, Benton County, Arkansas, married Lucy Belle Sisco June 19, 1928, Washington County, Arkansas. Lucy was born November 24, 1914, Arkansas and died May 11, 1994, Springdale, Arkansas. According to 1930, Chicago, Cook County, Illinois census Robert was a Clerk in a Drug Store. Since census records after 1930 have not been made public there is no record of where Robert and Lucy's children were born. Robert died July 22, 1984, at Springdale, Arkansas. Both Robert and Lucy are buried in the Friendship Cemetery, Springdale, Arkansas.

Children of Robert LaFayette Leach and Lucy Belle Sisco

#5-3-7-1-3-1.   Lu Ann Leach.
#5-3-7-1-3-2.   James Leach.

#4-3-7-1-4   SAMUEL HARRISON LEACH

Samuel Harrison Leach, born July 24, 1906, Benton County, Arkansas, married Mariam Schoenfeld, August 17, 1946, Chicago Illinois. No information on Mariam is known. Samuel died October 3, 1990, Mc Allen, Texas.

Children of Samuel Harrison Leach and Mariam Schoenfeld

#5-3-7-1-4-1.   David Charles Leach, born July 9, 1947.
#5-3-7-1-4-2.   Margaret Elizabeth Leach, born May 3, 1949.
#5-3-7-1-4-3.   Debra Sue Leach, born August 31, 1954.
#5-3-7-1-4-4.   Melody Joy Leach, born March 24, 1956.

#4-3-7-1-5   IRA LEACH

Ira Leach, born January 8, 1914, Benton County, Arkansas, married LaVerne Lucille Griggs, July 22, 1936, Benton County, Arkansas. LaVerne was born September 14, 1916, Elm Springs, Arkansas. Ira, like his father, was a farmer. Ira died June 7, 1997 Owasso, Oklahoma.

Children of Ira Leach and LaVerne Lucille Griggs

#5-3-7-1-5-1.   Richard Alan Leach, born May 19, 1939, Fayetteville, Arkansas.
#5-3-7-1-5-2.   Ronald Eugene Leach, born December 25, 1940, Logan, Benton County, Arkansas.
#5-3-7-1-5-3.   Judith Ann Leach, born October 2, 1942, Logan, Benton County, Arkansas.
#5-3-7-1-5-4.   Linda Kay Leach, born February 26, 1945, Logan, Benton County, Arkansas.

#4-3-7-2-1   ELMER MONROE LEACH

Elmer Monroe Leach, born 24 March 1894, Benton County, Arkansas, married Minty R. Robinson, 23 December 1915, Washington County, Arkansas. Minty was born 13 June, 1896, Washington County, Arkansas and died in December 1971 while a resident of Siloam Springs, Benton County, Arkansas. In the 1930 Benton County, Arkansas census Elmer stated he was a Salesman of Ford Cars. Elmer died 13 February 1977, Tulare County, California.

Children of Elmer Monroe Leach and Minty R. Robinson

#5-3-7-2-1-1.	Douglas A. Leach, born 1917, Benton County, Arkansas.
#5-3-7-2-1-2.	Silva B. Leach, born 1920, Benton County, Arkansas.
#5-3-7-2-1-3.	Raymond D. K. Leach, born 1922, Benton County, Arkansas.
#5-3-7-2-1-4.	Dallas E. Leach, born 8 June 1923, Benton County, Arkansas.

#4-3-7-2-3   NATHAN JESSE LEACH

Nathan Jesse Leach, born 19 November 1899, Benton County, Arkansas, married Velma Alice Clark, 5 January 1923, Benton County, Arkansas. Velma was born 16 December 1901 in Kansas and died January 1984, Benton County, Arkansas. According to the 1930, Nuckolls County, Nebraska census, Nathan was a Laborer in a Cement Plant.

Nathan died in March of 1977 in Benton County, Arkansas.

Child of Nathan Jesse Leach and Velma Alice Clark

#5-3-7-2-3-1.	Maurene F. Leach, born 1926 Benton County, Arkansas.

#4-3-7-4-1   LENA MAE LEACH

Lena Mae Leach born, 27 April 1903, Benton County, Arkansas, married Ray Story in 1922. Ray was born in Arkansas 1n 1902. According to 1930, Anaheim, Orange County, California, census Ray was a Rotary Man on a Oil Rig. Lena died 9 January 1983, Orange County, California.

#5-3-7-4-1-1.   Charles R. Story, born 6 February 1925, Orange County, California, Charles died 26 May 1994, Orange County, California.

#5-3-7-4-1-2.   Gordon H. Story, born 1929, Orange County, California.

#4-3-7-5-2   EVA VIOLA CARTER

Eva Viola Carter, born 5 January 1909, Benton County, Arkansas, married Jim Rich, 27 December 1927, Stilwell, Adair County, Oklahoma. Jim was born 20 November 1906 Mountain Home, Arkansas, and died 1 July 1992, Stilwell, Adair County, Oklahoma. Jim farmed and was an Automobile Mechanic. Eva died in November 1967, resulting from an automobile accident in Vega, Texas. Both Eva and Jim are buried in the Stilwell Cemetery, Stilwell, Oklahoma.

Children of Eva Viola Carter and Jim Rich

#5-3-7-5-2-1.   Jerald Rich, born 16 November 1928, Mulvane, Sumner County, Kansas.

#5-3-7-5-2-2.   Coleen Rich, born 9 August 1930, Adair County, Oklahoma.

#5-3-7-5-2-3.   Wanda Jean Rich, born 18 September 1932, Adair County, Oklahoma.

#5-3-7-5-2-4.   Harold Wesley Rich, born 26 December 1934, Adair County, Oklahoma.

#5-3-7-5-2-5.   Glenda Rose Rich, born 26 January 1940, Adair County, Oklahoma.

#5-3-7-5-2-6.   Burl Rich, born 22 November 1938, Adair County, Oklahoma.

#5-3-7-5-2-7.   Jimmie Dale Rich, born 31 January 1943, Adair County, Oklahoma.

#4-3-7-5-3   JOY VIOLA CARTER

Joy Viola Carter, born 13 November 1911, Benton County, Arkansas, married William Arnold McKay, 8 September 1933, Stilwell, Adair County, Oklahoma. William was listed in the 1920 and 1930 census as an American Indian. He was living in the Wauhillau Community, Adair County, Oklahoma. William died 17 August 1964, Yakima County, Washington.

Children of Joy Viola Carter and William Arnold McKay

#5-3-7-5-3-1.	Jerry Dennis McKay, born 1 May 1935, Stilwell, Adair County, Oklahoma.
#5-3-7-5-3-2.	Baby Girl McKay.
#5-3-7-5-3-3.	Leah Karen McKay, born 5 September 1941, Sunnyside, Yakima County, Washington.
#5-3-7-5-3-4.	Sherry Jean McKay, born December 1942, Sunnyside, Yakima County, Washington.

#4-3-7-5-4   AMZIE NATHAN CARTER

Amzie Nathan Carter, born 5 February 1914, Benton County, Arkansas, married Constance Quiroz, 15 February 1953. Constance was born 19 September 1910, in Mexico and died 28 April 1992, Grants Pass, Josephine County, Oregon. The children of Amzie and Constance are adopted. Amzie died 16 February 2002, Williams, Josephine County, Oregon.

Children of Amzie Nathan Carter and Constance Quiroz

#5-3-7-5-4-1.	Richard Arthur Carter, born 11 December 1954, Bremerhaven, Germany.
#5-3-7-5-4-2.	Linda Marie Carter, born 24 September 1956, Bremerhaven, Germany.

#4-3-7-5-5   ORIN WILLIAM CARTER

Orin William Carter, born 5 March 1916, Cherokee County, Oklahoma, married Frances Jeanette Brehm, 30 June 1950, Reno, Washoe County, Nevada. Frances was born 31 December 1923, Bostwick, Nuckolls County, Nebraska. Orin died in March 1998 at Grants Pass, Josephine County, Oregon.

Children of Orin William Carter and Frances Jeanette Brehm

#5-3-7-5-5-1.   Brian Orin Carter, born 25 February 1962, Concord, Contra Costa County, California.

#5-3-7-5-5-2.   Patricia Sue Carter, born 13 July 1964, Grants Pass, Josephine County, Oregon.

#4-3-7-5-6   JOHN WESLEY CARTER

John Wesley Carter, born 19 February 1918, Cherokee County, Oklahoma, married Mable Frances McDonald, 3 July 1941, Klamath Falls, Oregon. Mable was born 3 August 1921, Guymon, Texas County, Oklahoma and died 8 March 1994, Richland, Benton County, Arkansas.

Children of John Wesley Carter and Mable Frances McDonald

#5-3-7-5-6-1.   Levah May Carter, born 1 August 1942, Klamath Falls, Oregon.

#5-3-7-5-6-2.   Bonnie Jo Carter, born 16 July 1946, Klamath Falls, Oregon.

#4-3-7-5-7   LETHA NAOMI CARTER

Letha Naomi Carter, born 22 July 1920, Cherokee County, Oklahoma, married Charles Evan Hughes McKay, 15 March 1939. Charles was born 7 July 1917 at Stilwell, Adair County, Oklahoma, and died 5 December 1976, Klickitat, Oregon.

Children of Letha Naomi Carter and Charles Evan Hugher McKay

#5-3-7-5-7-1. Stanley Allen McKay, born 23 July 1942, Sunnyside, Yakima County, Washington.

#5-3-7-5-7-2. Gary Stephen McKay, born 3 February 1944, Seattle, King County, Washington.

#5-3-7-5-7-3. Anita Carol McKay, born 13 July 1945, Seattle, King County, Washington.

#5-3-7-5-7-4. Barbara Sue McKay, born 6 March 1947, Sunnyside, Yakima County, Washington.

#5-3-7-5-7-5. Daryl Evan McKay, born 18 January 1950, Sunnyside, Yakima County, Washington.

#5-3-7-5-7-6. Kiven Lee McKay, born 3 March 1961, Sunnyside, Yakima County, Washington.

#4-3-9-2-5   SARAH ESTER GRAY

Sarah Ester Gray, born 19 October 1917, Benton County, Arkansas, married Grady James Holmes, 10 June 1940, Selma, Fresno County, California. James was born 12 June 1912, Waldron, Scott County, Arkansas and died 3 January 1993, Fresno, Fresno County, California. Sarah died 16 October 1985 at Fresno, Fresno County, California.

Children of Sarah Ester Gray and Grady James Holmes

#5-3-9-2-5-1. Oleta Juanice Holmes, born 24 December 1940, Fresno County, California.

#5-3-9-2-5-2. Virginia Darlene Holmes, born 2 May 1942, Reedley, Fresno County, California.

#5-3-9-2-5-3. Gary Wayne Holmes, born 18 March 1944, Reedley, Fresno County, California, died 23 May 1944.

#5-3-9-2-5-4. Gerrell Dwight Holmes, born 13 March 1945, Reedley, Fresno County, California.

#5-3-9-2-5-5. James Carol Holmes, born 25 April 1946, Fresno, Fresno County, California.

#5-3-9-2-5-6.   Ilona Gail Holmes, born 18 October 1947, Fresno, Fresno County, California.

#5-3-9-2-5-7.   Douglas Wade Holmes, born 28 March 1949, Fresno, Fresno County, California.

#5-3-9-2-5-8.   Gloria Nadine Holmes, born 4 January 1951, Fresno, Fresno County, California.

#5-3-9-2-5-9.   Danny Erwin Holmes, born 26 May 1952, Fresno, Fresno County, California.

#5-3-9-2-5-10.   Esteven Ray Holmes, born 22 June 1956, Fresno, Fresno County, California.

#4-3-9-2-6   JASON RAY GRAY

Jason Ray Gray, born 25 January 1922, Benton County, Arkansas, married Virginia B. Franco, 26 October 1949 at Sparks, Nevada., Virginia was born 4 July 1924 and died 16 March 1994 at Oakland, Alameda County, California. Jason was an Automobile Mechanic. He died 15 May 2001, Oakland, Alameda County, California.

Child of Jason Ray Gray and Virginia B. Franco

#5-3-9-2-6-1.   Robert Jason Grey.

#4-3-9-3-1   OLIVE MARRS

Olive Marrs born, 4 January 1911, Benton County, Arkansas, married Wallace. Olive was married and living with her father in the 1930, California census. She died 11 November 1992 in San Diego County, California.

Child of Olive Marrs and Wallace

#5-3-9-3-1-1.   Lonnie Arlan Marrs, born 7 January 1930, Imperial County, California.

#4-3-11-1-1   ORIEN S. WOODS

Orien S. Woods, born 27 April 1898, Ardmore, Carter County, Oklahoma, married Myrtle W. in 1916. Myrtle was born in Texas in 1900. In the 1920 Grayson County, Texas census Orien was working for the M. K. & T Railroad. In the 1930 Dallas County, Texas census he was an automobile salesman. Orien died 30 March 1970 in Dallas County, Texas.

Children of Orien S. Woods and Myrtle S.

#5-3-11-1-1-1.   Dorothy E. Woods, born 1917, Grayson County, Texas.
#5-3-11-1-1-2.   Cecillie A. Woods, born 1919, Grayson County, Texas.
#5-3-11-1-1-3.   Warren V. Woods, born 1920, Grayson County, Texas.

#4-3-12-1-1   R. MCCOY SITTON

R. McCoy Sitton, born 14 February 1905, Benton County, Arkansas, married Laura Brandon in 1927. Laura was born in Rector Arkansas in 1912. In the 1930 census R. McCoy was farming in Benton County, Arkansas. He later obtained his Social Security Card in California.

Children of R. McCoy Sitton and Laura Brandon

#5-3-12-1-1-1.   Betty Joe Sitton, born June 1928, Benton County, Arkansas.
#5-3-12-1-1-2.   Donald D. Sitton, born 19 June 1931, Benton County, Atkansas, married Virginia Thompson.

#4-4-1-1-1   STELLA A. ALLEN

Stella A. Allen, born in July 1871 in Adams County, Illinois, married Ernest J. Grubb, 7 January 1892, Adams County, Illinois. Ernest was born October 1870 in Illinois. In the 1900 Adams County, Illinois census Ernest was a Blacksmith. In the 1910 census he was an Undertaker. Stella died between 1810 and 1820 census.

Children of Stella A. Allen and Ernest J. Grubb

#5-4-1-1-1-1.	Alta E. Grubb, born December 1892, Adams County, Illinois.
#5-4-1-1-1-2.	Frances L. Grubb, born April 1895, Adams County, Illinois.
#5-4-1-1-1-3.	Clara A. Grubb, born February 1899, Adams County, Illinois.

#4-4-1-1-3   LAWRENCE E. ALLEN

Lawrence E. Allen, born September1875, Adams County, Illinois, married Anna B. Henning, 22 February 1899, Adams County, Illinois. Anna was born in Adams County, Illinois April 1877. In 1900 Adams County, Illinois, census Lawrence was a Farmer. In 1810 and 1820 census he ran a Grocery Store.

Children of Lawrence E. Allen and Anna B. Henning

#5-4-1-1-3-1.	Alfred L. Allen, born 1902 in Adams County, Illinois.
#5-4-1-1-3-2.	Elva M. Allen, born 1903 in Adams County, Illinois.

#4-4-1-3-2   GEORGE A. LIERLE

George A. Lierle, born 21 November 1877 Adams County, Illinois, first married Susana. Susana was born in Illinois in 1878. In 1911 George married Laura. Laura was born in Illinois in 1879. George was a Physician and Surgeon.

Children of George A. Lierle and Laura

#5-4-1-3-2-1.   William R. Lierle, born 1911 in Adams County, Illinois.

#5-4-1-3-2-2.   Robert Lierle, born 1921 in Adams County, Illinois.

#4-4-1-3-4   WILLIAM R. LIERLE

William R. Lierle, born 22 November 1886, Adams County, Illinois, married Fanny M. Fanny was born in Illinois in 1893. William was a farmer in Adams County, Illinois. In 1820 he was living with his father, William B. Lierle.

Children of William R. Lierle and Fanny M.

#5-4-1-3-4-1.   Melvin E. Lierle, born 1913, Adams County, Illinois.

#5-4-1-3-4-2.   William R. Lierle, Jr., born June 1914 in Adams County, Illinois.

#4-4-1-6-2   ALBERT WILLIAM LIERLE

Albert William Lierle, born 30 November 1877, Adams County, Illinois, married Anna. Anna was born in 1883. Albert was a Farmer. The last record found of him was when he registered for draft in WWI, in Butler County, Kansas.

Children of Albert William Lierle and Anna

#5-4-1-6-2-1.   Ida Lierle, born 1907, Butler County, Kansas.

#5-4-1-6-2-2.   Paul Lierle, born 1910, Butler County, Kansas.

#5-4-1-6-2-3.   Allen Lierle, born 1911, Butler County, Kansas.

#5-4-1-6-2-4.   Luciel Lierle, born 1914, Butler County, Kansas.

#4-4-1-6-3   EMMA LIERLE

Emma Lierle, born September 1882, Adams County, Illinois, married Frank H. Howard 1815 in Butler County, Kansas. In the 1930, Butler County, Kansas census Emma was married to Frank H Varner. Emma's children were also using the name Varner. Frank H. Howard and Frank H. Varner were both born in Kansas in 1877. I believe Frank H. Varner and Frank H. Howard are the same person, both are Farmers.

Children of Emma Lierle and Frank H. Varner

#5-4-1-6-3-1.   Bernice Varner, born 1815, Butler County, Kansas.
#5-4-1-6-3-2.   Wilber Varner, born September 1817, Butler County, Kansas.

#4-4-1-6-4   CHARLES "BABE" LIERLE

Charles "Babe" Lierle, born 27 December 1885, Adams County, Illinois, married Vesta Frances, 1912, Butler County, Kansas. Vesta was born 1891 in Kansas. Charles was a Farmer. Charles died in March 1972 in Colorado Springs, Colorado.

Children of Charles "Babe" Lierle and Vesta Frances

#5-4-1-6-4-1.   Mildred W. Lierle, born 1916, Butler County, Kansas.
#5-4-1-6-4-2.   Ellen T. Lierle, born 1924, Butler County, Kansas.

#4-4-1-7-2   MAUDE LIERLE

Maude Lierle, born February 1879, Adams County, Illinois, married William Ruhl, 8 February 1899, Adams County, Illinois. William was born October 1868 in Illinois. Maude died between 1913 and 1920 while a resident in Adams County, Illinois. William was a Farmer in Adams County, Illinois.

Children of Maude Lierle and William Ruhl

#5-4-1-7-2-1.   Myron Ruhl, born November 1899, Adams County, Illinois.
#5-4-1-7-2-2.   Olof Ruhl, born 1903, Adams County, Illinois.
#5-4-1-7-2-3.   Freda Ruhl, born 1906, Adams County, Illinois.
#5-4-1-7-2-4.   Earl Ruhl, born 1909, Adams County, Illinois.
#5-4-1-7-2-5.   Elmer Ruhl, born 1913, Adams County, Illinois.

#4-4-1-7-4   CLIFFORD LIERLE

Clifford Lierle, born 3 March 1883, Adams County, Illinois, married Zelda in 1909. Zalda was born in 1988 in Illinois. In the 1910 and 1920, Adams County, Illinois census Clifford was a Farmer. In the 1930 census he was an Automobile Salesman. Clifford died in Adams County, Illinois in June 1969.

Child of Clifford Lierle and Zelda

#5-4-1-7-4-1.   Merle Lierle, born 1917 in Adams County, Illinois.

#4-4-2-1-3   HULDAH C. MILLER

Huldah C. Miller, born May 1863, Missouri, married, John J. Ashinhurst in 1882 in Missouri. John was born December 1859 in Missouri. John was a Wheelwright and Blacksmith. John died before 1930. Huldah was living in Cass County, Missouri with her brother, William in 1930.

Children of Huldah C. Miller and John J. Ashinhurst

#5-4-2-1-3-1.   Naome Ashinhurst, born May 1892, Benton County, Missouri.

#5-4-2-1-3-2.	Harold Ashinhurst, born 1908, Cass County, Missouri.

#4-4-2-3-2   EDWARD D. COOPER

Edward D. Cooper, born 9 September 1874, Crawford County, Missouri, married Lena L. Cook in 1898 in Missouri. Lena was born August 1874 in Missouri. In the 1910 Crawford County, Missouri, census Edward was a Carpenter and Builder. In 1930 census, he was a Furniture Merchant.

Child of Edward D. Cooper and Lena L. Cook

#5-4-2-3-2-1.	Maurice E. Cooper, born 1901, Crawford County, Missouri.

#4-4-2-4-1   SILAS MONROE HOLT

Silas Monroe Holt, born 28 February 1865 in Missouri, married Sarah Dugger, 19 October 1888 at Doswood, Douglas County, Missouri. Sarah was born in Tennessee in 1870. Silas and Sarah Farmed in Douglas County, Missouri.

Children of Silas Monroe Holt and Sarah Dugger

#5-4-2-4-1-1.	Newton A. Holt, born 1891, Douglas County, Missouri
#5-4-2-4-1-2.	Mabel L. Holt, born 1894, Douglas County, Missouri.
#5-4-2-4-1-3.	Maudie Holt, born 1899, Douglas County, Missouri.
#5-4-2-4-1-4.	Florence Holt, born 1903, Douglas County, Missouri.
#5-4-2-4-1-5.	Nora F. Holt, born 1904, Douglas County, Missouri.

#4-4-2-4-4   ALMIRA DIANA HOLT

Almira Diana Holt, born 15 April 1870, Missouri, married Cornelius D. Elliott, 17 March 1894, Harrisonville, Cass County, Missouri. Cornelius was born in 1853 in Illinois. In the 1910 and 1920, Douglas County, Missouri census, he was a Farmer.

Children of Almira Diana Holt and Cornelius D. Elliott

#5-4-2-4-4-1.	Noble Elliot, born 1899, Douglas County, Missouri.
#5-4-2-4-4-2.	Bula Elliott, born 1902, Douglas County, Missouri.
#5-4-2-4-4-3.	Clifford Elliott, born 1905, Douglas County, Missouri.

#4-4-2-4-5   ELIZA L. JANE HOLT

Eliza L. Jane Holt, born 23 December 1872, Missouri, married Richard B. Bird, 11 June 1891, Christian, Missouri. Richard was born in Texas in March1855 and died between the 1910 and 1920 census. In the 1900, Jasper County, Missouri, censes Richard was a Miner. In the 1910 census he was a Carpenter and Builder. In the 1920 Jasper County, Missouri census Eliza was working as a waitress in a restaurant.

Children of Eliza L. Jane Holt and Richard B. Bird

#5-4-2-4-5-1.	Emily A. Bird, born February 1891, Jasper County, Missouri.
#5-4-2-4-5-2.	Bessie B. Bird, born October 1894, Jasper County, Missouri.
#5-4-2-4-5-3.	Gertie E. Bird, born 1901, Jasper County, Missouri.
#5-4-2-4-5-4.	Grace M. Bird, born 1904 Jasper County, Missouri.
#5-4-2-4-5-5.	Florence R. Bird, born May 1909, Jasper County, Missouri.

#4-4-2-5-1   ADDIE L. STITES

Addie L. Stites, born 1886 in Missouri, married George W. Waggoner, 16 June 1907, Newton County, Missouri. George was born in 1880 in Missouri. In the 1920 and 1930 Newton County, Missouri, census he listed his occupation as a Farmer.

Children of Addie L. Stites and George W. Waggoner

#5-4-2-5-1-1.	May Waggoner, born 1909, Newton County, Missouri.
#5-4-2-5-1-2.	Eva Louetta Waggoner, born 1911, Newton County, Missouri.
#5-4-2-5-1-3.	William H. Waggoner, born 1914, Newton County, Missouri.
#5-4-2-5-1-4.	Clifford W. Waggoner, born July 1915, Newton County, Missouri.
#5-4-2-5-1-5.	Andrew J. "Zack" Waggoner, born September 1919, Newton County, Missouri.
#5-4-2-5-1-6.	Franklin L. Waggoner, born 1924, Newton County, Missouri.

#4-4-3-1-1   JOHN R. LEACH

John R. Leach, born 26 November 1869, Franklin County, Missouri, married Cora L. Cora was born in Missouri in 1875. According to 1900 and 1910 Crawford County, Missouri census, John was a Carpenter and House Builder. In the 1930 Cook County, Illinois census, Cora was living with her daughter Elsie and husband. John was probably deceased.

Children of John R. Leach and Cora L.

#5-4-3-1-1-1.	Loyd Leach, born February 1894, Crawford County, Missouri.
#5-4-3-1-1-2.	Elsie M. Leach, born 1907, Crawford County, Missouri.

#5-4-3-1-1-3.	Ben F. Leach, born August 1909, Crawford County, Missouri.

#4-4-3-5-1   BENJAMIN ANDREW LEACH

Benjamin Andrew Leach, born 9 November 1873, Missouri, married Gussie G. Gentry, 9 December 1899, Hickory County, Missouri. Gussie was born November 1882 in Missouri. In the 1900, Hickory County, Missouri census, Benjamin was a Farmer. In the 1910, Grady County, Oklahoma census, Benjamin was in Grady County Farming. In the 1920, Larimer County, Colorado census, Benjamin was operating a Retail Grocery Store.

Children of Benjamin Andrew Leach and Gussie G. Gentry

#5-4-3-5-1-1.	Vineta P. Leach, born 1902, Hickory County, Missouri.
#5-4-3-5-1-2.	Veneva B Leach, Born 1904, Hickory County, Missouri.
#5-4-3-5-1-3.	Robert T. Leach, born August 1926, Larimer County, Colorado.

#4-4-3-5-2   LEVI HENRY LEACH

Levi Henry Leach, born 30 January 1873, Missouri, married Eva L. Coffay, 26 March 1899, Hickory County, Missouri. Eva was born in August of 1879 in Missouri. In the 1900 Hickory County, Missouri census, Levi was a Farmer. In the 1910 Grady County, Oklahoma census he was a Farmer and Farm Equipment Dealer. In the 1920 Grady County, Oklahoma census, he operated a Retail Grocery Store. Levi died in March 1977 in Minco, Grady County, Oklahoma.

Children of Levi Henry Leach and Eva Coffay

#5-4-3-5-2-1.	Dorothy D. Leach, born 1903, Hickory County, Missouri.

#5-4-3-5-2-2	Eva M. Leach, born September 1918, Grady County, Oklahoma.

#4-4-3-5-3 FRANCIS MONROE LEACH

Francis Monroe Leach, born 12 October 1877, Missouri, married Augusta M. in Missouri in 1897. Augusta was born January 1879 in Missouri. Francis moved often. In 1900 he and Augusta were in Osage County, Missouri, where he listed himself as a Farm Laborer. In 1910 and 1920 census he was in Shannon County, Missouri, where he listed himself as a Farmer. In the1930 census he was in Franklin County, Missouri, where he listed himself as a Farmer.

Children of Francis Monroe Leach and Augusta M.

#5-4-3-5-3-1.	Clarence G. Leach, born December 1897 in Osage County, Missouri.
#5-4-3-5-3-2.	Maude F. Leach, born 1905, Shannon County, Missouri.
#5-4-3-5-3-3.	Thomas B. Leach, born 1909, Shannon County, Missouri.
#5-4-3-5-3-4.	Benjamin A. Leach, born 1911, Shannon County, Missouri.
#5-4-3-5-3-5.	Edith M. Leach, born 1915, Shannon County, Missouri.
#5-4-3-5-3-6.	Joseph M. Leach, born October 1919, Shannon County, Missouri. Joseph probably died before 1930 census.

#4-5-1-3-1 MALINDA B. GREEN

Malinda B. Green, born 13 May 1877, Holmes County, Mississippi, married Allen Tate, 28 July 1897, Holmes County, Mississippi. Allen was born in Mississippi in 1867 and died before the 1920 census. Melinda and Allen were in the Retail Grocery Business. Malinda died 15 November 1968 at Nashville, Davidson County, Tennessee.

Children of Malinda B. Green and Allen Tate

#5-5-1-3-1-1.	Norene E. Tate, born 1902, Holmes County, Mississippi.
#5-5-1-3-1-2.	Frank A. Tate, born 1904, Holmes County, Mississippi,
#5-5-1-3-1-3.	Nathel M. Tate, born 1905, Holmes County, Mississippi.
#5-5-1-3-1-4.	Marley C. Tate, born 1908, Holmes County, Mississippi.

#4-5-1-3-4   FANNIE G. GREEN

Fannie G. Green, born August 1886, Holmes County, Mississippi, married David Franklin Montgomery, 16 November 1909, Holmes County, Mississippi. David was born 26 June 1879 in Mississippi. He was a Farmer.

Children of Fannie G. Green and David Franklin Montgomery

#5-5-1-3-4-1.	Samuel Frances Montgomery, born 1904, Holmes County, Mississippi.
#5-5-1-3-4-2.	Alice Montgomery, born 1908, Holmes County, Mississippi.
#5-5-1-3-4-3.	Lucile Montgomery, born 1910, Holmes County, Mississippi.
#5-5-1-3-4-4.	John D. Montgomery, born 1916, Holmes County, Mississippi.

#4-5-1-3-6   JOHN WESLEY GREEN

John Wesley Green, born March 1889, Holmes County, Mississippi, married Alma G. in 1917. Alma was born in Pennsylvania in 1895. In the 1920, Woodward County, Oklahoma census John was there and declared himself a Physician, Surgeon and General Medical Practice. In the 1930, Hamilton County, Texas census he declared himself to be a Doctor and Surgeon.

Children of John Wesley Green and Alma G.

#5-5-1-3-6-1.   Jacquelyn C. Green, born 1921, Woodward County, Oklahoma.
#5-5-1-3-6-2.   Betty J. Green, born 1924, Woodward County, Oklahoma.

#4-5-3-2-1   LEONADES C. "LEE" RENSHAW

Leonades C. "Lee" Renshaw, born 12 June 1882, Texas, married Lillie Mae Griffin 1905. Lillie was born in 1887 in Texas and died 22 December 1962 in Kaufman County, Texas. Lee and Lillie lived their entire married life in Upshur County, Texas. In the 1910 census Lee was working in a Saw Mill. In the 1820 and 1830 census he was Farming. Lee died 26 June 1960 in Tarrant County, Texas.

Children of Leonades C. "Lee" Renshaw and Lillie Mae Griffin

#5-5-3-2-1-1.   Noble T. Renshaw, born 1906, Upshur County, Texas.
#5-5-3-2-1-2.   Velma M. Renshaw, born 1908, Upshur County, Texas.
#5-5-3-2-1-3.   Gladys Renshaw, born 1913, Upshur County, Texas.
#5-5-3-2-1-5.   Montie Lee Renshaw, born 1918, Upshur County, Texas.
#5-5-3-2-1-6.   Joyce Renshaw, born 1918, Upshur County, Texas.
#5-5-3-2-1-7.   Korraine Ima J. Renshaw, born 1920, Upshur County, Texas
#5-5-3-2-1-8.   Wilmer D. Renshaw, born 1924, Upshur County, Texas.
#5-5-3-2-1-9.   Joe Bill Renshaw, born 29 September 1928, Upshur County, Texas.

#4-6-4-1-3   HERBERT CARL MADDOX

Herbert Carl Maddox, born 28 February 1884, Jefferson County, Illinois, married Blanch H. Goodner in 1905. Blanch was born in Illinois in 1887. In 1910, Jefferson County, Illinois census, Herbert was a House Painter. In the 1920 Jefferson County, Illinois census he was a Business Agent for a Union.

Child of Herbert Carl Maddox and Blanche H. Goodner

#5-6-4-1-3-1.   Margorie M. Maddox, born November1909 in Jefferson County, Illinois

#4-6-4-4-1   WALTER CHAMBLISS

Walter Chambliss, born 13 September 1887, Jefferson County, Illinois, married Minnie H. in 1911. Minnie was born in Illinois, 8 June 1892 and died in February 1976, in Champaign County, Illinois. Walter and Minnie made their home in Champaign, Illinois. In 1920 he was a Station Agent for N. Y. C Railway. In 1930, he was a Telegrapher for N. Y. C. Railway. Minnie was a Seamctress and Dressmaker with her own shop.

Children of Walter Chambliss and Minnie H.

#5-6-4-4-1-1.   Marie H. Chambliss, born 1914, Champaign County, Illinois.
#5-6-4-4-1-2.   Delmar G. Chambliss, born 1920, Champaign County, Illinois.

#4-6-4-4-2   RAY CHAMBLISS

Ray Chambliss, born 6 April 1890, Jefferson County, Illinois, married Anna Mae about 1914. Anna was born in Illinois in 1893. Ray and Anna made their home in Champaign County, Illinois, where Ray Farmed.

#5-6-4-4-2-1.	Mary M. Chambliss, born July 1914, Champaign County, Illinois.
#5-6-4-4-2-2.	Charles Chambliss, born July 1916, Champaign County, Illinois.
#5-6-4-4-2-3.	Imogene Chambliss, born August 1918, Champaign County, Illinois.
#5-6-4-4-2-4.	Ray Chambliss, born 1921, Champaign County, Illinois.
#5-6-4-4-2-5.	Avanelle Chambliss, born 1922, Champaign County, Illinois.
#5-6-4-4-2-6.	Lawrence D. Chambliss, born 1926, Champaign County, Illinois.
#5-6-4-4-2-7.	Jack Chambliss, born 1928, Champaign County, Illinois.
#5-6-4-4-2-8.	Richard E. Chambliss, born March 1830, Champaign County, Illinois.

#4-6-4-4-4   HARRY CHAMBLISS

Harry Chambliss, born 24 November 1892, Jefferson County, Illinois, married Bessie in 1928. Bessie was born in Illinois in 1906. Harry and Bessie made their home in Champaign Illinois, where Harry farmed. Harry Died July 1971, Jefferson County, Illinois.

Child of Harry Chambliss and Bessie

#5-6-4-4-4-1.	Joseph J. Chambliss, born 1928, Champaign County, Illinois.

#4-6-4-4-5   OSCAR CHAMBLISS

Oscar Chambliss, born 30 July 1894 Jefferson County, Illinois, married Cora I. Cora was born in Illinois, 24 September 1896 and died at Iuka,

Marion County, Illinois in March 1986. Oscar and Cora made their home in Champaign Illinois. Oscar was a Carpenter.

Children of Oscar Chambliss and Cora I

#5-6-4-4-5-1.	Talmadge O. Chambliss, born 1916, Champaign County, Illinois.
#5-6-4-4-5-2.	Vivian Chambliss, born 1918, Champaign County, Illinois.
#5-6-4-4-5-3.	Juanita V. Chambliss, born 1920, Champaign County, Illinois.
#5-6-4-4-5-4.	Doris M. Chambliss, born 1922, Champaign County, Illinois.

#4-6-4-5-1   ARTHUR A. PULLIAM

Arthur A. Pulliam, born 9 July 1887, Jefferson County, Illinois married Mary S. in 1909. Mary was born in Jefferson County, Illinois in 1891. Arthur worked for the Railroad Company. He and Mary lived in Springfield, Sangamon, Illinois.

Children of Arthur A. Pulliam and Mary S.

#5-6-4-5-1-1.	Ralph R. Pulliam, born Sangamon County, Illinois.
#5-6-4-5-1-2.	Lucille M. Pulliam, born Sangamon County, Illinois.
#5-6-4-5-1-3.	Vivian M. Pulliam, born Sangamon County, Illinois.
#5-6-4-5-1-4.	Wilbur H. Pulliam, born Sangamon County, Illinois.

#4-6-4-5-2   GEORGE ELMER PULLIAM

George Elmer Pulliam, born 23 July 1889, Jefferson County, Illinois, Married Helen B. 1916. Helen was born in 1896 in Illinois. George was a School Teacher. In the 1820 census, George and Helen were living in Crawford County, Illinois. In 1930 census they were living in St Clair County, Illinois. George died 23 July 1975 in Rockford, Winnebago County, Illinois.

Children of George Elmer Pulliam and Helen B.

#5-6-4-5-2-1.   John P. Pulliam, born 1918, Crawford County, Illinois.

#5-6-4-5-2-2.   Elisabeth Pulliam, born 1920, Crawford County, Illinois.

SIXTH GENERATION

#5-1-1-1-2-1   RAYMOND EARNEST

Raymond Earnest, born 27 September 1895, Linn County, Kansas, married Jessie R. in 1914. Jessie R. was born in 1901 in Kansas and died between 1922 and 1930. Raymond was a Farmer in Linn County, Kansas. He died in January of 1973 at Fort Scott, Bourbon County, Kansas.

Children of Raymond Earnest and Jessie R.

#6-1-1-1-2-1-1.   John W. Earnest, born 1918 in Linn County, Kansas.

#6-1-1-1-2-1-2.   Kenneth L. Earnest, born 1922 in Linn County, Kansas.

#5-2-1-3-1-3   JOHN S. REEVES

John S. Reeves, born 24 October 1895, Kaufman County, Texas, first married Louise about 1916. Louise was born in Arkansas in 1899. John next married Sarah. Sarah was born in Texas in 1897. In the 1920, Choctaw County, Oklahoma census John was an Automobile Mechanic. In 1930, Live Oak County, Texas census John was an Oilfield Worker.

Child of John S. Reeves and Louise

#6-2-1-3-1-3-1.   Sherley Louise Reeves, born July 1917, Choctaw County, Oklahoma.

Children of John S. Reeves and Sarah

#6-2-1-3-1-3-2.   John J. Reeves, born 1924, Live Oak County, Texas.

#6-2-1-3-1-3-3.	Douglas B. Reeves, born September 1925, Live Oak County, Texas.

#5-2-2-1-6-4   MARION S. RENSHAW

Marion S. Renshaw, born 1901, Garvin County, Oklahoma Territory, married Etma in 1923. Etma was born in Tennessee in 1906. In the 1930 Limestone County, Texas, census Marion was a Oilfield Laborer.

Children of Marion S. Renshaw and Etma

#6-2-2-1-6-4-1.	Lavearn Renshaw, born 1925 in Limestone County, Texas.
#6-2-2-1-6-4-2.	Gradie Renshaw, born 1928 in Limestone County, Texas.

#5-2-2-1-6-5   ORVILLE L. RENSHAW

Orville L. Renshaw, born in 1904 in Garvin County, Texas, married Hazel in 1926. Hazel was born in Texas in 1910. In the 1930 Navarro County, Texas census, Orville was a Oilfield Laborer.

Child of Orville L. Renshaw and Hazel

#6-2-2-1-6-5-1.	James E. Renshaw, born 1928, Navarro County, Texas,

#5-2-3-1-1-2   GEORGE NEAL HENDREN

George Neil Hendren, born 29 January 1883, Dyer County, Tennessee, married Sallie A., May 20 October 1907, Dyer County, Tennessee. Sallie was born in 1887 in Tennessee. According to the 1930 Dyer County, Tennessee census, George was a Cotton Buyer. George died in May of 1969.

Children of George Neal Hendren and Sallie A. May

#6-2-3-1-1-2-1.	Nely D. Hendren, born 1910, Dyer County, Tennessee.
#6-2-3-1-1-2-2.	Winnie V. Hendren, born 1912, Dyer County, Tennessee.
#6-2-3-1-1-2-3.	Sarah A. Hendren, born 1916, Dyer County, Tennessee.

#5-2-3-1-1-4   ROBERT TAYLOR HENDREN

Robert Taylor Hendren, born 27 August 1888, Dyer County, Tennessee, married Mattie Palmer, 10 March 1920, Dyer County, Tennessee. Mattie was born in 1894 in Tennessee. Robert was a Farmer.

Children of Robert Taylor Hendren and Mattie Palmer

#6-2-3-1-1-4-1.	Dorothy M. Hendren, born 1922, Dyer County, Tennessee.
#6-2-3-1-1-4-2.	Robert C. Hendren, born 1924, Dyer County, Tennessee.
#6-2-3-1-1-4-3.	Beulah B. Hendren, born March 1928, Dyer County, Tennessee.
#6-2-3-1-1-4-4.	Rosyln A. Hendren, born January 1930, Dyer County, Tennessee.

#5-2-3-1-1-5   BEULAH ELLIS HENDREN

Beulah Ellis Hendren born June 1891 Dyer County, Tennessee, married Cleve E. Burks 14 March 1914 Dyer County, Tennessee. Cleve was born 21 October 1890 in Tennessee. According to the 1920 and 1930 Dyer County, Tennessee census Cleve was a Bookkeeper for a Wholesale Grocery Company. Beulah and Cleve lived their entire lives in Dyer County, Tennessee.

#6-2-3-1-1-5-1.　　　　Cleve E. Burks, Jr., born 1918 in Dyer County, Tennessee.

#5-2-3-1-4-1　　CHESTER W. HENDREN

Chester W. Hendren, born 4 December 1964, Dyer County, Tennessee, married Minter Pyles, 19 September 1910, Dyer County, Tennessee. Minter was born in Tennessee in 1894. Chester was a Farmer. Chester and Minter lived their entire married lives in Dyer County, Tennessee. Chester Died in July of 1964.

Children of Chester W. Hendren and Minter Pyles

#6-2-3-1-4-1-1.　　　　Kathryn Hendren, born 1911, Dyer County, Tennessee.

#6-2-3-1-4-1-2.　　　　Celia M. Hendren, born 1913, Dyer County, Tennessee.

#6-2-3-1-4-1-3.　　　　Cimon Hendren, born December 1915, Dyer County, Tennessee.

#6-2-3-1-4-1-4.　　　　Mabel C. Hendren, born September 1918, Dyer County, Tennessee.

#6-2-3-1-4-1-5.　　　　J. W. Hendren, born 1921, Dyer County, Tennessee.

#6-2-3-1-4-1-6.　　　　Geraldine Hendren, born 1924, Dyer County, Tennessee.

#6-2-3-1-4-1-7.　　　　Harold L. Hendren, born September 1927, Dyer County, Tennessee.

#5-2-3-1-4-3　　MARY OSCIE HENDREN

Mary Oscie Hendren, born May 1893, Dyer County, Tennessee, married James R. Marchant, 19 January 1918, Dyer County, Tennessee. James was born 13 June 1889 in Tennessee and died in July of 1865. James and Mary Farmed their entire lifetime in Dyer County, Tennessee.

Children of Mary Oscie Hendren and James R. Marchant

#6-2-3-1-4-3-1.	James R. Marchant, born 1919, Dyer County, Tennessee.
#6-2-3-1-4-3-2.	Doris Marchant, born 1921, Dyer County, Tennessee.
#6-2-3-1-4-3-3.	Martha A. Marchant, born 1926, Dyer County, Tennessee.
#6-2-3-1-4-3-4.	Jerry H. Marchant, born December 1928, Dyer County, Tennessee.

#-5-2-3-1-4-5   BEDFORD W. HENDREN

Bedford W. Hendren, born 29 December 1896, Dyer County, Tennessee, married Emma Lawler, 20 May 1916, Dyer County, Tennessee. Emma was born in 1900 in Tennessee. Bedford was a Farmer. In 1930 Bedford and Emma were divorced and she had married Alvin Johnson and living in Shelby County, Tennessee.

Children of Bedford W. Hendren and Emma Lawler

#6-2-3-1-4-5-1.	Sue F. Hendren, born 1917, Dyer County, Tennessee.
#6-2-3-1-4-5-2.	James L. Hendren, born 1924, Dyer County, Tennessee.

#5-2-3-1-5-2   CURRY V. HENDREN

Curry V. Hendren, born 20 May 1908, Dyer County, Tennessee, married Monnie Moore, 24 November 1928, Dyer County, Tennessee. Monnie was born in 1911 in Tennessee. Curry was a Farmer. Curry died 19 November 1994, Dyer County, Tennessee.

Child of Curry V. Hendren and Monnie Moore

#6-2-3-1-5-2-1.   John Hendren, born March 1930, Dyer County,
                        Tennessee.

#5-2-3-5-1-1   RICHARD PAUL HENDREN

Richard Paul Hendren, born 18 August 1900, Davie County, North
Carolina, married Lookie B. in 1924. Lookie was born in 1905 in North
Carolina. Richard and Lookie made their home in Charlotte County,
Virginia, where Richard Farmed. Richard died 28 December 1990 in
Charlotte County, Virginia.

Children of Richard Paul Hendren and Lookie B.

#6-2-3-5-1-1-1.   Katherine M. Hendren, born 1924, Charlotte
                        County, Virginia.
#6-2-3-5-1-1-2.   Charles R. Hendren, born October 1928,
                        Charlotte County, Virginia.

#5-3-1-2-2-1   ELZIE GILBERT LEACH

Elzie Gilbert Leach, born 9 May 1891, Oklahoma, Indian Territory,
married Daisy J. Lewis in 1919. Daisy was born in England in 1899.
In the 1920, Sonoma County, California census Elzie and Daisy were
living there where Elzie was a Laborer. In the 1930 Sonoma County,
California census Elzie and Daisy were living with Elzie's father and
working as a Laborer in Fruit Harvest.

Children of Elzie Gilbert Leach and Daisy J. Lewis

#6-3-1-2-2-1-1.   Franklin L. Leach, born 1 June 1920, Sonoma
                        County, California.
#6-3-1-2-2-1-2.   Lewis G. Leach, born 25 November 1921,
                        Sonoma County, California.

#6-3-1-2-2-1-3.	John Wesley Leach, born 15 October 1925, Sonoma County, California.
#6-3-1-2-2-1-4.	Herbert James Leach, born 20 December 1930, Sonoma County, California.

#5-3-1-2-2-4   ROY H. LEACH

Roy H. Leach, born 2 February 1899, Indian Territory, Oklahoma, Married Winifred K. Knipp in 1919. Winifred was born 14 December 1898 in California and died 15 February 1995 in San Diego, California. The 1930 Solano County, California census lists Roy as the Proprietor of a Grocery Store. Roy died 10 August 1965 at Tulare County, California.

Children of Roy H. Leach and Winifred K. Knipp

#6-3-1-2-2-4-1.	Jean Leach, born 10 October 1919, Sonoma County, California.
#6-3-1-2-2-4-2.	Bernice Leach, born 21 October 1921, Sonoma County, California.
#6-3-1-2-2-4-3.	Winifred Leach, born 6 October 1923, Solano County, California.
#6-3-1-2-2-4-4.	Warren Roy Leach, born 5 October 1925, Solano County, California.
#6-3-1-2-2-4-5.	Marie Leach, born 30 March 1928, Solano County, California.
#6-3-1-2-2-4-6.	Vernon Leach, born 22 July 1934, Los Angeles County, California.

#5-3-1-2-2-5   CARL WEST LEACH

Carl West Leach, born 4 April 1900, Siloam Springs, Arkansas, married, Opal Jean Wilson, 24 October 1931, Oakland, California. Opal was born 29 November 1915, Almyra, Arkansas and died 25 July 1990, Roseville, California. Carl died 13 March 1991, Sacramento, California.

Children of Carl West Leach and Opal Jean Wilson

#6-3-1-2-2-5-1.   Carl West Leach, Jr., born 17 June 1932, San Francisco, California.

#6-3-1-2-2-5-2.   Carol Jean Leach, born 25 December 1935, Alameda County, California.

#5-3-1-2-3-3   LELLAND GILBERT GARRISON

Leland Gilbert Garrison, born 6 July 1892, Crawford County, Arkansas, married Mary Bell Sifford in 1929. Mary was born in Texas, 27 July 1901 and died 11 September 1997, Mahave County, Arizona. According to the 1930 Fanning County, Texas census, Leland was the Caretaker for the National Guard Armory. Leland died 9 May 1973, Fanning County, Texas.

Children of Leland Gilbert Garrison and Mary Bell Sifford

#6-3-1-2-3-3-1.   Leland Gilbert Garrison, Jr., born 25 July 1936, Fanning County, Texas.

#6-3-1-2-3-3-2.   Robert Leach Garrison, born 1 May 1938, Fanning County, Texas.

#5-3-1-2-3-6   MARVIN GARRISON

Marvin G. Garrison, born 14 May 1902, Delta County, Texas, married Mabel Marie Scarborough, 1907. Mabel was born in 1907 in Texas. According to 1930, Fanning County, Texas census, Marvin was a Farmer. Marvin died 10 October 1966, Fanning County, Texas and is buried in the Willow Wild Cemetery.

Children of Marvin Garrison and Mabel Marie Scarborough

#6-3-1-2-3-6-1.   James W. Garrison, born 1925, Fanning County, Texas.

#6-3-1-2-3-6-2.	Doris Irene Garrison, born 29 December 1934, Fanning County, Texas.
#6-3-1-2-3-6-3.	Mary Merle Garrison, born 29 December 1934, Fanning County, Texas.
#6-3-1-2-3-6-4.	Paul Ray Garrison, born 3 July 1938, Fanning County, Texas.

#5-3-1-2-3-7   RAYMOND JACK GARRISON

Raymond Jack Garrison, born 16 August 1907, Orangeville. Fanning County, Texas, married Mattie D. Cockrill, 14 February 1931, Fanning County, Texas. Mattie was born in Texas in 1912. Raymond was a Farmer. Raymond died 11 September 1974, Fanning County, Texas and is buried in the Willow Wild Cemetery.

Child of Raymond Jack Garrison and Mattie D Cockrill

#6-3-1-2-3-7-1.	Sarah Anna Garrison, born 12 January 1939, Fanning County, Texas.

#5-3-1-2-3-8   JOHN CALVIN GARRISON

John Calvin Garrison, born 4 June 1910, Orangeville, Fanning County, Texas, married Lela Belle Taylor, 28 October 1928, Fanning County, Texas. Lela was born in Texas in 1911. According to 1930 Fanning County, Texas census, John was an Automobile Mechanic. John died 27 December 1993, Fanning County, Texas.

Children of John Calvin Garrison and Lela Belle Taylor

#6-3-1-2-3-8-1.	Elizabeth Louise Garrison, born 29 October 1931, Fanning County, Texas.
#6-3-1-2-3-8-2.	John Calvin Garrison, Jr., born 14 May 1935, Fanning County, Texas.

#5-3-1-2-4-1   FAYE ONA LEACH

Faye Ona Leach, born 15 September 1896, Sequoyah County, Oklahoma, married Robert Lloyd Riddle, 31 October 1915, Sequoyah County, Oklahoma. Robert was born 9 July 1900 in Arkansas and died 21 February 1978 in Detroit, Wayne County, Michigan. According to the 1930, Wayne County, Michigan census, Robert was a Welder for a Factory. Faye died 4 February 1981 in Detroit, Wayne County, Michigan.

Child of Faye Ona Leach and Robert Lloyd Riddle

#6-3-1-2-4-1-1.   Lloyd Riddle, born after 1930, in Detroit, Michigan.

#5-3-1-2-4-2   RAYMOND CISCO LEACH

Raymond Cisco Leach, born 5 July 1898, Sequoyah County, Oklahoma, married Ruby F. Ruby was born 8 August 1902 in Oklahoma and died 2 November 1996 in Sequoyah County, Oklahoma. According to 1930 Sequoyah County, Oklahoma census, Raymond was a Automobile Mechanic. Raymond died 12 August 1983, Sequoyah County, Oklahoma.

Child of Raymond Cisco Leach and Ruby F.

#6-3-1-2-4-2-1.   Iris C. Leach, born 1922, Sequoyah County, Oklahoma.

#5-3-1-2-4-3   CAROLINE "CARRIE" LEACH

Caroline "Carrie" Leach, born 5 February 1900, Sequoyah County, Oklahoma, married William Lester Martin, 16 May 1918, Sequoyah County, Oklahoma. William was born 17 October 1893 in Indiana and died April 1972 in Salt Lake City, Utah. William was a Telegraph Operator for Western Union. Caroline died 29 March 1985 in Salt

Lake City, Utah. Her ashes were scattered from an Airplane across a Mountain Range.

Children of Caroline "Carrie" Leach and William Lester Martin

#6-3-1-2-4-3-1.   William Charles Martin, born March 1919, Sequoyah County, Oklahoma.

#6-3-1-2-4-3-2.   Amy Martin, born 1921, Wallace County, Kansas.

#5-3-1-2-4-5   MAY MARIE LEACH

May Marie Leach, born 29 August 1904, Sequoyah County, Oklahoma married Gilbert Clyde Strickland in 1925. Gilbert was born 21 September 1903 in Logan County, Arkansas and died in 1959. Gilbert is buried in the Highland Park Cemetery, Crawford County, Kansas. According to the 1930, Newton County, Missouri census, Gilbert was a Telegraph Operator for the Kansas City Southern Railroad. May died in 1959 in Sequoyah County, Oklahoma.

Children of May Marie Leach and Clyde C. Strickland

#6-3-1-2-4-5-1.   Gilbert Wood Strickland, born May 1926, Sequoyah County, Oklahoma.

#6-3-1-2-4-5-2.   Clyde Edmond Strickland, born August 1929, Newton County, Missouri.

#5-3-1-2-4-6   VERNA MARGARET LEACH

Verna Margaret Leach, born 10 July 1907, Sequoyah County, Oklahoma, married James Samuel Patterson, 5 September 1927, Sequoyah County, Oklahoma. James was born 23 October 1905 in Carlton, Kansas and died 30 January 1991, Okaloosa County, Florida. According to 1930, Tulsa County, Oklahoma census, James worked Constructing Telephone Lines. Verna died 19 March 2001 Shalimar, Okaloosa County, Florida.

Children of Verna Margaret Leach and James Samuel Patterson

#6-3-1-2-4-6-1.   Anna Belle Patterson, born 31 January 1929, Sequoyah County, Oklahoma.

#6-3-1-2-4-6-2.   James Samuel Patterson, born 17 November 1932, Shawnee, Oklahoma and died on the same day.

#6-3-1-2-4-6-3.   Jerry Ray Patterson, born 4 January 1936, Shawnee, Oklahoma.

#5-3-1-3-3-2   DICK HALE LEACH

Dick Hale Leach, born 14 July 1931, Imperial County, California, married Ramel Mae Ludwig 14 July 1956, Reno Washoe County, Nevada.

Children of Dick Hale Leach and Ramel Mae Ludwig

#6-3-1-3-3-2-1.   Deborah Ann Leach, born 28 January 1957, Shasta County, California.

#6-3-1-3-3-2-2.   Diana Lynn Leach, born 15 February 1959, Shasta County, California.

#5-3-1-3-4-1   NORMA JEAN LEACH

Norma Jean Leach, born 10 January 1935, Ft Smith, Sebastian County, Arkansas, married Kenneth Ray Bartlett, 7 September 1957, Coffeyville, Montgomery County, Kansas.

Children of Norma Jean Leach and Kenneth Ray Bartlett

#6-3-1-3-4-1-1.   Laura Beth Bartlett, born 23 January 1958, Oklahoma City, Oklahoma.

#6-3-1-3-4-1-2.   Gregory Wade Bartlett, born 19 September 1961, Oklahoma City, Oklahoma.

#6-3-1-3-4-1-3.   Stephen Miles Bartlett, born 24 June 1963, Oklahoma City, Oklahoma.

#5-3-1-3-4-2   PEGGY JOYCE LEACH

Peggy Joyce Leach, born 11 December 1936, Ft Smith, Sebastian County, Arkansas, married Donald Albert Dalton, 30 December 1960, Littleton, Arapahoe County, Colorado. Donald was born 23 February 1931, Riffle, Garfield County, Colorado.

Children of Peggy Joyce Leach and Donald Albert Dalton

#6-3-1-3-4-2-1.   Shelly Dawn Dalton, born 18 January 1963, Wheat Ridge, Colorado.
#6-3-1-3-4-2-2.   Donald Albert Dalton, Jr., born 10 October 1965, Riffle, Garfield County, Colorado.

#5-3-1-3-4-3   DONALD BOYCE LEACH

Donald Boyce Leach, born 11 December 1936, Ft Smith, Sebastian County, Arkansas, married Betty Ann Bell.

Children of Donald Boyce Leach and Betty Ann Bell

#6-3-1-3-4-3-1.   Mark Edwin Leach, born 8 July 1957.
#6-3-1-3-4-3-2.   Scott Delane Leach, born 31 August 1962.
#6-3-1-3-4-3-3.   Michel Don Leach, born 27 April 1968.

#5-3-1-3-5-1   BOB G. LEACH

Bob G. Leach, born 21 December 1934, Muldrow, Sequoyah County, Oklahoma, married Edna Spore, 14 August 1965, Senora, Mexico. Edna was born 31 May 1937, Senora, Mexico.

Children of Bob G. Leach and Edna Spore

#6-3-1-3-5-1-1.   Elizabeth Leach, born 14 March 1966, El
                      Centro, Imperial County, California.
#6-3-1-3-5-1-2.   Stephen Edward Leach, born 21 January 1969,
                      El Centro, Imperial County, California.

#5-3-1-3-5-2   BETTY ANN LEACH

Betty Ann Leach, born 19 August 1932, Muldrow, Sequoyah County,
Oklahoma, married, John Walter Fields, 18 January 1958, Las Vegas,
Clark County, Nevada. John was born 30 September 1928 at Baker,
Baker County, Oregon.

Children of Betty Ann Leach and John Walter Fields

#6-3-1-3-5-2-1.   Douglas Lloyd Fields, born 25 October 1952,
                      San Diego County, California.
#6-3-1-3-5-2-2.   David Scott Fields, born 15 October 1958,
                      Imperial County, California.
#6-3-1-3-5-2-3.   Richard Walter Fields, born 30 June 1960, San
                      Diego County, California.
#6-3-1-3-5-2-4.   Patrick John Fields, 15 June 1964, San Diego
                      County, California.

#5-3-1-5-3-4   ELSIE FAY GRIFFITH

Elsie Fay Griffith, born December 1898, Logan County, Oklahoma,
married Edward Mulhall, 20 July 1929, Colorado Springs, Colorado.
Edward was born 9 June 1892, Logan County, Oklahoma Territory
and died 15 April 1970, Tulsa, Oklahoma. Elsie died 21 March 1991,
Harrison, Arkansas.

Child of Elsie Fay Griffith and Edward Mulhall

#6-3-1-5-3-4-1.   Edward Mulhall, Jr., born 19 March 1933, Tulsa
                       County, Oklahoma.

#5-3-1-5-7-2   OTIS S. STOUT

Otis S. Stout, born 1906, Logan County, Oklahoma Territory, married
Grace about 1926. Grace was born in Oklahoma in 1909.

Children of Otis S. Stout and Grace

#6-3-1-5-7-2-1.   Ruth Stout, born 1927, Logan County,
                       Oklahoma.
#6-3-1-5-7-2-2.   Imogene Stout, born 1928, Logan County,
                       Oklahoma.
#6-3-1-5-7-2-3.   Mary Jane Stout, born October 1929, Logan
                       County, Oklahoma.

#5-3-1-6-4-1   LUTHER SINGLETON

Luther Singleton, born 1907, Benton County, Arkansas, married
Martha. According to 1930 census Luther was living with his step father
in Franklin County, Kansas and working in a Cleaners.

Children of Luther Singleton and Martha.

#6-3-1-6-4-1-1.   Richard Singleton, married Sharon
#6-3-1-6-4-1-2.   James H. Singleton, born 1/28/1950, married
                       Carol.
#6-3-1-6-4-1-3.   Gary Singleton.
#6-3-1-6-4-1-4.   Donald Gregory Singleton, 9 February 1954,
                       Washington D. C., married Laura Lee Burch.
                       Donald died 30 December 1992, Silver Springs,
                       Marylang.

#5-3-1-6-4-2   EULIA ANN CHULUFAS

Eulia Ann Chulufas, born 14 December 1916, Ottawa, Franklin County, Kansas, married George Hubert Gast in 1932. George died in October 1968 in Kansas City, Missouri. After the death of George Eulia married Claborn Beard, 11 December 1971 in Kansas City, Missouri.

Children of Eulia Ann Chulufas and George Gast

#6-3-1-6-4-2-1.	Georgiana Gast, born 3 March 1936, Kansas City, Missouri, married Harold Brokaw 26 June 1954 Kansas City, Missouri.
#6-3-1-6-4-2-2.	Eugune Gast.
#6-3-1-6-4-2-3.	Gerald Gast, born 20 June 1942, Kansas City, Missouri, married Janet Kay Thomas.
#6-3-1-6-4-2-4.	Tommy Dean Gast, born 1 August 1944, Kansas City, Missouri, Tommy died 26 June 2010, Kansas City, Missouri.

#5-3-1-6-4-3   DOROTHY ELLEN CHULUFAS

Dorothy Ellen Chulufas, born 19 January 1918, Franklin County, Kansas, married Paul Neergaard, 20 January 1938, Kansas City, Missouri. Paul died 30 November 1966, Milwaukee, Wisconsin. Dorthy next married Allen C. Warr, 21 June 1940, Independence, Missouri.

Children of Dorothy Ellen Chaufas and Allen C. Warr

#6-3-1-6-4-3-1.	Gary R. Warr, born5 July 1943, Kansas City, Missouri, married Janet L. Gaither, 2 March 1968, Los Angeles, California.
#6-3-1-6-4-3-2.	Denise Warr.

#5-3-1-6-4-4   JAMES MORRIS CHULUFUS

James Morris Chulufus, born 2 February 1922, Franklin, Ottawa County, Kansas, married Kathy Virginia Thompson, 21 March 1942, Ottawa County, Kansas. Kathy was born 12 March 1926, Carnegie, Kiowa County, Kansas.

Children of James Morris Chulufus and Kathy Virginia Thompson

#6-3-1-6-4-4-1.   Linda Dean Chulufus, born 12 March 1944, Kern County, California.

#6-3-1-6-4-4-2.   Jimmy Charles Chulufus, born 19 February 1948, Sedan, Kansas.

#5-3-1-6-4-5   CATHERINE JANE CHULUFUS

Catherine Jane Chulufus, born 14 October 1923, Franklin County, Kansas, married Edward William Reddick, 9 January 1945 Topeka, Shawnee County, Kansas. Catherine died 30 December 2011, Grand Haven, Michigan.

Children of Catherine Jane Chulufus and Edward William Reddick

#6-3-1-6-4-5-1.   Edward Reddick, born 21 December 1945, Frankfort, Michigan.

#6-3-1-6-4-5-2.   Sharon Reddick, born 24 November 1946, Muskegon, Michigan.

#6-3-1-6-4-5-3.   Richard Reddick, born 9 November 1948, Muskegon, Michigan.

#6-3-1-6-4-5-4.   William Reddick, born 16 January 1950, Muskegon, Michigan.

#5-3-1-6-4-6   GENEVIVE LORRAINE CHULUFAS

Genevive Lorraine Chulufas, born 14 July 1925, Ottawa, Franklin County, Kansas, married Buddy Janes Harding, 30 September 1947. Buddy died 20 January 1988, Grover City, San Louis Obispo County, California,

Children of Genevive Lorraine Chulufas and Buddy James Harding

#6-3-1-6-4-6-1.   Christopher James Harding, born 29 May 1948, Los Angelus, California. Christopher died 29 September 1968.

#6-3-1-6-4-6-2.   Gary Lee Harding, born 22 June 1952, Los Angeles, California.

#5-3-1-6-4-7   RICHARD FRANKLIN CHULUFUS

Richard Franklin Chulufus, born 9 January 1927, Franklin County, Kansas, married Elizabeth Jane Keith, 20 June 1950, District of Columbia. Elizabeth was born 23 June 1926, Miami, Dade County, Florida.

Children of Richard Franklin Chulufus and Elizabeth Jane Keith

#6-3-1-6-4-7-1.   Richard Franklin Chaufus, Jr., born 23 July 1953, Independence, Missouri.

#6-3-1-6-4-7-2.   Karen Elizabeth Chaufus, born 3 September 1951, Washington, D.C.

#5-3-1-11-1-1-1   BONITA R. LEACH

Bonita R. Leach, born 23 April 1917, Washington County, Arkansas, married Homer Lewis Sparks, 10 July 1949. Homer was born 4 September 1911, Kentucky, Newton County, Arkansas and died 23

September 1984, Haskell, Muskogee County, Oklahoma. Bonita died 23 October 1984, Dallas, Texas, as a result of an automobile accident in Haskell County, Oklahoma.

Child of Bonita R. Leach and Homer Lewis Sparks

#-6-3-1-11-1-1-1.   Martha Ruth Sparks, born 15 April 1952, Muskogee County, Oklahoma.

#5-3-1-11-1-2   DORTHA ANN LEACH

Dortha Ann Leach, born 20 April 1925, Washington County, Arkansas, married Glenn Allen Dickson, 17 June 1948. Glenn is a Doctor.

Child of Dortha Ann Leach and Glenn Allen Dickson

#6-3-1-11-1-2-1.   Glen Raymond Dickson, born 21 May 1951.

#5-3-1-11-3-1   CHARLES HAROLD LEACH

Charles Harold Leach, born 24 October 1924, Washington County, Arkansas, first married Lavon Waites in 1946. Harold later married Pat Mars, 22 October 1975 in Tahlequah, Oklahoma. Pat was born 10 May 1932 in Oklahoma City, Oklahoma. Harold ran an upholstery business in Siloam Springs, Arkansas.

Child of Charles Harold Leach and Lavon Waites

#6-3-1-11-3-1-1.   Charles Harold Leach, Jr., born 8 December 1949, Washington County, Arkansas. Charles died 6 May 2008, Washington County, Arkansas.
#6-3-1-11-3-1-2.   Larry Leach, born 14 August 1954, Washington County, Arkansas.

#5-3-1-11-3-2   HOWARD LEE LEACH

Howard Lee Leach, born 21 February 1932, Washington County, Arkansas, first married Nora Keck. Howard later married Ruby Ellen Laughlin, 19 September 1961 Stilwell, Oklahoma. Howard married a third time but her name is unknown. Howard was a Trucker, he died from a stroke, 30 July 1974, Kansas City, Missouri.

Children of Howard Lee Leach and Nora Keck

#6-3-1-11-3-2-1.   Vickie Lee Leach, born 19 September 1951, Washington County, Arkansas.
#6-3-1-11-3-2-2.   Dennis Leach, born in Washington County, Arkansas.

Children of Howard Lee Leach and Ruby Ellen "Heck" Laughlin

#6-3-1-11-3-2-3.   Howard Lee Leach, born 22 October 1965, Washington County, Arkansas.
#6-3-1-11-3-2-4.   Acey Leach, born 3 April 1968, Washington County, Arkansas.

Child of Howard Lee Leach and unknown wife

#6-3-1-11-3-2-5.   Phillip Leach, born Washington County, Arkansas.

#5-3-1-11-3-4   JAMES LEACH

James Leach, born 27 September 1943, Washington County, Arkansas, married Elsie Skeeme in 1963. James farmed Apple and Peach Orchards Near Lincoln, Washington County, Arkansas. James later had a child out of wedlock.

Children of James Leach and Elsie Skeeme

#6-3-1-11-3-4-1.   Lisa Leach, born Washington County, Arkansas.

#6-3-1-11-3-4-2.   Paul Leach, born Washington County, Arkansas.

Child of James Leach born out of wedlock

#6-3-1-11-3-4-3.   Charlie Charles Leach, born Benton County, Arkansas.

#5-3-2-1-4-2   HERBERT M. SMITH

Herbert M. Smith, born October 1895, King County, Washington, married Ruth in 1928. Ruth was born in Washington in 1907. According to the 1930, King County, Washington census, Herbert was a Road Worker for the County.

Child of Herbert M. Smith and Ruth

#6-3-2-1-4-2-1.   Charles Smith, born May 1929, King County, Washington.

#5-3-2-1-6-1   WILBUR M. SMITH

Wilbur M. Smith, born 1894, Washington, married Mary E. in 1918. Mary E. was born in 1903 in Oregon. According to the 1930, Cowlitz County census Wilbur was a Shingle Maker at a Shingle Mill.

Children of Wilbur M. Smith and Mary E.

#6-3-2-1-6-1-1.   Wilbur M. Smith, born 1922, Cowlitz County, Washington.
#6-3-2-1-6-1-2.   Clara L. Smith, born 1924, Cowlitz County, Washington.
#6-3-2-1-6-1-3.   Dennis M. Smith, born October 1928, Cowlitz County, Washington.

#5-3-2-2-9-2   RALPH WALDO BLASIER

Ralph Waldo Blasier, born 5 March 1904, Mulhall, Logan County, Oklahoma Territory, married Emma Johanna Ille, 13 April 1926, Walters, Cotton County, Oklahoma. Emma was born 15 September 1906, Lexington, Cleveland County, Oklahoma and died 24 December 1973, Ft Smith Sebastian County, Arkansas and is buried at Prairie Grove, Arkansas. Ralph died 7 September 1960, Lawton, Comanche County, Oklahoma.

Children of Ralph Waldo Blasier and Emma Johanna Ille

#6-3-2-2-9-2-1.   Joan Blasier, born 4 October 1930, Byres, Clay County, Texas.
#6-3-2-2-9-2-2.   Ralph Blasier, born 26 December 1931, Byres, Clay County, Texas.

#5-3-2-5-1-1   JAMES ELZA GLIDEWELL

James Elza Glidewell, born 18 October 1890, Washington County, Arkansas, married Lula May "Mary" Freeman, 12 December 1909, Washington County, Arkansas. Mary was born in Washington County, Arkansas 9 April 1892 and died 16 February Washington County, Arkansas. Elza died 23 December 1947 Washington County, Arkansas. Elza and Mary were lifetime farmers in Washington County, Arkansas.

Children of James Elza Glidewell and Lula May "Mary" Freeman

#6-3-2-5-1-1-1.   Loyce Glidewell, born 21 December 1910, Washington County, Arkansas.
#6-3-2-5-1-1-2.   Ardith Glidewell, born 22 July 1912, Washington County, Arkansas.
#6-3-2-5-1-1-3.   Hollie Glidewell, born 17 November 1916 Washington County, Arkansas.
#6-3-2-5-1-1-4.   Ray Glidewell, born 22 August 1918, Washington County, Arkansas.

#6-3-2-5-1-1-5.	Wilma Glidewell, born 17 November 1920, Washington County, Arkansas.
#6-3-2-5-1-1-6.	Rudy Glidewell, born 4 October 1922, Washington County, Arkansas.
#6-3-2-5-1-1-7.	Billy Glidewell, born 20 June 1925, Washington County, Arkansas.

#5-3-2-5-1-3   OLVA EARLS GLIDEWELL

Olva Earls Glidewell, born 21 October 1894, Washington County, Arkansas, married Laura Jettie Freeman, 29 November 1914, Washington County, Arkansas. Laura was born in Washington County, Arkansas, October of 1897. Olva and Laura were lifetime farmers in Washington County, Arkansas.

Children of Olva Earls Glidewell and Laura Jettie Freeman

#6-3-2-5-1-3-1.	Thelma Glidewell, born 7 November 1915, Washington County, Arkansas.
#6-3-2-5-1-3-2.	Johnnie Belle Glidewell, born 14 April 1917, Washington County, Arkansas.
#6-3-2-5-1-3-3.	Joy Glidewell, born 18 July 1919, Washington County, Arkansas.
#6-3-2-5-1-3-4.	James Glidewell, born 18 February 1922, Washington County, Arkansas.
#6-3-2-5-1-3-5.	Leland Glidewell, born 1 September 1928, Washington County, Arkansas.
#6-3-2-5-1-3-6.	June Glidewell, born 21 July 1934, Washington County, Arkansas.

#5-3-2-5-4-2   BENNETT HENRY LEACH

Bennett Henry Leach, born 11 June 1897, Washington County, Arkansas first married Jewel A. Whinery, 17 May 1919, Washington County, Arkansas. Jewel was born in 1902 in Morrow, Washington County, Arkansas. On 30 August 1935, Bennett married Weata Ryder in Washington County, Arkansas. Weata was born 2 August 1900, Adair County, Oklahoma and died 8 January 1970 in Tulsa, Tulsa County, Oklahoma. According to 1920 census Benton was employed by DuPont Chemical Engineering Company in Tennessee. In 1930 he was farming in Washington County, Arkansas. Benton died 31 March 1931 at Sunnyside, Washington and is buried in the Cox Cemetery, Washington County, Arkansas.

Child of Bennett Henry Leach And Jewel A. Whinery

#6-3-2-5-4-2-1.   Marabelle Leach, born 1921, Washington County, Arkansas.

Children of Bennett Henry Leach and Weata Mayme Ryder

#6-3-2-5-4-2-2.   Bennett Henry Leach, Jr., born 3 September 1937, Adair County, Oklahoma.
#6-3-2-5-4-2-3.   Bobby Joe Leach, born 25 January 1937, Adair County, Oklahoma.

#5-3-2-5-4-3   LUTHER DALE LEACH

Luther Dale Leach, born 3 September 1899, Washington County, Arkansas, married Tichie E. Marshall about 1920. Tichie was born in Arkansas in 1902. Luther was a lifetime Farmer and Cattle Buyer in Washington County, Arkansas. Luther died in January of 1964.

Children of Luther Dale Leach and Tichie E. Marshall

#6-3-2-5-4-3-1.   Lowell Leach, born 19 October 1922, Washington County, Arkansas.
#6-3-2-5-4-3-2.   Donald Leach, born March 1926, Washington County, Arkansas.

#5-3-2-5-4-4   AUDREY RAY LEACH

Audrey Ray Leach, born 22 June 1901, Washington County, Arkansas, married Otto L. Robinson, 7 August 1919, Washington County, Arkansas. Otto was born in Palaski County, Arkansas, 23 December 1899, and died Adair County, Oklahoma in November 1981. Otto operated a Barber Shop in Stilwell, Oklahoma, for many years.

Children of Audrey Ray Leach and Otto L. Robinson

#6-3-2-5-4-4-1.   Marjorie Robinson, born 4 January 1920, Washington County, Arkansas.
#6-3-2-5-4-4-2.   Imogene Robinson, born 12 April 1926, Los Angeles, California.

#5-3-2-5-4-5   WINNIE LEACH

Winnie Leach, born 13 June 1903, Washington County, Arkansas, married Joe W. Price, 1 November 1921, Stilwell, Adair County, Oklahoma. Joe was born in Adair County, Indian Territory 1n 1900. Joe Farmed and ran a Country Store.

Children of Winnie Leach and Joe E. Price

#6-3-2-5-4-5-1.   Grady Price, born 13 October 1922, Washington County, Arkansas.
#6-3-2-5-4-5-2.   Jalora Price, born 28 February 1926, Washington County, Arkansas.

#5-3-2-5-6-2   ERNEST LEACH

Ernest Leach, born 16 May 1910, Washington County, Arkansas, married Anna Muriel Snodgrass, 9 September 1930, Westville, Adair County, Oklahoma. Anna was born 1911 in Washington County, Arkansas According to 1930, Washington County, Arkansas census, Ernest was a Carpenter.

Child of Ernest Leach and Anna Muriel Snodgrass

#6-3-2-5-6-2-1.   Ernastine Leach, born 19 September 1931, Washington County, Arkansas.

#5-3-2-5-7-1   OPAL R. RINEHART

Opal R. Rinehart, born 18 November 1900, Washington County, Arkansas, married Myrtle King, 5 March 1923. Myrtle was born in Arkansas in 1907 and died 27 February 1929, Stilwell, Adair County, Oklahoma. According to the 1930 Washington County, Arkansas census, Opal was a Farmer. Opal died in Washington County, Arkansas in May of 1963.

Child of Opal R. Rinehart and Myrtle

#6-3-2-5-7-1.   Bobbie C. Rinehart, born May 1929, Washington County, Arkansas.

#5-3-2-5-7-2   HARLEY RINEHART

Harley Rinehart, born 19 December 1902, Washington County, Arkansas, married Lena Glidewell, 13 December 1930, Washington County, Arkansas. Lena was born 1915 in Washington County, Arkansas.

Children of Harley Rinehart and Lena Glidewell

#6-3-2 5-7-2-1.   Kenneth Rinehart, born 25 June 1933, Washington County, Arkansas.

#6-3-2-5-7-2-2.   Ronnie Rinehart, born 19 January 1936, Washington County, Arkansas.

#6-3-2-5-7-2-3.   Carolyn Rinehart, born 7 August 1942, Washington County, Arkansas.

#5-3-2-5-7-3   JAMES RINEHART

James Rinehart, born 19 October 1904, Washington County, Arkansas, married Burmah Freeman, 3 August 1929, Washington County, Arkansas. Burmah was born 13 June 1910, Washington County, Arkansas and died 1 January 1990, Adair County, Oklahoma. James Operated a Grocery and Filling Station in Morrow, Washington County, Arkansas. James died 26 June 1979, Washington County, Arkansas.

Children of James Rinehart and Burmah Freeman

#6-3-2-5-7-3-1.   Roy Gene Rinehart, born 28 June 1932 Washington County, Arkansas.
#6-3-2-5-7-3-2.   Irmalee Rinehart, born 9 March 1939 Washington County, Arkansas.

#5-3-2-5-7-4   ORVIL LEE RINEHART

Orvil Lee Rinehart, born 14 November 1906, Washington County, Arkansas, married Oklahoma Fletcher, 8 February 1931. Oklahoma was born 8 March 1910 in Oklahoma and died 21 April 1995, Orange County, California. Orvil died 29 December 1960, Los Angeles County, California.

Children of Orvil Lee Rinehart and Okla Fletcher

#6-3-2-5-7-4-1.   Charles Edwin Rinehart, born 28 January 1932, Los Angeles, California.
#6-3-2-5-7-4-2.   Albert Henry Rinehart, born 2 February 1934, Oklahoma.
#6-3-2-5-7-4-3.   Don Rinehart, born 10 August 1935, Oklahoma.

#5-3-2-5-7-5   LILLUS RINEHART

Lillus Rinehart, born 6 June 1909, Washington County, Arkansas, married Fay B. Reed, 11 December 1927. Fay was born 30 May 1906, Washington County, Arkansas and died October 1986, Stilwell, Adair County, Oklahoma. Fay Operated a Hardware and Furniture Store in Stilwell, Oklahoma. Lillus died 5 March 1995, at Stilwell, Adair County, Oklahoma.

Children of Lillus Rinehart and Fay B. Reed

#6-3-2-5-7-5-1.	Emma Dean Reed, born 31 October 1930, Stilwell, Adair County, Oklahoma.
#6-3-2-5-7-5-2.	Dennis Fay Reed, 21 February 1933, Stilwell, Adair County, Oklahoma.

#5-3-2-5-9-1   JOHN WALTER REED

John Walter Reed, born 25 April 1901, Washington County, Arkansas, married Annie D. Simpson, 22 August 1921, Washington County, Arkansas. Annie was born 1904 in Arkansas. John and Annie moved to Washington prior to 1925. According to the 1930, Grays Harbor County, Washington census, John was not employed at that time.

Children of John Walter Reed and Annie D. Simpson

#6-3-2-5-9-1-1.	James Garland Reed, born 1922, Washington County, Arkansas.
#6-3-2-5-9-1-2.	Curtis Robert Reed, born 1925, Gray Harbor County, Washington.
#6-3-2-5-9-1-3.	Virgil Grady Reed, born 22 September 1927, Gray Harbor County, Washington.

#5-3-2-5-9-2   ROSCOE KING ABSHIRE

Roscoe King Abshire, born 2 February 1912, Washington County, Arkansas, married Irene Loftin, 30 September 1930, Washington County, Arkansas. Irene was born 23 September 1910, Washington County, Arkansas.

Children of Roscoe King Abshire and Irene Loftin

#6-3-2-5-9-2-1.	Merle Dean Abshire, born 11 November 1933, Washington County, Arkansas, died 22 October 1937, Washington County, Arkansas.
#6-3-2-5-9-2-2.	Darrell Wayne Abshire, born 8 February 1935, Washington County, Arkansas.
#6-3-2-5-9-2-3.	Billy Gene Abshire, born 21 August 1936, Washington County, Arkansas.
#6-3-2-5-9-2-4.	Wanda Lee Abshire, born 30 March 1939, Washington County, Arkansas.
#6-3-2-5-9-2-5.	Phyllis Sue Abshire, born 28 July 1948, Washington County, Arkansas.

#5-3-2-5-9-3   DOW LEACH ABSHIRE

Dow Leach Abshire, born 24 March 1914, Washington County, Arkansas, married Francis Lucille Keck, 19 August 1939. Francis was born 2 November 1922.

Children of Dow Leach Abshire and Francis Lucille Keck

#6-3-2-5-9-3-1.	Bobby Joel Abshire, born 4 March 1944, Washington County, Arkansas.
#6-3-2-5-9-3-2.	James Leroy Abshire, born December 1946, Washington County, Arkansas.
#6-3-2-5-9-3-3.	Donald Lee Abshire, born 31 January 1953, Washington County, Arkansas.
#6-3-2-5-9-3-4.	Debra Kay Abshire, born 3 August 1957, Washington County, Arkansas.

#5-3-2-5-9-4   ELIZABETH DORCAS ABSHIRE

Elizabeth Dorcas Abshire, born 22 February 1920, Washington County, Arkansas, married Glen Loftin, 29 March 1941, Washington County, Arkansas. Glen was born 23 October 1922, Washington County, Arkansas.

Children of Elizabeth Dorcas Abshire and Glen Loftin

#6-3-2-5-9-4-1.   Etsel Glen Loftin, born 23 October 1942, Washington County, Arkansas.

#6-3-2-5-9-4-2.   Annette Loftin, born 11 March 1945, Washington County, Arkansas.

#6-3-2-5-9-4-3.   Keith Loftin, born 23 November 1947, Washington County, Arkansas.

#6-3-2-5-9-4-4.   Bruce Loftin, born 14 September 1950, Washington County, Arkansas.

#5-3-2-5-9-5   DOROTHY ELLEN ABSHIRE

Dorothy Ellen Abshire, born 29 July 1924, Washington County, Arkansas, married Robert Gene Minick, 31 August 1943. Robert was born 27 June 1921, Tennessee and died 24 October 1999, San Lois Obispo County, California. Dorothy died 18 July 2004, San Bernardino County, California.

Children of Dorothy Ellen Abshire and Bob Gene Minick

#6-3-2-5-9-5-1.   Roger Lail Minick, born 31 July 1944, Romana, Oklahoma.

#6-3-2-5-9-5-2.   Mary Linn Minick, born 28 January 1951, Benton County, Arkansas.

#6-3-2-5-9-5-3.   Alecia Ann Minick, born 31 August 1952, Benton County, Arkansas.

#6-3-2-5-9-5-4.   Storm Sterling Minick, born 18 September 1957, Fontana, San Bernardino County, California.

#5-3-2-5-9-6   CONNIE LAVERNE ABSHIRE

Connie Laverne Abshire, born 8 January 1928 Washington County, Arkansas, married Lucrissie Runabout, 6 February 1951. Lacrissie died 9 July 1978.

Children of Connie Laverne Abshire and Lacrissie Runabout

#6-3-2-5-9-6-1.   Patricia Ann Abshire, born 9 March 1952, Oklahoma.
#6-3-2-5-9-6-2.   Larry Eugene Abshire, born 24 February 1954, Wichita, Kansas.
#6-3-2-5-9-6-3.   Anita Sue Abshire, born 10 August 1956, Wichita, Kansas.
#6-3-2-5-9-6-4.   Connie Joe Abshire, born 10 February 1961, Wichita, Kansas.
#6-3-2-5-9-6-5.   Joseph David Abshire, born 14 October 1964, Wichita, Kansas.

#5-3-2-7-1-2   GILBERT GERALD SHELTON

Gilbert Gerald Shelton, born 20 October 1902, Oklahoma City, Oklahoma Territory, married Arvella Mae Manning, 25 April 1936. Arvella was born 11 August 1910. Gilbert died 8 November 1983, Oklahoma City, Oklahoma and is buried in the Memorial Park Cemetery.

Children of Gilbert Gerald Shelton and Arvella Manning

#6-3-2-7-1-2-1.   Charles Shelton, born.
#6-3-2-7-1-2-2.   Lorna Shelton, born.
#6-3-2-7-1-2-3.   Loretta Shelton, born.

#5-3-2-7-1-3 LILLIAN INA SHELTON

Lillian Ina Shelton, born 11 February 1905, Oklahoma City, Oklahoma Territory, married Oscar Lee Grahm, 1 March 1924, Oklahoma City, Oklahoma. Oscar was born 1 November 1899 in Oklahoma and died 8 June 1968, Oklahoma City, Oklahoma. According to 1930 Oklahoma County, Oklahoma census, Oscar worked in Railroad Freight. Lillian died 5 February 1990, Oklahoma City, Oklahoma and is buried in Memorial Park Cemetery.

Children of Lillian Ina Shelton and Oscar Lee Grahm

#6-3-2-7-1-3-1.	William Leroy Grahm, born 1926, Oklahoma County, Oklahoma.
#6-3-2-7-1-3-2.	Wanda Louis Grahm, born 1929, Oklahoma County, Oklahoma.
#6-3-2-7-1-3-3.	Bob Grahm, born Oklahoma County, Oklahoma.
#6-3-2-7-1-3-4.	Tommy Grahm, born Oklahoma County, Oklahoma.
#6-3-2-7-1-3-5.	Jack Grahm, born Oklahoma County, Oklahoma.

#5-3-2-7-1-4 THELMA M. SHELTON

Thelma M. Shelton, born 21 January 1908, Oklahoma City, Oklahoma, married Earl Ray Link, 6 December 1924, Oklahoma City, Oklahoma. Earl was born 21 June 1908, Oklahoma. According to the 1930 Oklahoma County, Oklahoma census, Earl was a Baptist Clergyman.

Children of Thelma M. Shelton and Earl Ray Link

#6-3-2-7-1-4-1.	Elvona Lee Link, born November 1926, Oklahoma County, Oklahoma.
#6-3-2-7-1-4-2.	Emory Link, born Oklahoma County, Oklahoma.

#5-3-2-7-1-5   CLARA BERNICE SHELTON

Clara Bernice Shelton, born 15 January 1915, Oklahoma City, Oklahoma, married Ralph Austin Weinscott, 31 May 1931 Oklahoma City, Oklahoma. Ralph was born 15 June 1915.

Child of Clara Bernice Shelton and Ralph Austin Weinscott

#6-3-2-7-1-5-1.   Ralph Gerald Weinscott, born Oklahoma County, Oklahoma.

#5-3-2-7-1-6   LAVITA MARIE SHELTON

Lavita Marie Shelton, born 18 January 1918, Oklahoma City, Oklahoma, married Martin Bean. Lavita died 26 February 1984, and had her ashes scattered over Northern California.

Child of Lavita Marie Shelton and Martin Bean

#6-3-2-7-1-6-1.   Barbara Bean, born.

#5-3-2-7-6-5   JOSEPH DECATUR LONGWITH

Joseph Decatur Longwith, born 24 March 1925, Bluejacket, Oklahoma, married Helen Marie Berry, 1 March 1947, Oklahoma City, Oklahoma. Helen was born 1 August 1926, Oklahoma City, Oklahoma.

Children of Joseph Decatur Longwith and Helen Marie Berry

#6-3-2-7-6-5-1.   Dale Eugene Longwith, born 26 August 1951, Oklahoma City, Oklahoma.
#6-3-2-7-6-5-2.   Barbara Jean Longwith, born 17 March 1954, Oklahoma City, Oklahoma.

#5-3-3-1-1-1   VELMA LENORE EDMISTON

Velma Lenore Edmiston born 3 June 1907 Tulare County, California, married Meryl Seldomn Chatten in 1926. Meryl was born 12 April 1902 California and died 7 July 1992 in Tulare County, California. According to the 1930 Tulare County California census, Meryl was a Truck Driver for a Creamery. Velma died 3 June 1996 Tulare County, California.

Children of Velma Lenore Edmiston and Meryl Seldomn Chatten

#6-3-3-1-1-1-1.	Rayford Eugene Chatten, born 16 January 1927, Tulare County, California.
#6-3-3-1-1-1-2.	Dorothy Evelyn Chatten, born 7 July 1931, Tulare County, California.
#6-3-3-1-1-1-3.	Donna Earlene Chatten, born 16 September 1935, Tulare County, California.
#6-3-3-1-1-1-4.	Thomas Arthur Chatten, born 1 January 1940, Tulare County, California.

#5-3-3-1-3-1   FRANK RIKER EDMISTON

Frank Riker Edmiston, born 23 December 1909, Tulare County, California, married Clara Delta Kloss, 24 June 1992. Clara was born 16 May 1915 in North Dakota. Frank and Clara were fruit farmers in Tulare County, California. Frank died 24 June 1992, Tulare County, California.

Children of Frank Riker Edmiston and Clara Delta Kloss

#6-3-3-1-3-1-1.	Nancy Emma Edmiston, born 26 July 1937, Tulare County, California.
#6-3-3-1-3-1-2.	Raymond Frank Edmiston, born 7 February 1939, Tulare County, California, died in his infancy.
#6-3-3-1-3-1-3.	Norma Della Edmiston, born 8 November 1940, Tulare County, California.

#6-3-3-1-3-1-4.   Gloria Ann Edmiston, born 28 February 1945, Contra Costa County, California.

#5-3-3-1-3-2   FREDERICK DELZELL EDMISTON

Frederick Delzell Edmiston, born 19 April 1911, Tulare County, California, married Eleanor Frances Van Hoy about 1938. Eleanor was born 24 June 1918, and died 13 September 2002, Tulare County, California. Frederick were involved in Fruit Farming in Tulare County, California. Frederick died 3 February 1992, Fresno County, California.

Children of Frederick Delzell Edmiston and Eleanor Frances Van Hoy

#6-3-3-1-3-2-1.   Robert Allen Edmiston, born 11 October 1939, Tulare County, California. Robert married Mrs. Trisler, 25 March 1989. No Children of marriage.
#6-3-3-1-3-2-2.   Eleanor Margaret Edmiston, born 15 June 1947, Tulare County, California.

#5-3-3-1-3-3   MARIAN ELIZABETH EDMISTON

Marian Elizabeth Edmiston, born 14 July 1912, Tulare County, California, married Vernon Earl Haury about 1938. Vernon was born 7 August 1910 in California and died 20 March 1995 in Ventura County, California. Marian died 13 April 1995 in Ventura California.

Children of Marian Elizabeth Edmiston and Vernon Earl Haury

#6-3-3-1-3-3-1.   Marianna Haury, born 23 April 1939, Alameda County, California.
#6-3-3-1-3-3-2.   Eugene Vernon Haury, born 15 March 1943, Alameda County, California.

| #6-3-3-1-3-3-3. | John Frederick Haury, born 24 April 1947, Alameda County, California. |
| #6-3-3-1-3-3-4. | Steven Earl Haury, born 29 October 1953, Ventura County, California. |

#5-3-3-1-3-4   RICHARD THOMAS EDMISTON

Richard Thomas Edmiston, Born 9 December 1923, Tulare County, California, married Ruth Elaine Kress. Richard and Ruth were involved in Agriculture in Tulare County, California.

Children of Richard Thomas Edmiston and Ruth Elaine Kress

#6-3-3-1-3-4-1.	Susan Elaine Edmiston, born 24 January 1948, Tulare County, California.
#6-3-3-1-3-4-2.	Rebecca Ruth Edmiston, born 30 June 1951, Tulare County, California.
#6-3-3-1-3-4-3.	Thomas James Edmiston, born 9 June 1955, Tulare County, California,

#5-3-4-2-1-3   HAROLD MURRAY

Harold Murray, born 1905, Los Angeles, California, married Gertrude about 1927. Gertrude was born in Oklahoma in 1910. According to the 1930 Okmulgee County, Oklahoma census, Harold was a Mechanic for an Auto Agency.

Child of Harold Murray and Gertrude

| #6-3-4-2-1-3-1. | Gertrude C. Murray, born January 1927, Okmulgee County, Oklahoma. |

#5-3-4-3-1-1   LEE EDMISTON

Lee Edmiston, born July 1892, Washington County, Arkansas, married Maggie about 1913. Maggie was born 1897 in North Carolina. According to the 1930 Tulsa County, Oklahoma census, Lee was employed in Maintenance for a Bus Line.

Children of Lee Edmiston and Maggie

#6-3-4-3-1-1-1.	Pauline Edmiston, born 1916, Washington County, Arkansas.
#6-3-4-3-1-1-2.	Rayburn Edmiston, born 1917, Washington County, Arkansas.
#6-3-4-3-1-1-3.	Lee Edmiston, born 1923, Washington County, Arkansas.
#6-3-4-3-1-1-4.	Louise Edmiston, born October 1927, Washington County, Arkansas.

#5-3-4-3-1-2   CLIFFORD EDMISTON

Clifford Edmiston, born May 1894, Washington County, Arkansas, married Elsie about 1915. Elsie was born in Arkansas in 1897. According to 1930 Adair County, Oklahoma census, Clifford was a Farmer, living at Westville, Oklahoma.

Children of Clifford Edmiston and Elsie

#6-3-4-3-1-2-1.	Gratie Edmiston, born 1916, Adair County, Oklahoma.
#6-3-4-3-1-2-2.	Gussie Edmiston, born 1918, Washington County, Arkansas.
#6-3-4-3-1-2-3.	Genevive Edmiston, born 1922, Washington County, Arkansas.

#5-3-4-3-2-2   RETA E. MORROW

Reta E. Morrow, born 20 April 1894, Tulare County, California, married Joseph E. Lilly about 1919. Joseph E. Lilly was born 2 October 1887 in Kansas and died 25 December 1960, Los Angeles County, California. According to the 1930 Los Angeles County, California census, Joseph was a Rancher.

Children of Reta E. Morrow and Joseph E. Lilly

#6-3-4-3-2-2-1.   Earlene Lilly, born 1920, Los Angeles County, California.

#6-3-4-3-2-2-2.   Ralph Ervin Lilly, born 20 October 1926, Los Angeles County, California.

#5-3-4-3-6-1   ORVAL H. EDMISTON

Orval H. Edmiston, born 1908, Washington County, Arkansas, married Theresa in 1924. Theresa was born in Utah in 1905. According to the 1930 Iron County, Utah census, Orval was a Yard Man For the Railroad.

Children of Orval H. Edmiston and Theresa

#6-3-4-3-6-1-1.   Norma Edmiston, born October 1925 in Iowa.

#6-3-4-3-6-1-2.   D. Clyde Edmiston, born December 1927 in Iowa.

#6-3-4-3-6-1-3.   Howard C. Edmiston, born May 1929 Iron County, Utah.

#5-3-5-1-2-2   HOWARD M. ERWIN

Howard M. Erwin, born 19 March 1906 in Oregon, married Florence Irene Rittenhouse in 1927. Florence was born 8 May 1910 in New Mexico and died 1 March 1989, Los Angeles County, California. According to 1930, Los Angeles County, California census Howard was a Gas Flow Contract Superintendent. Howard died 17 October 1973, Los Angeles County, California.

Children of Howard M. Erwin and Florence Irene Rittenhouse

#6-3-5-1-2-2-1.   Virginia Erwin, born May 1928, Los Angeles County, California.

#6-3-5-1-2-2-2.   Carol Jean Erwin, born 28 September 1930, Los Angeles, California.

#5-3-5-1-4-3   RUTH HALSTEAD

Ruth Halstead, born 25 April 1907, Los Angeles County, California, married Harry L. Vatcher in 1926. Harry was born in England, 2 September 1905, and died 19 March 1968, Los Angeles County, California. According to 1930 Los Angeles County, California, Census, Harry was a Salesman for Wholesaler. Ruth Died 20 September 1984, Los Angeles County, California.

Child of Ruth Halstead and Harry L. Vatcher

#6-3-5-1-4-3-1.   Bruce Halstead Vatcher, born 10 June 1933, Los Angeles County, California.

#5-3-5-2-1-1   BAILEY G. ROGERS

Bailey G. Rogers, born September 1896, Guadalupe County, Texas, married Oma Bandy in 1919. Oma was born April 1898 in Crocket County, Texas.

Child of Bailey G. Rogers and Oma Bandy

#6-3-5-2-1-1-1.   James E. Rogers, born 2 January 1927, Medina County, Texas.

#5-3-5-2-1-2   EMORY GRAYFORD ROGERS

Emory Grayford Rogers, born 1906, Medina County, Texas, married Ethel P. Harlee in 1926. Ethel was born 1910 in Texas.

Child of Emory Grayford Rogers and Ethel P. Harlee

#6-3-5-2-1-2-1.   Ora Jaradene Rogers, born 21 June 1940, Medina County, Texas.

#5-3-5-2-2-1   ANNIE FLORENCE BUTLER

Annie Florence Butler, born 1907, Medina County, Texas, married Samuel Gilbert Hutchinson about 1933.

Children of Annie Florence Hutchinson and Samuel Gilbert Hutchinson

#6-3-5-2-2-1-1.   Mary Lois Hutchinson, born 31 July 1935, Hays County, Texas.
#6-3-5-2-2-1-2.   Patricia Anne Hutchinson, born 30 September 1942, Hays County, Texas.

#5-3-5-2-2-3   FRED WALKER BUTLER, JR.

Fred Walker Butler, Jr., born 1910, Medina County, Texas, married Vedith Edith Belver, 3 December 1933. Vedith was born 20 July 1914, and died 21 April 2003, Hayes County, Texas. Fred died 26 January 1993, Hays County, Texas.

Children of Fred Walker Butler, Jr. and Vedith Edith Belver

#6-3-5-2-2-3-1.   Betty Marie Butler, born 3 October 1934, Hays County, Texas.
#6-3-5-2-2-3-2.   Velma Ann Butler, born 2 October 1940, Hays County, Texas.

#5-3-5-4-1-1   BLEAKLEY ASHLEY WALKER

Bleakley Ashley Walker, born 3 June 1924, Texas, married Dora Beverly McNulty about 1946. Dora was born 18 March 1929, Crocket County, Texas. Bleakley died 30 July 1975, San Bernardino County, Calicornia.

Children of Bleakley Ashley Walker and Dora Beverly McNulty

#6-3-5-4-1-1-1.   Sylvia Sue Walker, born 24 December 1948, Jefferson County, Texas.
#6-3-5-4-1-1-2.   Barry Winston Walker, born 13 October 1950, Parker County, Texas.

#5-3-5-4-1-2   WILLIE LILBURN WALKER

Willie Lilburn Walker, born 27 August 1925, Texas, married Catherine June Walker about 1950. Willie died 6 March 2004, Jonesboro, Arkansas.

Children of Willie Lilburn Walker and Catherine June Walker

#6-3-5-4-1-2-1.   Warren Lilburn Walker, born 21 September 1952, Grayson County, Texas.
#6-3-5-4-1-2-2.   Melody Aline Walker, born 16 January 1955, Grayson County, Texas.

#5-3-5-4-2-3   MARY OPHELIA WALKER

Mary Ophelia Walker, born 6 January 1919, Williamson County, Texas, married Thomas Maxon Whitley about 1941. Mary died 5 December 1980, Austin, Travis County, Texas.

Child of Mary Ophelia Walker and Thomas Maxon Whitley

#6-3-5-4-2-3-1.   Nilburn Allen Whitley, born 19 January 1943, Travis County, Texas.

#5-3-5-4-2-4   VIVIAN LUCILLE WALKER

Vivian Lucille Walker, born 22 July 1920, Williamson County, Texas, married Arthur Raney Daugherty about 1941. Arthur was born 28 October 1918, and died 20 June 1992, Austin, Travis County, Texas. Vivian died 4 June 1975, Austin, Travis County, Texas.

Children of Vivian Lucille Walker and Arthur Raney Daugherty

#6-3-5-4-2-4-1.   Alice Lucille Daugherty, born 9 June 1943, Travis County, Texas.

#6-3-5-4-2-4-2.   Barbara Jean Daugherty, born 1 November 1944, Travis County, Texas.

#5-3-5-4-2-5   VERNA GENE WALKER

Verna Gene Walker, born 1 October 1925, Williamson County, Texas, married Joe Fuhrman about 1949. Joe was born 19 January 1915, and died 9 May 1968, Austin, Travis County, Texas. Verna died 20 January 1998, Dallas, Dallas County, Texas.

Children of Verna Gene Walker and Joe Fuhrman

#6-3-5-4-2-5-1.   Marilyn Jean Fuhrman, born 14 September 1950, Travis County, Texas.

#6-3-5-4-2-5-2.   Joe Scott Fuhrman, born 28 November 1952, Travis County, Texas.

#5-3-5-4-3-2   JAMES WALTER WILLIAMS

James Walter Williams, born 21 July 1922, Williamson County, Texas, married Lillie Mae Zieschang, 11 April 1947, Lampasas, Texas. Lillie was born 22 December 1928, Guadalupe County, Texas. James died 8 June 2008, Austin, Travis County, Texas.

Children of James Walter Williams and Lillie Mae Zieschang

#6-3-5-4-3-2-1.   Carol Ann Williams, born 12 August 1953, Travis County, Texas.

#6-3-5-4-3-2-2.   Bryan Keith Williams, born 23 August 1956, Travis County, Texas.

#5-3-5-5-1-2   ELIZABETH NELL WALKER

Elizabeth Nell Walker, born 30 October 1925, Uvalde, Uvalde County, Texas, married Vernon Leo Rankin about 1941. Vernon was born 11 February 1918, and died 15 November 1999, Carrizo Springs, Dimmit County, Texas. Elizabeth died 26 June 1979, Uvalde, Uvalde County, Texas.

Children of Elizabeth Nell Walker and Vernon Leo Rankin

#6-3-5-5-1-2-1.   Carolyn Knox Rankin, born 29 July 1943, Uvalde County, Texas.

#6-3-5-5-1-2-2.   Sharon Elizabeth Rankin, born 30 August 1946, Uvalde County, Texas.

#6-3-5-5-1-2-3.   Robert Edward Rankin, born 17 December 1949, Uvalde County, Texas.

#5-3-5-5-1-3   SAM ALLEN WALKER

Sam Allen Walker, born 3 November 1928, Uvalde, Uvalde County, Texas, married Eleanor Gladine Shaw about 1951. Eleanor was born 28 January 1932, and died 8 March 2001, Bandera, Bandera County, Texas. Sam died 25 November 1984.

Children of Sam Allen Walker and Eleanor Gladine Shaw

#6-3-5-5-1-3-1.   Stanley Maurice Walker, born 23 August 1952, Uvalde County, Texas.

#6-3-5-5-1-3-2.   Gregory Stewart Walker, born 19 September
                       1955, Uvalde County, Texas.

#5-3-5-5-1-4   JACK PAUL WALKER

Jack Paul Walker, born 7 January 1932, Uvalde, Uvalde County, Texas,
married, Betty Sue Etheridge about 1955. Betty was born 27 February
1934, Bexar County, Texas.

Children of Jack Paul Walker and Betty Sue Etheridge

#6-3-5-5-1-4-1.   Jeffrey Paul Walker, born 13 June 1957, Uvalde
                       County, Texas.
#6-3-5-5-1-4-2   Lynn Evan Walker, born 10 January 1962,
                       Uvalde County, Texas.

#5-3-5-5-1-5   JOE ANN WALKER

Joe Ann Walker born, 27 December 1932 Uvalde, Uvalde County, Texas,
married Clyde Claude Alexander 30 May 1972 Harding County, Texas.
Clyde was born 29 April 1934 Jefferson County, Texas.

Child of Joe Ann Walker and Clyde Claude Alexander

#6-3-5-5-1-5-1.   Claudette Rachelle Alexander, born 29 October
                       1972, Jefferson County, Texas.

#5-3-5-5-2-1   CAROLYN MARIE WALKER

Carolyn Marie Walker, born 11 December 1948, Grayson County,
Texas, married Michael Thomas King, 9 May 1969, Dallas, Dallas
County, Texas. Michael was born in 1947.

Children of Carolyn Marie Walker and Michael Thomas King

#6-3-5-5-2-1-1.   James Michael King, born 9 November 1970, Dallas County, Texas.

#6-3-5-5-2-1-2.   Jeffrey Thomas King, born 9 January 1976, Dallas County, Texas.

#5-3-5-5-2-3   KATHERINE JEAN WALKER

Katherine Jean Walker, born 10 January 1952, Dallas, Dallas County, Texas, married David Paul Mays, 19 December 1970, Dallas, Dallas County, Texas. David was born 10 October 1948, Hopkins County, Texas.

Children of Katherine Jean Walker and David Paul Mays

#6-3-5-5-2-3-1.   John Paul Mays, born 3 February 1975, Tarrant County, Texas.

#6-3-5-5-2-3-2.   Joseph David Mays, born 12 October 1977, Tarrant County, Texas.

#6-3-5-5-2-3-3.   Timothy Isaac Mays, born 23 March 1980, Tarrant County, Texas.

#5-3-5-5-2-4   RONALD LYNN WALKER

Ronald Lynn Walker, born 22 January 1957, Dallas, Dallas County, Texas, married Amy Candida Pate, 31 July 1976, Hunt County, Texas. Amy was born in 1958.

Children of Ronald Lynn Walker and Amy Candida Pate

#6-3-5-5-2-4-1.   Matthew Ryan Walker, born 17 September 1978, Hunt County, Texas.

#6-3-5-5-2-4-2.   Dustin Michael Walker, born 31 October 1980, Hunt County, Texas.

| #6-3-5-5-2-4-3. | Corey Daniel Walker, born 30 December 1982, Hopkins County, Texas. |
| #6-3-5-5-2-4-4. | Colby Aaron Walker, born 4 March 1986, Hopkins County, Texas. |

#5-3-5-6-1-1   JAMES WILLIS DOCKERY

James Willis Dockery, born November 1903, Uvalde County, Texas, married Cynthia Lee Dockery in 1929. Cynthia was born 21 January 1906, in Texas and died 16 January 1985, Bexar County, Texas. James died 27 May 1991, Bexar County, Texas.

Children of James Willis Dockery and Cynthia Lee Dockery

#6-3-5-6-1-1-1.	James Willis Dockery, Jr., born 13 October 1929, Bexar County, Texas.
#6-3-5-6-1-1-2.	Allen Daniel Dockery, born 6 September 1931, Bexar County, Texas.
#6-3-5-6-1-1-3.	Richard Lee Dockery, born 28 August 1933, Bexar County, Texas.
#6-3-5-6-1-1-4.	Ted Edwin Dockery, born 31 December 1935, Bexar County, Texas.

#5-3-5-6-1-4   ALVIN ALLEN DOCKERY

Alvin Allen Dockery, born 19 August 1910, Uvalde County, Texas, married Laura Etta Wheeler about 1931. Laura was born 5 October 1909, and died 16 February 2001, Los Angeles, Los Angeles County, California. Alvin died December 1970 in Missouri.

Children of Alvin Allen Dockery and Laura Etta Wheeler

| #6-3-5-6-1-4-1. | Allen Wheeler Dockery, born 12 January 1933, Hays County, Texas. |

| #6-3-5-6-1-4-2. | Jo Ann Dockery, born 10 May 1935, Uvalde County, Texas. |

#5-3-6-2-3-1   GEORGE H. SANDS

George H. Sands, born 21 December 1912, Charleston, Mississippi County, Missouri, married Lavace Brazel, 23 October 1937, Benton, Scott County, Missouri. Lavace was born in 1923 in Missouri. George was a heavy machinery operator and followed construction projects.

Child of George H. Sands and Lavace Brazel

| #6-3-6-2-3-1-1. | Betty Sue Sands, born 5 August 1938. |

#5-3-6-2-3-5   ALBERTA SANDS

Alberta Sands, born April 1918, Charleston, Mississippi County, Missouri, first married James Chester Elliott about 1946. James was born 28 July 1922, Graves County, Kentucky. Alberta later married Dale Chamnis.

Children of Alberta Sands and James Chester Elliott

#6-3-6-2-3-5-1.	James Chester Elliot, born 28 September 1947, Cairo, Illinois.
#6-3-6-2-3-5-2.	Regina Elliott, born 19 September 1948, Mississippi County, Missouri.
#6-3-6-2-3-5-3.	Gilbert Elliott, born March 1950, Mississippi County, Missouri.

Child of Alberta Sands and Dale Chamnis

| #6-3-6-2-3-5-4. | Bobby Chamnis, born March 1960, Alton, Illinois. |

#5-3-6-2-3-7   HERBERT MARSHAL 'JAKE' SANDS

Herbert Marshall 'Jake' Sands, born 8 January 1922, Charleston, Mississippi County, Missouri, married Margie Marie Morgan, 7 February 1942, Mississippi County, Missouri. Margie was born in Buncombe, Illinois 12 January 1928.

Children of Herbert Marshall 'Jake' Sands and Margie Morgan

#6-3-6-2-3-7-1.   Margie Ellen Sands, born 15 December 1942, Mississippi County, Missouri.

#6-3-6-2-3-7-2.   Lovace Ann Sands, born 17 September 1945, Cairo, Illinois.

#6-3-6-2-3-7-3.   Herbert Harrison Sands, born 7 August 1949, Cairo, Illinois.

#6-3-6-2-3-7-4.   Gary Lee Sands, born 21 August 1952, Cairo, Illinois.

#5-3-6-2-3-8   MINNIE PEARL SANDS

Minnie Pearl Sands, born 8 May 1927, Charleston, Mississippi County, Missouri, married Lawrence Quertermous, 25 September 1943, Mississippi County, Missouri. Lawrence was born 26 November 1923, at Double Springs, Alabama. Lawrence has Farmed and Raised Livestock for many years in Union County, Illinois.

Children of Minnie Pearl Sands and Lawrence Quertermous

#6-3-6-2-3-8-1.   Sandra Lee Quertermous, born 21 March 1945, Union County, Illinois.

#6-3-6-2-3-8-2.   Larry Joe Quertermous, born 7 January 1947, Union County, Illinois.

#5-3-6-2-3-9   REGENA ELLEN SANDS

Regena Ellen Sands, born 30 June 1930, Scott County, Missouri, married Lyle Waldron, 3 December 1947, Charleston, Mississippi County, Missouri. Lyle was born about 1926.

Children of Regena Ellen Sands and Lyle Waldron

#6-3-6-2-3-9-1.	Thomas Eugene Waldron, born 29 October 1948, Hammond, Indiana.
#6-3-6-2-3-9-2.	Robert Waldron, born 28 August 1950, Charleston, Missouri.
#6-3-6-2-3-9-3.	Curtis Waldron, born 2 September 1953, Charleston, Missouri, died 2006, Indianapolis, Indiana.
#6-3-6-2-3-9-4.	Talbert Waldron, born 27 October 1957, East Chicago, Indiana.
#6-3-6-2-3-9-5.	Linda Sue Waldron, born 4 May 1961, Hammond, Indiana.

#5-3-6-2-7-1   HELEN MAXINE LEACH

Helen Maxine Leach, born 26 September 1922, Washington County, Arkansas, married Ralph Walter Burris, 6 August 1947, Sidney, Nebraska. Ralph was born 20 September 1922, in Scott City, Kansas and died 3 January 1990, in Malene, Kansas, (a small town near Elk Falls). Ralph is buried in the Ganderville Cemetery, Washington County, Arkansas. Ralph moved many times and held many jobs over the years of the marriage. Maxine died 9 December 1997, Piersonville, Cass County, Missouri.

Children of Helen Maxine Leach and Ralph Walter Burris

#6-3-6-2-7-1-1.	Max Walter Burris, born 18 July 1948, Garden City, Kansas.
#6-3-6-2-7-1-2.	William Clarence Burris, born 19 December 1950, Wichita, Kansas.

#6-3-6-2-7-1-3.   Katherine Ann Burris, born 18 October 1954, Harris County, Texas.

#6-3-6-2-7-1-4.   Lee Roy Burris, born 14 February 1957, Phoenix, Arizona.

#6-3-6-2-7-1-5.   Harvey Joseph Burris, born 7 January 1960, Yakima, Washington, died 5 November 1962, Prairie Grove, Washington County, Arkansas.

#5-3-6-2-7-2   WILLIAM PAUL "BILL" LEACH

William Paul "Bill" Leach, born 14 February 1925, Washington County, Arkansas, married Flora Irene Holmes, 1 November 1952, Tahlequah, Cherokee County, Oklahoma. Irene was born 11 April 1933, Boone County, Arkansas. Bill worked in the Logging Industry in Northern California. He died from Leukemia which he probably got from a period of time he worked in an Atomic Energy Plant. Bill died 29 December 1972, in Mendocino County, California and is buried in the Russian River Cemetery.

Children of William Paul "Bill" Leach and Flora Irene Holmes

#6-3-6-2-7-2-1.   William Paul Leach, born 5 January 1954, Washington County, Arkansas.

#6-3-6-2-7-2-2.   Carolyn Isabell Leach, born 15 May 1955, Mendocino County, California.

#6-3-6-2-7-2-3.   Cheryl Rose Leach, born 30 October 1958, Mendocino County, California.

#5-3-6-2-7-3   ANNA PHYLLIS LEACH

Anna Phyllis Leach, born 6 February 1927, Washington County, Arkansas, married Clinton "Shorty" Sargent, 22 November 1952, Washington County, Arkansas. Shorty was born 24 August 1922, Washington County, Arkansas. He worked for the Forrest Department Controlling Fires and farmed near West Fork, Arkansas.

Children of Anna Phyllis Leach and Clinton "Shorty" Sargent

#6-3-6-2-7-3-1.	John Paul Sargent, born 5 June 1954, Washington County, Arkansas.
#6-3-6-2-7-3-2.	James Henry Sargent, born 2 February 1956, Washington County, Arkansas.
#6-3-6-2-7-3-3.	Thomas Lynn Sargent, born 3 September 1961, Washington County, Arkansas.

#5-3-6-2-7-4   HATTIE LILLUS LEACH

Hattie Lillus Leach, born 6 February 1927, Washington County, Arkansas, married Howard Franklin Evans, 28 November 1957, Yakima, Washington. Howard was born 18 September 1929, Deep Water, Missouri. Lillus worked as a Nurse in Yakima, Washington for many years.

Children of Hattie Lillus Leach and Howard Franklin Evans

#6-3-6-2-7-4-1.	Sharon Kay Evans, born 10 December 1927, Yakima, Washington.
#6-3-6-2-7-4-2.	Karen Fay Evans, born 11 August 1960, Yakima, Washington.
#6-3-6-2-7-4-3.	LeAnna Lynn Evans, born 6 January 1963, Yakima, Washington.
#6-3-6-2-7-4-4.	LaDonna Lee Evans, born 6 January 1963, Yakima, Washington.
#6-3-6-2-7-4-5.	Rachel Denise Evans, born 26 February 1965, Yakima, Washington.

#5-3-6-2-7-5   HENRY HARRISON "JACK" LEACH

Henry Harrison "Jack" Leach, born 26 September 1922, Washington County, Arkansas, married Ruby Mae Ormsbee, 24 April 1953, Yakima, Washington. Jack died from Cancer probably resulting from years earlier when he worked at a Atomic Energy Plant. Jack's employment was as a Labeling Machine Operator for a canning plant in or around Yakima Washington.

Children of Henry Harrison "Jack" Leach and Ruby Mae Ormsbee

#6-3-6-2-7-5-1.   Brenda Kay Leach, born 13 September 1954, Yakima, Washington.

#6-3-6-2-7-5-2.   Larry 'Dean' Leach, born 14 November 1955, Yakima, Washington.

#5-3-6-2-7-6   JOHN RALPH LEACH

John Ralph Leach, born 5 December 1933, Washington County, Arkansas, married Wanda Loughridge, 1 May 1957, Tahlequah, Cherokee County, Oklahoma. Wanda was born 8 August 1940, Washington County, Arkansas. John first retired from the United States Navy and later retired from a Chicken Hatchery.

Children of John Ralph Leach And Wanda Loughridge

#6-3-6-2-7-6-1.   Gail Lea Leach, born 17 September 1963, Green Cove Springs, Florida.

#6-3-6-2-7-6-2.   John Ralph Leach, Jr., born 11 September 1968, Pensacola, Florida.

#5-3-6-2-8-1   CHARLES WEBB HANES, JR.

Charles Webb Hanes, Jr., born 20 January 1923, Charleston Mississippi County, Missouri, married Elsie M. Morgan, 3 November 1941, East Prairie, Mississippi County, Missouri. Elsie was born 12 January 1926, Buncombe, Illinois and died 1 November 1981, Los Angeles County, California. Charles died 8 February 1975, Los Angeles County, California. Charles was buried in Mississippi County, Missouri.

Child of Charles Webb Hanes, Jr. and Elsie M. Morgan

#6-3-6-2-8-1.   Phyllis Jean Hanes, born 25 August 1943,
                       Mississippi County, Missouri.

#5-3-6-2-8-2   MAXINE HANES

Maxine Hanes, born 5 August 1924, Charleston, Mississippi County,
Missouri, married Alfred Buddy Hill, 20 September 1941, Charleston,
Missouri. Buddy was born 7 February 1918, Cairo, Illinois.

Children of Maxine Hanes and Alfred Buddy Hill

#6-3-6-2-8-2-1.   Betty Lou Hill, born 9 January 1943, Mississippi
                       County, Missouri.
#6-3-6-2-8-2-2.   Gary Michael Hill, born 18 March 1947,
                       Mississippi County, Missouri.
#6-3-6-2-8-2-3.   Charles Alfred Hill, born 26 January 1948,
                       Mississippi County, Missouri.

#5-3-6-2-8-3   LULA MAE HANES

Lula Mae Hanes, born 25 August 1926, Charleston, Mississippi County,
Missouri, married Edward Delane Morgan, 31 January 1944, Tampa
Florida. Edward was born 5 September 1923, Buncombe, Illinois. Lula
Mae retired after working a lifetime at Brown Show Factory, Charleston,
Missouri.

Children of Lula Mae Hanes and Edward Morgan

#6-3-6-2-8-3-1.   Edward Delane Morgan, born 11 April 1946,
                       Mississippi County, Missouri.
#6-3-6-2-8-3-2.   Dennis Morgan, born 30 June 1947, Mississippi
                       County, Missouri.
#6-3-6-2-8-3-3.   Danny Morgan, born 30 September 1949,
                       Mississippi County, Missouri.

#6-3-6-2-8-3-4.	David Morgan, born 30 July 1954, Mississippi County, Mississippi.
#6-3-6-2-8-3-5.	Diana Morgan, born 2 September 1955, Mississippi County, Missouri.
#6-3-6-2-8-3-6.	Dale Morgan, born 30 December 1956, Mississippi County, Missouri.
#6-3-6-2-8-3-7.	Deborah Morgan, born 14 December 1957, Mississippi County, Missouri.

#5-3-6-2-9-1   ETHEL ELLEY BIGGS

Ethel Elley Biggs, born 11 January 1922, Washington County, Arkansas, married Donald Edward Lockwood, 10 July 1948, Minneapolis, Hennepin County, Minnesota. Donald was born 1 May 1921, Minneapolis, Minnesota and died 26 December 2004, Minneapolis, Minnesota.

Children of Elizabeth Elley Biggs and Donald Edward Lockwood

#6-3-6-2-9-1-1.	Jeffrey Allen Lockwood, born 6 June 1949, Hennepin County, Minnesota.
#6-3-6-2-9-1-2.	Cheryl Christine Lockwood, born 4 July 1951, Hennepin County, Minnesota.
#6-3-6-2-9-1-3.	Peggy Jo Ann Lockwood, born 20 April 1953, Hennepin County, Minnesota.
#6-3-6-2-9-1-4.	Patrick Arthur Lockwood, born 16 October 1954, Hennepin County, Minnesota, died 21 November 2003 Hennepin County, Minnesota.
#6-3-6-2-9-1-5.	Patricia Arleva Lockwood, born 16 October 1954, Hennepin County, Minnesota.

#5-3-6-2-9-3   LOUISE BIGGS

Louise Biggs, born 9 December 1932, Washington County, Arkansas, First married Randal Wayne Pharr, 7 July 1950, Washington County, Arkansas. Wayne was born 14 December 1930, Washington County,

Arkansas. Wayne and Louise grew chickens and Turkeys in Washington County, Arkansas. Louise later married James Sturdy, 28 March 1986, Washington County, Arkansas. Louise died 20 November 2007, Washington County, Arkansas, from complications following Cancer treatment.

Children of Louise Biggs and Wayne Pharr

#6-3-6-2-9-3-1.   Linda Pharr, born 8 April 1952, Washington County, Arkansas.

#6-3-6-2-9-3-2.   Michael Wayne Pharr, born 22 May 1953, Washington County, Arkansas.

#6-3-6-2-9-3-3.   Marsha Pharr, born 20 January 1957, Washington County, Arkansas.

#5-3-6-2-9-4   GEORGE RAY BIGGS

George Ray Biggs, born 31 December 1934, Washington County, Arkansas, married Hazel McCracken, 30 August 1954, Tahlequah, Cherokee County, Oklahoma. Hazel was born 9 January 1934, Washington County, Arkansas. George Farmed, raised Turkeys, Chickens and had an Egg Farm Near Lincoln, Arkansas.

Children of George Ray Biggs and Hazel McCracken

#6-3-6-2-9-4-1.   Denise Biggs, born April 24 1957, Washington County, Arkansas.

#6-3-6-2-9-4-2.   Carl Biggs, born 8 February 1959, Washington County, Arkansas.

#6-3-6-2-9-4-3.   Curtis Paul Biggs, born 26 March 1963, Washington County, Arkansas.

#5-3-6-2-10-1   MARSHALL WEBB LEACH

Marshall Webb Leach, born 1 April 1924, Memphis, Shelby County, Tennessee, married Rose Mary Elaine SanFilippo, 4 November 1950,

San Francisco, California. Rose Mary was born 20 December 1934, San Diego, California. Marshall was raised by his grand parents in Washington County. Served a tour of duty in the Navy in WW ll, after which he drove a bus in the San Francisco area until retirement. Marshall died 18 January 2008, Los Altos, Santa Clara County, California.

Children of Marshall Webb Leach and Rose Mary Elaine SanFilippo

#6-3-6-2-10-1-1.   Sharon Ann Leach, born 6 August 1951, Oakland, California.

#6-3-6-2-10-1-2.   Paula Jo Leach, born 3 October 1957, Redwood City, California.

#5-3-6-2-11-1   REVA MAE LEACH

Reva Mae Leach born, 1 January 1934, Washington County, Arkansas, married Johnny Ray Etheridge, 19 April 1953, Stilwell, Adair County, Oklahoma. John was born 5 September 1930, Stilwell, Adair County, Oklahoma. John was a Radar Technician with FAA. After divorcing John, Reva married A. D. Paine, 30 August 1996, Guymon, Texas County, Oklahoma.

Children of Reva Mae Leach And Johnny Ray Etheridge

#6-3-6-2-11-1-1.   Johnny Ray Etheridge, Jr., born 13 April 1954, Prairie Grove, Arkansas.

#6-3-6-2-11-1-2.   Lou Ann Etheridge, born 23 October 1957, Stillwater, Oklahoma.

#6-3-6-2-11-1-3.   Patricia Gail Etheridge, born 26 June 1959, Norman, Oklahoma

#5-3-6-2-11-2   FRANCES LEACH

Frances Leach, born 30 January 1936, Washington County, Arkansas, married Patrick Eugene Brown, 23 January 1956, Tahlequah, Cherokee

County, Oklahoma. Pat was born 11 September 1934, Oklahoma City, Oklahoma and died 18 January 2000, Oklahoma City, Oklahoma. Pat is buried in the Rose Hill Burial Park in Oklahoma City. Pat was a lifetime attorney in Oklahoma City with Frances working in his office.

Children of Frances Leach and Patrick Eugene Brown

#6-3-6-2-11-2-1.	Patrick Eugene Brown ll, born 23 March 1963, Oklahoma City, Oklahoma.
#6-3-6-2-11-2-2.	Michael Leach Brown, born 31 August 1963, Oklahoma City, Oklahoma.
#6-3-6-2-11-2-3.	Sarita Frances Brown, born 29 July 1965, Oklahoma City, Oklahoma.

#5-3-6-2-11-3   GEORGE HARRISON LEACH II

George Harrison Leach II, born Washington County, Arkansas, married Norma Lee Brock, 26 May 1959, Tahlequah, Cherokee County, Oklahoma. Norma was born 21 June 1942, Stilwell, Adair County, Oklahoma. George operated a Canning Plant in Plainview Texas until 1974, when he sold out to go to Law School. After Law at Oklahoma City University, he served as Assistant District Attorney in Cimarron County, Oklahoma for six years, then as Associate District Judge until 1991. In 1991 he was appointed as District Judge where he served until retirement in September of 2000. After divorcing Norma George married Iolline Jo Pitcock, 26 April 1995, in Stinnett, Texas.

Children of George Harrison Leach II and Norma Lee Brock

#6-3-6-2-11-3-1.	George Harrison Leach 111, born 6 July 1961, Plainview, Texas.
#6-3-6-2-11-3-2.	Debra Lynn Leach, born 2 March 1963, Washington County, Arkansas.
#6-3-6-2-11-3-3.	Catherine Marie Leach, born 14 July 1964, Washington County, Arkansas, died 14 July

1964, Washington County, Arkansas, buried at Stilwell, Oklahoma.

#5-3-6-2-13-1   ALFRED ANDREW SPRATT

Alfred Andrew Spratt, born 30 October 1928, Washington County, Arkansas, married Edith Elizabeth Caldwell October 1950.

Children of Alfred Andrew Spratt and Edith Caldwell

#6-3-6-2-13-1-1.   Carl Spratt, born 15 February 1952, Carbondale, Illinois

#6-3-6-2-13-1-2.   Kathy Spratt, born 10 September 1954, Salem, Illinois

#5-3-6-2-13-2   GENE DERALD SPRATT

Gene Derald Spratt, born 4 August 1930, Drumright, Oklahoma, married Rosemary Pursley, 15 June 1951, Mount Vernon, Illinois. Rosemary was born 21 May 1932 Salem, Illinois. Gene retired as a School Teacher and moved to Arizona.

Children of Gene Derald Spratt and Rosemary Pursley

#6-3-6-2-13-2-1.   Donald Eugene Spratt, born 7 April 1953, Tacoma Washington.

#6-3-6-2-13-2-2.   Thomas Gerald Spratt, born 29 March 1954, Carbondale, Illinois.

#6-3-6-2-13-2-3.   Scott Spratt, born 15 December 1958, Carmi, Illinois.

#5-3-6-2-13-3   EUGENE JERALD SPRATT

Eugene Jerald Spratt, born 4 August 1930, Drumright, Oklahoma, married Peggy Goff, 2 December 1956, Bloomington, Illinois. Peggy was born 18 January 1936, Bloomington, Illinois. Eugene retired from U. S. Military after 28 years service.

Children of Eugene Jerald Spratt and Peggy Goff

#6-3-6-2-13-3-1. Jim Spratt, born 28 August 1970, Panama City, Florida.

#6-3-6-2-13-3-2. David Spratt, born 28 December 1972, Great Falls, Montana.

#5-3-6-2-13-4   WILLIAM WALTER SPRATT

William Walter Spratt, born 4 January 1933, Washington County, Arkansas, married Betty ElJean Costilow, 4 August 1953, Salem, Illinois. Betty was born 23 October 1933, in Salem, Illinois.

Children of William Walter Spratt and Betty ElJean Costlow

#6-3-6-2-13-4-1. Tracy Kay Spratt, born 28 January 1959, Carmi, Illinois.

#6-3-6-2-13-4-2. William Walter Spratt, born 8 March 1963, New Iberia, Louisiana.

#6-3-6-2-13-4-3. Elsie Anne Spratt, born 20 January 1967, Little Rock, Arkansas.

#6-3-6-2-13-4-4. Nancy Spratt, born 4 December 1968, New Iberia, Louisiana.

#5-3-6-4-1-1   VERNA BELL CAVIN

Varna Bell Cavin, born 9 October 1914, in Cherokee County, Oklahoma, married Clifford C. Stephens about 1939 in Texas. Clifford died about 1971. Varna died 19 September 1997, in Safford, Graham County, Arizona.

Children of Verna Bell Cavin and Clifford C. Stephens

#6-3-6-4-1-1-1.	Robert Eugene Stephens, born 26 September 1940, El Paso, Texas.
#6-3-6-4-1-1-2.	James Thomas Stephens, born 29 November 1943, Terry County, Texas
#6-3-6-4-1-1-3.	Sharron Stephens. (married Ferguson).
#6-3-6-4-1-1-4.	Beverly Stephens. (married Flint).
#6-3-6-4-1-1-5.	Verna Stephens. (married Sharp).
#6-3-6-4-1-1-6.	Joan Stephens. (married Oldaker).

#5-3-6-4-1-2   HAZEL MAE CAVIN

Hazel Mae Cavin, born 13 November 1919, in Tulsa County, Oklahoma, married William C. McIntire. William was born 15 June 1909, and died 16 October 2000, at Hot Springs, Arkansas. Hazel died 12 January 2008, in Hot Springs, Arkansas.

Child of Hazel Mae Cavin and William C. McIntire

#6-3-6-4-1-2-1.	John David McIntire born about 1949.

#5-3-7-1-1-2   BOBBY GENE GUTHREY

Bobby Gene Guthrey born, 13 November 1927, Gentry, Benton County, Arkansas, married Arlene Louella Yocham, 9 January 1950, Gentry, Benton County, Arkansas. Arlene was born 14 June 1929, Preston, Oklahoma.

Children of Bobby Gene Guthrey and Arlene Louella Yocham

#6-3-7-1-1-2-1.	Brenda Christine Guthrey, born 15 April 1952, Tulsa, Oklahoma.
#6-3-7-1-1-2-2.	Marcia Elsie Guthrey, born 19 February 1955, Searcy, Arkansas.

#6-3-7-1-1-2-3.   Letitia Elsie Guthrey, born 11 February 1966, died 6 June 1977.

#5-3-7-1-1-3   PATRICIA LOUISE GUTHREY

Patricia Louisa Guthrey, born 3 December 1932, Gentry, Benton County, Arkansas, married Donald Kent Marts, 24 July 1958. Donald was born 21 October 1928, at Cimarron, Gray County, Kansas.

Children of Patricia Louise Guthrey and Donald Kent Marts

#6-3-7-1-1-3-1.   Andy Thomas Marts, born 2 March 1961.
#6-3-7-1-1-3-2.   Michael Kent Marts, born 17 March 1963.

#5-3-7-1-1-4   MARY RUTH GUTHREY

Mary Ruth Guthrey, born 29 March 1941, Benton County, Arkansas, married David Frederick Shomberg. David was born 27 July 1942.

Children of Mary Ruth Guthrey and David Frederick Shomberg

#6-3-7-1-1-4-1.   Sheryl Lyn Schomberg, born 19 April 1969.
#6-3-7-1-1-4-2.   Suzanne Lea Schomberg, born 23 February 1971.

#5-3-7-5-2-1   JERALD E. RICH

Jerald E. Rich, born 16 November 1928, Mulvane, Sumner County, Kansas, married Lorna Stucke, 24 January 1954, Santa Clara, Utah. Lorna was born 29 October 1933, Santa Clara, Utah and died 4 July 1986, Las Vegas, Nevada. Jerald spent four years in the United States Air Force, Then Operated a Service Station for two years, Then worked for the Air Force Base for eight years, afterwards he operated his own Automotive Shop in the Las Vegas, Nevada area until retirement.

Children of Jerald E. Rich and Lorna Stucke

#6-3-7-5-2-1-1.   Kenneth Jerald Rich, born 24 January 1960, Las Vegas, Nevada.

#6-3-7-5-2-1-2.   Michael Alan Rich, born 19 October 1971, Las Vegas, Nevada.

#5-3-7-5-2-2   COLEEN RICH

Coleen Rich born, 9 August 1930, Adair County, Oklahoma, married Kenneth W. Murray, 23 April 1953, Stilwell, Adair County, Oklahoma. Kenneth was born 13 April 1916, Okfuskee County, Oklahoma and died 19 January 1997, Muskogee, Muskogee County, Oklahoma. Kenneth worked for years in the Meat Market at Blackard's IGA in Stilwell, Oklahoma. Coleen first worked for Carson Loan Company in Stilwell, Oklahoma, and later for the Rural Electric Service, Stilwell, Oklahoma.

Child of Coleen Rich and Kenneth W. Murray

#6-3-7-5-2-2-1.   Virginia Murray, born April 30 1955, Stilwell, Adair County, Oklahoma.

#5-3-7-5-2-3   WANDA JEAN RICH

Wanda Jean Rich, born 18 September 1932, Adair County, Oklahoma, first married James Lee Murray, 21 May 1959, Stilwell, Adair County, Oklahoma. James was born 5 October 1930. Wanda later married Clarence Breshears.

Child of Wanda Jean Rich and James Lee Murray

#6-3-7-5-2-3-1.   James Lee Murray, born 16 March 1968, Stilwell, Adair County, Oklahoma.

#5-3-7-5-2-4　　　HAROLD WESLEY RICH

Harold Wesley Rich, born 26 December 1934, Adair County, Oklahoma, first married Betty Nevells, 16 January 1956, Stilwell, Adair County, Oklahoma. Betty was born 11 July 1936, Tulsa, Oklahoma and Died of Cancer 11 March 1984 at Tulsa, Oklahoma. Harold was employed as a technician for Chevron Oil Company. After the death of Betty, Harold married Mary Ann Patterson, 16 February 1985, Tulsa, Oklahoma.

Children of Harold Wesley Rich and Belly Nevells

#6-3-7-5-2-4-1.	Pamela Sue Rich, born 20 October 1956, Muskogee County, Oklahoma.
#6-3-7-5-2-4-2.	Sharon Lanett Rich, born 6 November 1962, Muskogee County, Oklahoma.

#5-3-7-5-2-5　　　GLENDA ROSE RICH

Glenda Rose Rich, born 26 January 1937, Adair County, Oklahoma, married Leon Bolin in December 1970, at Stilwell, Adair County, Oklahoma.

Child of Glenda Rose Rich and Leon Bolin

#6-3-7-5-2-5-1.	Tracy Bolin, born 15 April 1973, Ft Smith, Sebastian County, Arkansas.

#5-3-7-5-2-6　　　BURL RICH

Burl Rich, born 22 November 1938, Adair County, Oklahoma, first married Lydia Earlene Maner, Muskogee, Oklahoma. Burl, later, on 14 February 1964, married Eva Green, Muskogee, Oklahoma. Eva was born 22 September 1946, Okemah, Oklahoma Burl worked for the Veterans Administration.

Children of Burl Rich and Eva Green

#6-3-7-5-2-6-1.   Shelly Rich, born 16 June 1965, St Louis, Missouri.

#6-3-7-5-2-6-2.   Fincher Burl Rich, born 8 April 1968, Muskogee, Oklahoma.

#5-3-7-5-6-1   LEVAH MAY CARTER

Levah May Carter, born 1 August 1942, Klamath Falls, Oregon, married Ronald Lee Worley, 19 May 1962, Klamath Falls. Oregon. Ronald was born 21 November 1940, Rogersville, Webster County, Missouri.

Children of Levah May Carter and Ronald Lee Worley

#6-3-7-5-6-1-1.   Wesley Cleo Worley, born 28 May 1967, Seattle, King County, Washington.

#6-3-7-5-6-1-2.   Levahna Lee Worley, born 12 January 1969, Seattle, King County, Washington.

#5-3-7-5-6-2   BONNIE JO CARTER

Bonnie Jo Carter, born 16 July 1946, Klamath Falls, Oregon, married David John Born 7 August 1971, Klamath Falls, Oregon. David was born 4 April 1947, Klamath Falls, Oregon.

Children of Bonnie Jo Carter and David John Born

#6-3-7-5-6-2-1.   Julie Jo Born, born 3 November 1973, Apple Valley, San Bernardino County, California.

#6-3-7-5-6-2-2.   John Daniel Born, born 17 November 1976, Richland, Benton County, Arkansas.

#6-3-7-5-6-2-3.   Alva Vian Born, born 21 October 1984, Klamath Falls, Oregon.

#5-3-9-2-5-1   OLETA JUANICE HOLMES

Oleta Juanice Holmes, born 24 December 1940, Fresno, Fresno County, California, first married Doyle Ray Hurst. Doyle was born 5 April 1938, Santa Cruz, California. Oleta later married Robert Arlen Yocum, 22 January 1966, Fresno, Fresno County, California. Robert was born 18 May 1934, Holdenville, Seminole County, Oklahoma.

Children of Oleta Juanice Holmes and Doyle Ray Hurst

#6-3-9-2-5-1-1.   Debra Marlene Hurst, born 3 October 1957, Fresno, California.
#6-3-9-2-5-1-2.   Kerry Dianne Hurst, born 5 September 1960, Fresno, California.

Children of Oleta Juanice Holmes and Robert Arlen Yocum

#6-3-9-2-5-1-3.   Kristi Ann Yocum, born 2 September 1964, Fresno, California.
#6-3-9-2-5-1-4.   Robert James Yocum, born 10 December 1972, Fresno, California.

#5-3-9-2-5-2   VIRGINIA DARLENE HOLMES

Virginia Darlene Holmes, born 2 May 1942, Reedley, Fresno County, California, married Alfred Roger Mawhinney, 21 October 1967, Carson City, Nevada. Alfred was born 7 August 1936, Emeryville, California.

Child of Virginia Darlene Holmes and Alfred Roger Mawhinney

#6-3-9-2-5-2-1.   John Eric Mawhinney, born 1 August 1970, Alameda County, California.

#5-3-9-2-5-4   GERRELL DWIGHT HOLMES

Gerrell Dwight Holmes, born 13 March 1945, Reedly, Fresno County, California, married Virginia Joyce Brown, 4 March 1967, Fresno County, California. Virginia was born 25 July 1950, California and died in 1994.

Children of Gerrell Dwight Holmes and Virginia Joyce Brown

#6-3-9-2-5-4-1.   Christina M. Holmes, born 12 November 1967, Fresno County, California.
#6-3-9-2-5-4-2.   Sherri Lynn Holmes, born 10 November 1970, Fresno County, California.

#5-3-9-2-5-5   JAMES CAROL HOLMES

James Carol Holmes, born 25 April 1946, Fresno, Fresno County, California, first married Deborah Ann Hemmeigarn. Deborah was born in 1951. James later married Elizabeth Higgs, 6 October 1978, Kaysville, Davis County, Utah. Elizabeth was born in 1953.

Child of James Carol Holmes and Deborah Ann Hemmeigarn

#6-3-9-2-5-5-1.   Brian James Holmes, Born 1972 Utah.

Child of James Carol Holmes and Elizabeth Higgs

#6-3-9-2-5-5-2.   Joshua Leroy Holmes Born in Utah.

#5-3-9-2-5-6   ILONA GAIL HOLMES

Ilona Gail Holmes, born 18 October 1947, Fresno, Fresno County, California, married Dale Lee Evans 30 May 1975, Fresno County, California.

Child of Ilona Gail Holmes and Dale Lee Evans

#6-3-9-2-5-6-1.   Larry Douglas Evans, born 7 May 1971.

#5-3-9-2-5-9   DANNY ERWIN HOLMES

Danny Erwin Holmes, born 26 May 1952, Fresno, Fresno County, California, married Barbara Sue Martin, 23 October 1973, Fresno, Fresno County, California. Barbara was born 14 April 1958, Fresno County, California.

Children of Danny Erwin Holmes and Barbara Sue Martin

#6-3-9-2-5-9-1.   Stephani Ann Holmes, born 15 February 1974, Fresno County, California.
#6-3-9-2-5-9-2.   Jonathan Daniel Holmes, born 11 February 1976, Fresno County, California.

#5-3-9-2-5-10   ESTEVEN RAY HOLMES

Esteven Ray Holmes, born 22 June 1956, Fresno, Fresno County, California, married Deborah Louise Bjork, 24 May 1980, Fresno, Fresno County, California. Deborah was born in 1959.

Children of Esteven Ray Holmes and Deborah Louise Bjork

#6-3-9-2-5-10-1.   Crystal Elizabeth Holmes, born 25 September 1981, Fresno County, California.
#6-3-9-2-5-10-2.   Ashley Marie Holmes, born 3 March 1985, Fresno County, California.
#6-3-9-2-5-10-3.   Brianna Ellen Holmes, born 22 May 1991, Fresno County, California.

#5-4-1-7-2-1   MYRON RUHL

Myron Ruhl, born November 1899, Adams County, Illinois, married Edna M. in 1924. Edna was born in 1901, Illinois. According to 1930, Warren County, Illinois census, Myron was a Farmer.

Child of Myron Ruhl and Edna M.

#6-4-1-7-2-1-1.   William K. Ruhl, born 1925, Illinois.

#5-4-2-4-4-1   NOBLE ELLIOT

Noble Elliot, born 1899, Douglas County, Missouri, married Erma in 1919. Erma was born in Missouri in 1900.

Child of Noble Elliot and Erma

#6-4-2-4-4-1-1.   Maxine L. Elliot, born December 1926, Missouri.

#5-4-3-1-1-2   ELSIE M. LEACH

Elsie M. Leach born 1907, Crawford County, Missouri. Married Karl E. Vetter. Karl was born in 1902.

Child of Elsie E. Leach and Karl E. Vetter

#6-4-3-1-1-2-1.   Donald E. Vetter, born 1928, Cook County, Illinois.

SEVENTH GENERATION

#6-3-1-2-4-5-1   GILBERT WOOD STRICKLAND

Gilbert Wood Strickland born 6 May 1926, Sequoyah County, Oklahoma, married Betty.

Children of Gilbert Wood Strickland and Betty

#7-3-1-2-4-5-1-1.   Mark Strickland, born. Married Nancy.
#7-3-1-2-4-5-1-2.   Shannon Strickland, born. Married Maria Las De Mercedes, 16 November 1984.
#7-3-1-2-4-5-1-3.   Kimberly Strickland, born. Married Douglas Lawson, 2 June 1979.

#6-3-1-2-4-6-1   ANNA BELLE PATTERSON

Anna Belle Patterson born 31 January 1929, Sequoyah County, Oklahoma, married William Winsor 29 October 1947.

Children Of Anna Belle Patterson and William Winsor

#7-3-1-2-4-6-1-1.   Sheri Lynn Winsor, born. Married Darriel G. Hallstrom.
#7-3-1-2-4-6-1-2.   Patrick Ray Winsor, born. Married Joy Elizabeth.
#7-3-1-2-4-6-1-3.   Michael James Winsor, born. Married Cheryl Ann.

#6-3-1-2-4-6-3   JERRY RAY PATTERSON

Jerry Ray Patterson born 4 January 1936, Shawnee, Oklahoma, married Jeanie Faye Trimmer 6 May 1956.

Children of Jerry Ray Patterson and Jeanie Faye Trimmer

#7-3-1-2-4-6-3-1.	Tami Lynn Patterson, born. Married Dan Catania.
#7-3-1-2-4-6-3-2.	Valerie Ann Patterson, born. Married Bill Davies.
#7-3-1-2-4-6-3-3.	Rebecca Kay Patterson, born.

#6-3-1-3-4-1-3   STEPHEN JAMES BARTLETT

Stephen James Bartlett, born 24 June 1963, Oklahoma City, Oklahoma, married Tracy Lee Warner, 12 June 1981, Del City, Oklahoma. Tracy was born 22 February 1963, Oklahoma City, Oklahoma.

Children of Stephen James Bartlett and Tracy Lee Warner

#7-3-1-3-4-1-3-1.	Jerrod Miles Bartlett, Born 16 January 1983, Oklahoma City, Oklahoma.
#7-3-1-3-4-1-3-2.	Tyler Lee Bartlett, born 2 August 1985, Oklahoma City, Oklahoma.

#6-3-1-3-4-2-1   SHELLY DAWN DALTON

Shelly Dawn Dalton, born 18 January 1963, Wheat Ridge, Colorado, married first John Goggin. Shelly later married David Gerging, 15 February 2002, in Juno, Alaska. David was born 15 February 1956.

Children of Shelly Dawn Dalton and John Gerging

#7-3-1-3-4-2-1-1.	Ian Gerging, born 10 July 2003, Denver, Colorado.
#7-3-1-3-4-2-1-2.	Benjamin Gerging, born 25 February 2006, Denver, Colorado.

#6-3-1-5-3-4-1   EDWARD MULHALL, JR.

Edward Mulhall, Jr., born 19 March 1933, Tulsa, Tulsa County, Oklahoma, married Janet Elizabeth Breffle, 28 November 1959, Evergreen, Colorado. Janet was born 18 August 1936, Estes Park, Colorado.

Children of Edward Mulhall, Jr. and Janet Elizabeth Breffle

#7-3-1-5-3-4-1-1.   Mitchell Edward Mulhall, born 15 September 1960, Ft Carson, Colorado.

#7-3-1-5-3-4-1-2.   Jill Elizabeth Mulhall, born 2 June 1962, Ft Carson, Colorado.

#6-3-1-6-4-4-1   LINDA DEAN CHULUFUS

Linda Dean Chulufus, born 12 March 1944, Bakersfield, Kern County, California, married Dennis Albert Erikson, 4 June 1967, Granada Hill, California. Dennis was born 9 March 1939, Las Angeles County, California.

Children of Linda Dean Chulufus and Dennis Albert Erikson

#7-3-1-6-4-4-1-1.   Karl Dean Erikson, born 28 November 1968, Los Angeles, California.

#7-3-1-6-4-4-1-2.   Craig Adam Erikson, born 19 August 1970, Los Angeles, California.

#6-3-1-6-4-7-1   RICHARD FRANKLIN CHULUFUS, JR.

Richard Franklin Chaufus, Jr., born 23 July 1953, Independence, Missouri, married Cindy Broderson in 1977 in Vancouver, Clark County, Washington.

Children of Richard Franklin Chulufas, Jr., and Cindy Broderson

#7-3-1-6-4-7-1-1.   Richard Franklin Chulufas lll, born 28 October 1977.

#7-3-1-6-4-7-1-2.   Jennifer Lee Ann Chulufas, born 19 February 1979.

#6-3-1-6-4-7-2   KAREN ELIZABETH CHULUFAS

Karen Elizabeth Chulufas, born 3 September 1951, Washington D.C. married Roger Allen Moberg, 22 July 1972, Battleground, Clark County, Washington.

Children of Karen Elizabeth Chulufas and Roger Allen Moberg

#7-3-1-6-4-7-2-1.   Lisa Louise Moberg, born 28 March 1974.

#7-3-1-6-4-7-2-2.   Carla Marie Moberg, born 13 January 1976.

#6-3-2-2-9-2-2   RALPH BLASIER

Ralph Blasier born, 26 December 1931, Byres, Clay County, Texas, married Tama Fern Talley, 21 November 1953 Kansas City, Missouri. Tama was born 29 June 1932, Chigley, Murray County, Oklahoma.

Children of Ralph Blasier and Tama Fern Talley

#7-3-2-2-9-2-2-1.   Karen Lyne Blasier, born 1 July 1954, Sulphur, Murray County, Oklahoma.

#7-3-2-2-9-2-2-2.   Tony Ralph Blasier, born 22 October 1956, Ardmore, Carter County, Oklahoma.

#6-3-2-5-1-1-1   LOYCE GLIDEWELL

Loyce Glidewell, born 21 December 1910, Washington County, Arkansas married Naomi A. Burgess 29 November 1930. Naomi was born in 1915 in Washington County, Arkansas. Loyce later married Wilma Henter, Loyce died 10 February 1997, Washington County, Arkansas.

Children of Loyce Glidewell and Naomi A. Burgess

#7-3-2-5-1-1-1-1.   Nadine Glidewell, born 1932, Crawford County, Arkansas.

#7-3-2-5-1-1-1-2.   Jeanine Glidewell, born 18 July 1933, Crawford County, Arkansas, died 26 March 2012, Fort Smith, Arkansas, married Sam m. Peoples, 9 Seprember 1953.

Child of Loyce Glidewell and Wilma Hunter

#7-3-2-5-1-1-1-3   Nathan Loyce Glidewell, born July 22 1938, Orange County, California.

#6-3-2-5-1-1-2   ARDITH GLIDEWELL

Ardath Glidewell, born 22 July 1914, Washington County, Arkansas, married Orval Keck. Orval was born 26 November 1913 Crawford County, Arkansas and died 29 July 1993 Washington County, Arkansas According to 1930 Crawford County, Arkansas census, Orval was employed as a farm laborer. Ardath died 7 May 1969 Washington County, Arkansas.

Child of Ardith Glidewell and Orval Keck

#7-3-2-5-1-1-2-1.   Alice Lee Keck, born Washington County, Arkansas.

#6-3-2-5-1-1-3   HOLLIE GLIDEWELL

Hollie Glidewell, born 17 July 1916, Washington County, Arkansas, married Othal Howard. Othal was born 12 July 1910 in Okmulgee,

Oklahoma and died 21 December 1984, Lincoln, Arkansas. Othal was a Farmer and Apple Grower near Lincoln, Arkansas. Hollie died 11 August 2002, Lincoln, Arkansas.

Children of Hollie Glidewell and Othal Howard

#7-3-2-5-1-1-3-1.   Bob Howard, born 27 February 1936, Washington County, Arkansas.

#7-3-2-5-1-1-3-2.   Theda Jean Howard, born 22 February 1938, Los Angeles County, California.

#6-3-2-5-1-1-7   BILL F. GLIDEWELL

Bill F. Glidewell, born 20 June 1925, Washington County, Arkansas, married Ruby Prince at Huntsville, Arkansas. Ruby was born 6 June 1936 at Waurika, Oklahoma. Bill Farmed and Raised Poultry in Washington County, Arkansas.

Children of Bill F. Glidewell and Ruby Prince

#7-3-2-5-1-1-7-1.   Bobby Gene Glidewell, born 1 May 1954, Berea, Ohio.

#7-3-2-5-1-1-7-2.   Janet Fay Glidewell, born 15 August 1957, Washington County, Arkansas.

#6-3-2-5-1-3-2   JOHNNIE BELLE GLIDEWELL

Johnnie Belle Glidewell, born 14 April 1917, Washington County, Arkansas, married Forrest Rodgers, 28 July 1934 in Lincoln, Washington County, Arkansas. Forrest was born 15 January 1916, Washington County, Arkansas and died 21 January 2002, Washington County, Arkansas. Forrest was a very prosperous and successful business man in Lincoln, Arkansas.

#7-3-2-5-1-3-2-1.	Gale Rodgers, born 3 May 1939, Washington County, Arkansas.
#7-3-2-5-1-3-2-2.	Pamela Rodgers, born 19 September 1949, Washington County, Arkansas.

#6-3-2-5-1-3-3 JOY GLIDEWELL

Joy Glidewell, born 18 July 1919, Washington County, Arkansas, married Richard D. Butzback. Richard was born 3 July 1914, Pueblo, Colorado and died in June 1995 in Banning, Riverside County, California. Joy died 25 September 1971, Los Angeles County, California.

Child of Joy Glidewell and Richard D. Butzback

#7-3-2-5-1-3-3-1.	James Richard Butzbock, born 27 January 1943, Los Angeles County, California.

#6-3-2-5-1-3-4 JAMES GLIDEWELL

James Glidewell, born 18 February 1922, Washington County, Arkansas, married Dorothy Cate. James and Dorothy moved from Arkansas to Los Angeles County, California about 1950.

Children of James Glidewell and Dorothy Cate

#7-3-2-5-1-3-4-1.	Judith Glidewell, born in 1948.
#7-3-2-5-1-3-4-2.	Jane Ann Glidewell, born 17 March 1953, Los Angeles County, California
#7-3-2-5-1-3-4-3.	Lisa Gaye Glidewell, born 17 September 1958, Los Angeles County, California.

#6-3-2-5-1-3-5   LELAND GLIDEWELL

Leland Glidewell, born 1 September 1928, Washington County, Arkansas, married Arlene Breitenbach. Leland moved from Arkansas to Los Angeles, California about 1950.

Children of Leland Glidewell and Arlene Breitenback

#7-3-2-5-1-3-5-1.   Timothy Gene Glidewell, born 31 July 1951, Los Angeles County, California.

#7-3-2-5-1-3-5-2.   Michael E. Glidewell, born 22 January 1956, Orange County, California.

#6-3-2-5-4-2-2   BENNETT HENRY LEACH, JR.

Bennett Henry Leach, Jr., born 3 September 1937, Adair County, Oklahoma first married Jean. Bennett, later married Darlyne Sue Cook. Darlyne was born 23 July 1938, Tulsa, Oklahoma. Bennett was a Farm Machinery Salesman who made his home in Broken Arrow, Oklahoma.

Child of Bennett Henry Leach, Jr. and Jean

#7-3-2-5-4-2-2-1.   Suzanna Leach, born 27 January 1978, Tulsa, Oklahoma.

#6-3-2-5-4-2-3   BOBBY JOE LEACH

Bobby Joe Leach, born 25 January 1940, Adair County, Oklahoma, married Sharon L. Skitt, 13 October 1961, Riverside County, California. Sharon was born in 1946.

Children of Bobby Joe Leach and Sharon L. Skitt

#7-3-2-5-4-2-3-1.   Billy J. Leach, born 10 March 1962, Alameda County, California.

#7-3-2-5-4-2-3-2.   William J. Leach, born 10 March 1962, Alameda County, California.

#7-3-2-5-4-2-3-3.   Jeffrey D. Leach, born 15 July 1963, Alameda County, California.

#7-3-2-5-4-2-3-4.   Brian L. Leach, born 28 October 1970, Riverside County, California.

#6-3-2-5-4-5-2   JALORA PRICE

Jalora Price, born 28 February 1926, Evansville, Washington County, Arkansas, married James Tibbits, 19 July 1946, Hot Springs, Arkansas. James was born 1 September 1925, Davidson, Arkansas.

Child of Jalora Price and James Tibbits

#7-3-2-5-4-5-2-1.   Dennis D. Tibbits, born 15 August 1953, Tulsa, Oklahoma. Dennis married Kathy Carter, 16 February 2004, Negril, Jamaica.

#6-3-2-5-7-1-1   BOBBIE CURTIS RINEHART

Bobbie Curtis Rinehart, born 25 June 1933, Washington County, Arkansas, married Velma Louise Boyd, 24 February 1948. Velma was born 9 August 1930, Okmulgee, Oklahoma.

Children of Bobbie Curtis Rinehart and Velma Louise Boyd

#7-3-2-5-7-1-1-1.   Curtis Rinehart, born 1 February 1949, Washington County, Arkansas.

#7-3-2-5-7-1-1-2.   Bobby Dean Rinehart, born 22 September 1950, Washington County, Arkansas.

#6-3-2-5-7-2-1　　KENNETH RINEHART

Kenneth Rinehart, born 25 June 1933, Washington County, Arkansas, married Elaine Johnson.

Children of Kenneth Rinehart and Elaine Johnson

#7-3-2-5-7-2-1-1.   Jami Dee-Anne Rinehart, born 10 February 1960, Tulsa, Oklahoma.

#7-3-2-5-7-2-1-2.   Kenneth Brent Rinehart, born 12 June 1964, Tulsa, Oklahoma.

#6-3-2-5-7-2-3　　CAROLYN RINEHART

Carolyn Rinehart, born 7 August 1942, Washington County, Arkansas, married David Holder.

Children of Carolyn Rinehart and David Holder

#7-3-2-5-7-2-3-1.   Angelia Diane Holder, born 1 February 1966, Washington County, Arkansas.

#7-3-2-5-7-2-3-2.   Gregory Scott Holder, born 10 May 1968, Washington County, Arkansas.

#6-3-2-5-7-3-1　　ROY GENE RINEHART

Roy Gene Rinehart, born 28 June 1932, Washington County, Arkansas, married Evanell Fralicks, 28 December 1951, Clovis, New Mexico. Evanell was born 4 May 1935, Ector, Texas.

Children of Roy Gene Rinehart and Evanell Fralicks

#7-3-2-5-7-3-1-1.   Lynn Rinehart, born 24 August 1955, Ft Worth, Texas.

#7-3-2-5-7-3-1-2.   Kellye Janette Rinehart, born 2 November 1960, Hollywood, California.

#6-3-2-5-7-3-2   IRMALEE RINEHART

Irmalee Rinehart, born 9 March 1939, Washington County, Arkansas, first married Donald Reed, 8 March 1958, Adair County, Oklahoma. Donald was born 17 June 1932. After the tragic death of Donald in a traffic accident near Carthage, Missouri, 26 October 1959, Irmalee married Neal Ambrose Reed, 23 November 1960 in Tulsa, Oklahoma. Neal was a Poultry farmer in Washington County, Arkansas. Neil adopted the child of Irmalee's first marriage and raised him as his own child.

Child of Irmalee Rinehart and Donald Reed

#7-3-2-5-7-3-2-1.   Paul Don Reed, born 4 December 1958, Washington County, Arkansas.

Children of Irmalee Rinehart and Neal Ambrose Reed

#7-3-2-5-7-3-2-2.   Clark Neal Reed, born 25 March 1962, Washington County, Arkansas.
#7-3-2-5-7-3-2-3.   Timothy Gene Reed, born 17 April 1965, Washington County, Arkansas.

#6-3-2-5-7-4-1   CHARLES EDWIN RINEHART

Charles Edwin Rinehart, born 28 January 1932, Los Angeles County, California, married Barbara S. Roark, 25 August 1962, Imperial County, California. Barbara was born in 1943. Charles died 7 March 1987, Riverside County, California.

Children of Charles Edwin Rinehart and Barbara S. Roark

#7-3-2-5-7-4-1-1.   Jeff A. Rinehart, born 8 September 1965, Orange County, California.
#7-3-2-5-7-4-1-2.   Geoffrey A. Rinehart, born 8 September 1965, Orange County, California.

#6-3-2-5-7-4-3   DONALD L. RINEHART

Donald L. Rinehart, born 10 August 1935, Oklahoma, married Marjorie R. Hlavnick, 20 August 1960, Los Angeles County, California.

Children of Donald L. Rinehart and Marjorie R. Hlavnick

#7-3-2-5-7-4-3-1.   Cheryl L. Rinehart, born 3 April 1963, Los Angeles County, California.
#7-3-2-5-7-4-3-2.   Todd D. Rinehart, born 12 January 1965, Orange County, California. Todd died 8 April 1965, Los Angeles County, California.
#7-3-2-5-7-4-3-3.   Ryan L. Rinehart, born 18 June 1966, Orange County, California.

#6-3-2-5-7-5-1   EMMA DEAN REED

Emma Dean Reed, born 31 October 1930, Stilwell, Adair County, Oklahoma, married Ivory Clinton Painter, 1 November 1951. Clinton was born 6 November 1922. Clinton Died 28 October 1990, Ft Smith, Arkansas.

Children of Emma Dean Reed and Ivory Clinton Painter

#7-3-2-5-7-5-1-1.   Stephen Clinton Painter, born 29 July 1953.
#7-3-2-5-7-5-1-2.   Melissa Dean Painter, born 29 September 1957.
#7-3-2-5-7-5-1-3.   Julie Ann Painter, born 28 February 1963.

#6-3-2-5-7-5-2   DENNIS FAY REED

Dennis Fay Reed, born 21 February 1933, Stilwell, Adair County, Oklahoma, married Ercelyn June Rodgers, 8 June 1958. Dennis died 26 June 1990, Tulsa, Oklahoma.

Child of Dennis Fay Reed and Ercelyn June Rodgers

#7-3-2-5-7-5-2-1.   Russell Warren Reed, born 3 February 1965.

#6-3-2-5-9-1-3   VIRGIL GRADY REED

Virgil Grady Reed, born 22 September 1927, Gray Harbor County, Washington, married Nora Sprague in 1962. Virgil died 12 February 1978.

Children of Virgil Grady Reed and Nova Sprague

#7-3-2-5-9-1-3-1.   Laura Ann Read, born 15 January 1963.
#7-3-2-5-9-1-3-2.   Carolyn Reed, born 15 August 1964.

#6-3-2-5-9-2-2   DARRELL WAYNE ABSHIRE

Darrell Wayne Abshire, born 8 February 1935, Washington County, Arkansas, married Dorothy Nell McWilliams, 26 August 1960. Dorothy was born 8 September 1935, in Kingston, Oklahoma.

Children of Darrell Wayne Abshire and Dorothy Nell McWilliams

#7-3-2-5-9-2-2-1.   Gayla Nell Abshire, born 18 August 1961, Washington County, Arkansas.
#7-3-2-5-9-2-2-2.   Janna Lynn Abshire, born 1 August 1963, Washington County, Arkansas.
#7-3-2-5-9-2-2-3.   Treva Irene Abshire, born 22 December 1965, Washington County, Arkansas.

#6-3-2-5-9-2-3   BILLY GENE ABSHIRE

Billy Gene Abshire born 21 August 1936, Washington County, Arkansas, married Barbara Ann Stephens, 28 December 1956. Barbara was born 10 September 1939. Bill was a Cabinet Builder and Co-owner of Abshire and Bell Construction Company.

Children of Billy Gene Abshire and Barbara Ann Stephens

#7-3-2-5-9-2-3-1.   Royce Steven Abshire, born 7 April 1959, Washington County, Arkansas.

#7-3-2-5-9-2-3-2.   Lance Dean Abshire, born 11 July 1962, Washington County, Arkansas.

#7-3-2-5-9-2-3-3.   Sherri Roxanne Abshire, born 26 July 1967, Washington County, Arkansas.

#6-3-2-5-9-2-4   WANDA LEE ABSHIRE

Wanda Lee Abshire, born 30 March 1939, Washington County, Arkansas, first married Eugene Ball. Wanda later married Dale H. Bell, 24 January 1965. Dale was born 22 August 1937. Dale was Co-owner of Abshire and Bell Construction Company of Rogers, Arkansas.

Child of Wanda Lee Abshire and Dale H. Bell

#7-3-2-5-9-2-4-1.   Lisa Ann Bell, born 24 September 1965, Washington County, Arkansas.

#6-3-2-5-9-2-5   PHYLLIS SUE ABSHIRE

Phyllis Sue Abshire, born 28 July 1948, Washington County, Arkansas, first married Hugh Thomas Reed, 30 September 1966. Hugh was born 1 February 1943, Lincoln, Washington County, Arkansas. Hugh and Phylis grew chickens in Washington County, Arkansas. Phylis later married James Leo Rock. James was born in 1939 in McAlister, Oklahoma. James ran an iron and metal business in Stilwell, Oklahoma.

Children of Phyllis Sue Abshire and Hugh Thomas Reed

#7-3-2-5-9-2-5-1.   John Thomas Reed, born 20 January 1974, Washington County, Arkansas.

#7-3-2-5-9-2-5-2.   David Wayne Reed, born 1975, Washington County, Arkansas.

#6-3-2-5-9-3-2   JAMES LEROY ABSHIRE

James Leroy Abshire, born 6 December 1946, Washington County, Arkansas, married Pamela Whinery, 27 May 1966. Pamela was born 26 January 1948, Washington County, Arkansas. James and Pamela made their home in Lincoln, Washington County, Arkansas.

Children of James Leroy Abshire and Pamela Whinery

#7-3-2-5-9-3-2-1.   Rodney Wayne Abshire, born 5 January 1969, Washington County, Arkansas.

#7-3-2-5-9-3-2-2.   Jason Brent Abshire, born 26 December 1970, Washington County, Arkansas.

#6-3-2-5-9-3-4   DEBRA KAY ABSHIRE

Debra Kay Abshire, born 3 August 1957, Washington County, Arkansas, married Jerry Yeager.

Children of Debra Kay Abshire and Jerry Yeager

#7-3-2-5-9-3-4-1.   Brandy Kaye Yeager, born 31 December 1976, Washington County, Arkansas.

#7-3-2-5-9-3-4-2.   Britney Kaye Yeager, born 7 July 1979, Washington County, Arkansas.

#6-3-2-5-9-4-1   ETSEL GLEN LOFTIN

Etsel Glen Loftin, born 23 October 1942, Washington County, Arkansas, married Nita Langham, in 1964. Etsel served in the United States Navy and later divorced and lived in Fayetteville and Ozark Arkansas.

Children of Etsel Glen Loftin and Nita Langham

#7-3-2-5-9-4-1-1.   Brock Tyler Loftin, born 11 July 1965, Merced County, California.

#7-3-2-5-9-4-1-2.   Chandra Elizabeth Loftin, 17 September 1966, San Diego County, California.

#6-3-2-5-9-4-2   ANNETTE CAROL LOFTIN

Annette Carol Loftin, born 11 March 1945, Washington County, Arkansas, married Edd Neal Miller, Kansas City, Kansas on 5 June 1964. Edd is a Minister. He and Annette made their home in McAlister, Oklahoma, where he pastured a church.

Children of Annette Carol Loftin and Edd Neal Miller

#7-3-2-5-9-4-2-1.   Kelly Lynn Miller, born 8 May 1957, Oklahoma.

#7-3-2-5-9-4-2-2.   Kyle Dorance Miller, born 20 April 1972, Oklahoma.

#6-3-2-5-9-4-3   JIMMY KEITH LOFTIN

Jimmy Keith Loftin, born 23 November 1947, Washington County, Arkansas, married Barbara Ann Jones, Prairie Grove, Arkansas, on 28 December 1965.

Children of Jimmy Keith Loftin and Barbara Ann Jones

#7-3-2-5-9-4-3-1.   Mannie Lee Loftin, born 6 January 1968, Washington County, Arkansas.

#7-3-2-5-9-4-3-2.   Todd Aaron Loftin, born 1 January 1971, Washington County, Arkansas.

#6-3-2-5-9-4-4   JERRY BRUCE LOFTIN

Jerry Bruce Loftin, born 14 September 1950, Washington County, Arkansas, married Jamie Holtzclaw of Fayetteville, Washington County, Arkansas.

Children of Jerry Bruce Loftin and Jamie Holtzclaw

#7-3-2-5-9-4-4-1.   Shannon "Stacy" Loftin, born 9 October 1968, Washington County, Arkansas.

#7-3-2-5-9-4-4-2.   Melissa Renee Loftin, born 3 June 1972, Washington County, Arkansas.

#6-3-2-5-9-5-1   ROGER LAIL MINICK

Roger Lail Minick, born 31 July 1944, Romana, Oklahoma, Married Joyce Carrol Johnson, 2 April 1972, Alameda, California. Joyce was born in 1951.

Child of Roger Lail Minick and Joyce Carrol Johnson

#7-3-2-5-9-5-1-1.   Allison Norjane Minick, born 19 February 1988, Alameda County, California.

#6-3-2-5-9-5-2   MARY LYNN MINICK

Mary Lynn Minick, born 28 January 1951, Benton County, Arkansas, married James D. Wood, 18 December 1979, San Bernardino County, California. James was born in 1951.

Children of Mary Lynn Mynick and James D. Wood

#7-3-2-5-9-5-2-1.   Junnifer Minick Wood, born 20 March 1982, San Bernardino County, California.
#7-3-2-5-9-5-2-2.   Martin Douglas Wood, born 5 February 1985, San Bernardino County, California.

#6-3-2-5-9-5-3   ALECIA ANN MINICK

Alicia Ann Minick, born 31 August 1952, Benton County, Arkansas, married Jackson M. Dodge, 4 September 1976, Siskiyou, California. Jackson was born in 1952.

Children of Alicia Ann Minick and Jackson M. Dodge

#7-3-2-5-9-5-3-1.   Lilaann Millberry Dodge, born 26 January 1987, Alameda County, California.
#7-3-2-5-9-5-3-2.   Aidanansell Dinsmore Dodge, born 30 August 1990, Santa Barber County, California.

#6-3-2-5-9-5-4   STORM STERLING MINICK

Storm Sterling Minick, born 18 September 1957, Fontana, San Bernardino County, California, married Allena J. Floodman, 21 June 1975, San Bernardino County, California. Allena was born 24 December 1957.

Children of Stormy Sterling Minick and Allena J. Floodman

#7-3-2-5-9-5-4-1.   Aman Tuk Minick, born 3 January 1976, Fontana, San Bernardino County, California.
#7-3-2-5-9-5-4-2.   Sterling Roscoe Minick, born 13 February 1979, Portland, Oregon.
#7-3-2-5-9-5-4-3.   Stormy Alene Minick, born 9 November 1981, San Bernardino County, California.

#6-3-2-5-9-6-1   PATRICIA ANN ABSHIRE

Patricia Ann Abshire, born 9 March 1952, Oklahoma Married Gary Dean Rhiner.

Children of Patricia Ann Abshire and Gary Dean Rhiner

#7-3-2-5-9-6-1-1.   Lida Diane Rhiner, born 9 December 1969.
#7-3-2-5-9-6-1-2.   Gary Shawn Rhiner, born 15 July 1972.
#7-3-2-5-9-6-1-2.   Lana Michele Rhiner, born 24 June 1974.

#6-3-2-5-9-6-3   ANITA SUE ABSHIRE

Anita Sue Abshire, born 10 August 1956, Wichita, Kansas, married Richard Gene Webb.

Children of Anita Sue Abshire and Richard Gene Webb

#7-3-2-5-9-6-3-1.   Christine Webb, born 13 January 1974.
#7-3-2-5-9-6-3-2.   Isen Andrea Webb, born 1 April 1979.

#6-3-2-5-9-6-4   CONNIE JOE ABSHIRE

Connie Joe Abshire, born 10 February 1961 Wichita, Kansas, married Albert Pena.

Child of Connie Joe Abshire and Albert Pena

#7-3-2-5-9-6-4-1.   Alexander Laverne Pena, born 19 November 1980.

#6-3-2-7-6-5-2   BARBARA JEAN LONGWITH

Barbara Jean Longwith, born 17 March 1954 Oklahoma City, Oklahoma, married Richard Joe Cottrell 1 October 1972 Midwest City, Oklahoma. Richard was born 20 August 1951 in Shawnee, Oklahoma. Barbara later married Orin Allen Kimball.

Children of Barbara Jean Longwith and Richard Joe Cottrell

#7-3-2-7-6-5-2-1.   Justin Cottrell, born 12 November 1973, Oklahoma City, Oklahoma.
#7-3-2-7-6-5-2-2.   Travis John Cottrell, born 17 September 1976, Oklahoma City, Oklahoma.

#6-3-3-1-3-1-1   NANCY ERMA EDMISTON

Nancy Emma Edmiston, born 26 July 1937 Tulare County, California, married Shackleford. Nancy died 18 September 1989, Tulare County, California.

Children of Nancy Erma Edmiston and Shackleford

#7-3-3-1-3-1-1-1.   Deborah L. Shackleford, born 19 July 1956, Tulare County, California.
#7-3-3-1-3-1-1-2.   Diane G. Shackleford, born 24 October 1958, Tulare County, California.
#7-3-3-1-3-1-1-3.   Denise L. Shackleford, born 31 December 1961, Tulare County, California.

#6-3-3-1-3-1-3 NORMA DELLA EDMISTON

Norma Della Edmiston, born 8 November 1940, Tulare County, California, married John Rodes.

Child of Norma Della Edmiston and John Rhodes

#7-3-3-1-3-1-3-1. Mark E. Rhodes, born 12 August 1968, Tulare County, California.

#6-3-3-1-3-1-4 GLORIA ANN EDMISTON

Gloria Ann Edmiston, born 28 February 1945, Contra Costa County, California, married Stephen W. Fischer, 24 November 1965, Tulare County, California. Stephen was born in Tulare County, California 20 October 1944.

#6-3-3-1-3-3-1 MARIANNA HAURY

Marianna Haury, born 23 April 1939, Alameda County, California, married Jack B. Omeara, 14 April 1962, Ventura County, California.

Children of Marianna Haury and Jack B. Omeara

#7-3-3-1-3-3-1-1. Jacquely Omeara, born 4 May 1966, Fresno County, California.
#7-3-3-1-3-3-1-2. Kevin S. Omeara, born 19 January 1968, Stanislaus County, California.

#6-3-3-1-3-3-2 EUGENE VERNON HAURY

Eugene Vernon Haury, born 15 March 1943, Alameda County, California, first Married Patricia Ann Hopkins, 17 June 1967, Santa Barbara, California. Patricia was born 10 July 1945, San Bernardino,

California and died 20 June 1970, Santa Barbara County, California. Eugene next married Asenath Gail Campbell, 7 August 1971, Ventura County, California. This Marriage ended in a divorce 20 January 1984. Eugene married a third time.

Child of Eugene Vernon Haury and Patricia Anne Hopkins

#7-3-3-1-3-3-2-1.   Elizabeth Louise Haury, born 1968, Santa Barbara County, California.

#6-3-3-1-3-3-4   STEVEN EARL HAURY

Steven Earl Haury, born 29 October 1953, Ventura County, California, married Windy Schuman. Steven and Windy made their home in New Mexico

Child of Steve Earl Haury and Windy Shuman

#7-3-3-1-3-3-4-1.   Lynea Haury, born New Mexico.

#6-3-5-1-4-3-1   BRUCE HALSTEAD VATCHER

Bruce Halstead Vatcher, born 10 June 1933, Los Angeles, Los Angeles County, California, married Barbara Lee Boss, 5 August 1961, Kern County, California. Barbara was born 5 November 1935, San Bernardino County, California.

Children of Bruce Halstead Vatcher and Barbara Lee Boss

#7-3-5-1-4-3-1-1.   Brian L. Vatcher, born 21 April 1962, San Diego County, California.
#7-3-5-1-4-3-1-2.   David M. Vatcher, born 24 January 1967, San Diego County, California.

#6-3-5-2-2-3-1   BETTY MARIE BUTLER

Betty Marie Butler, born 3 October 1934, Hays County, Texas, married Alvin Leroy Williamson about 1957. Alvin was born 11 April 1933, Hays County, Texas.

Children of Betty Marie Butler and Alvin Leroy Williamson

#7-3-5-2-2-3-1-1.   Cindy Lee Williamson, born 10 January 1959, Hays County, Texas.

#7-3-5-2-2-3-1-2.   Kristi Lee Williamson, born 10 October 1960, Hays County, Texas.

#7-3-5-2-2-3-1-3.   Kathi Ann Williamson, born 14 April 1963, Hays County, Texas.

#6-3-5-2-2-3-2   VELMA ANN BUTLER

Velma Ann Butler, born 2 October 1940, Hays County, Texas, married Robert Owen Blackburn, 25 November 1970, Travis County, Texas. Robert was born in 1940.

Child of Velma Ann Butler and Robert Owen Blackburn

#7-3-5-2-2-3-2-1.   Robin Ann Blackburn, born 12 October 1972, Travis County, Texas.

#6-3-5-4-1-1-1   SYLVIA SUE WALKER

Sylvia Sue Walker, born 24 December 1948, Jefferson County, Texas, married David Carter Branch, 20 May 1972, San Diego County, California. David was born 28 February 1948, Bosque County, Texas.

Children of Sylvia Sue Walker and David Carter Branch

#7-3-5-4-1-1-1-1.   William Ashley Branch, born 23 September 1985, McLennan County, Texas.

#7-3-5-4-1-1-1-2.   Katherine Rode Branch, born 14 December 1987, McLennan County, Texas.

#6-3-5-4-1-1-2   BARRY WINSTON WALKER

Barry Winston Walker, born 13 October 1950, Parker County, Texas, married Patricia C. Guthrie, 3 August 1974, McLennan County, Texas. Patricia was born in 1957.

Children of Barry Winston Walker and Patricia C. Guthrie

#7-3-5-4-1-1-2-1.   Tarra E. Walker, born 8 August 1976, Kern County, California.
#7-3-5-4-1-1-2-2.   Ashley C. Walker, born 8 December 1977, Kern County, California.

#6-3-5-4-2-4-1   ALICE LUCILLE DOUGHERTY

Alice Lucille Dougherty, born 9 June 1943, Travis County, Texas, married Henry B. Jenkins about 1960. Henry was born 14 August 1941, Hopkins County, Texas.

Children of Alice Lucille Dougherty and Henry B. Jenkins

#7-3-5-4-2-4-1-1.   William Milburn Jenkins, born 16 April 1962, Travis County, Texas.
#7-3-5-4-2-4-1-2.   Barbara Marie Jenkins, born 12 May 1970, Dallas County, Texas.

#6-3-5-4-2-4-2   BARBARA JEAN DOUGHERTY

Barbara Jean Dougherty, born 1 November 1944, Travis County, Texas, married Mack Ervin Green about 1967.

Children of Barbara Jean Dougherty and Mack Ervin Green

#7-3-5-4-2-4-2-1.   Stacy Evonne Green, born 2 February 1969, Hays County, Texas.

#7-3-5-4-2-4-2-2.   Lisa Benaye Green, born 27 December 1973, Hays County, Texas.

#7-3-5-4-2-4-2-3.   Quiana Lynn Green, born 3 March 1978, Travis County, Texas.

#6-3-5-4-2-5-1   MARILYN JEAN FUHRMAN

Marilyn Jean Fuhrman, born 14 September 1950, Travis County, Texas, first married Eural Roy Dearing, Jr., 11 January 1968, Travis County, Texas. Eural was born 5 July 1947, Lubbock County, Texas. Marilyn and Eural were divorced 14 November 1969, Travis County, Texas. Marilyn's second marriage was to John Wayne Jacobie, 12 August 1977, Travis County, Texas.

Child of Marilyn Jean Fuhrman and Eural Roy Dearing, Jr.

#7-3-5-4-2-5-1-1.   Roy Gilbert Dearing, born 8 August 1968, Travis County, Texas.

Child of Marilyn Jean Fuhrman and John Wayne Jacobie

#7-3-5-4-2-5-1-2.   John Robert Jacobie, born 27 January 1978, Dallas County, Texas.

#6-3-5-4-2-5-2   JOE SCOTT FUHRMAN

Joe Scott Fuhrman, born 28 November 1952, Travis County, Texas, married Kathy Lynn Edwards, 28 February 1976, Bastrop County, Texas. Kathy was born 9 April 1956, Gregg County, Texas.

#7-3-5-4-2-5-2-1.   Monica Lynn Fuhrman, born 25 June 1976, Bastrop County, Texas.

#7-3-5-4-2-5-2-2.   Levi Scott Fuhrman, born 8 November 1978, Travis County, Texas.

#6-3-5-4-3-2-1   CAROL ANN WILLIAMS

Carol Ann Williams, born 12 August 1953, Travis County, Texas, first married Joe Bruce Walker, 21 September 1973, Travis County, Texas. Joe was born 21 May 1946, Jefferson County, Texas. Joe and Carol were divorced 3 March 1988, Travis County, Texas. On 8 April 1988, Carol married Gary Lynn Lilja at Williamson County, Texas. Gary was born 8 December 1939, Travis County, Texas.

Children of Carol Ann Williams and Joe Bruce Walker

#7-3-5-4-3-2-1-1.   Clinton Dean Walker, born 17 December 1974, Travis County, Texas.

#7-3-5-4-3-2-1-2.   Casey Joe Walker, born 13 July 1978, Travis County, Texas.

#6-3-5-4-3-2-2   BRYAN KEITH WILLIAMS

Bryan Keith Williams, born 23 August 1956, Travis County, Texas, first married Deborah Darlene Hawes, 2 May 1981, Travis County, Texas. Deborah was born15 November 1955, Aransas County, Texas. Bryan and Deborah obtained a divorce 18 July 1997, Travis County, Texas. On 20 February 1998, Bryan Married Elizabeth Anna Williams. Elizabeth was born 9 April 1970, Travis County, Texas.

Child of Bryan Keith Williams and Deborah Darlene Hawes

#7-3-5-4-3-2-2-1.   Alicia Nichole Williams, born 18 August 1986, Travis County, Texas.

Children of Bryan Keith Williams and Elizabeth Anna Williams

#7-3-5-4-3-2-2-2.   Anna Elizabeth Williams, born 7 January 2004, Travis County, Texas.

#7-3-5-4-3-2-2-3.   Zackary James "Zeke" Williams, born 3 May 2007, Travis County, Texas.

#6-3-5-5-1-2-1   COROLYN KNOX RANKIN

Carolyn Knox Rankin, born 29 July 1943, Uvalde County, Texas, married Elmer Fayne Driver about 1961. Elmer was born 13 April 1942, Eastland County, Texas.

Children of Carolyn Knox Rankin and Elmer Fayne Driver

#7-3-5-5-1-2-1-1.   Terry Yvonne Driver, born 29 June 1962, Winkler County, Texas.

#7-3-5-5-1-2-1-2.   Deanna Kim Driver, born 30 December 1863, Reeves County, Texas.

#6-3-5-5-1-2-2   SHARON ELIZABETH RANKIN

Sharon Elizabeth Rankin, born 30 August 1946, Uvalde County, Texas, married Jack Edward Easley about 1964. Jack was born 18 July 1945, Uvalde County, Texas.

Children of Sharon Elizabeth Rankin and Jack Edward Easley

#7-3-5-5-1-2-2-1.   Jack Edward Easley, Jr., born 18 March 1965, Uvalde County, Texas.

#7-3-5-5-1-2-2-2.   James Vernon Easley, born 7 January 1968, Uvalde County, Texas.

#7-3-5-5-1-2-2-3.   Joseph Alvin Easley, born 16 January 1973, Uvalde County, Texas.

#6-3-5-5-1-2-3 ROBERT EDWARD RANKIN

Robert Edward Rankin, born 17 December 1949, Uvalde County, Texas, married Deborah Jean Petty, 17 June 1972, Uvalde County, Texas. Deborah was born 4 November 1951, Bell County, Texas.

Children of Robert Edward Rankin and Deborah Jean Petty

#7-3-5-5-1-2-3-1.   Patrick Scott Rankin, born 14 November 1977, Denton County, Texas.
#7-3-5-5-1-2-3-2.   Meridith Nicole Rankin. Born 5 September 1979, Denton County, Texas.

#6-3-5-5-1-3-1 STANLEY MAURICE WALKER

Stanley Maurice Walker, born 23 August 1952, Uvalde County, Texas, married Nina Eileen Smith, 4 July 1975, Bexar County, Texas. Nina was born 1956 in Orlando, Florida.

Children of Stanley Maurice Walker and Nina Eileen Smith

#7-3-5-5-1-3-1-1.   Julie Lynn Walker, born 17 January 1978, Bexar County, Texas.
#7-3-5-5-1-3-1-2.   Cynthia Mae Walker, born 30 January 1981, Bexar County, Texas.

#6-3-5-5-1-4-1 JEFFREY PAUL WALKER

Jeffrey Paul Walker, born 13 June 1957, Uvalde County, Texas, married Cheryl Jean Walker, 9 June 1978, Uvalde County, Texas. Cheryl was born 13 September 1958, Uvalde County, Texas.

Children of Jeffrey Paul Walker and Cheryl Jean Walker

#7-3-5-5-1-4-1-1.   Cale Jeffrey Walker, born 26 September 1982, Bexar County, Texas.

#7-3-5-5-1-4-1-2.   Cara Jean Walker, born 29 January 1987, Bexar
County, Texas.

#6-3-5-5-1-4-2   LYNN EVAN WALKER

Lynn Evan Walker, born 10 January 1962, Uvalde County, Texas,
married Linda Sue Perry, 27 July 1988, Uvalde County, Texas. Linda was
born in 1960.

Child of Lynn Evan Walker and Linda Sue Perry

#7-3-5-5-1-4-2-1.   Kendall Lynn Walker, born 22 October 1995,
Uvalde County, Texas.

#6-3-5-5-1-5-1   CLAUDETTE RACHELLE
ALEXANDER

Claudette Rachelle Alexander, born 29 October 1972, Jefferson County,
Texas.

Child of Claudette Rachelle Alexander

#7-3-5-5-1-5-1-1.   Kristen Nicara Alexander, born 16 September
1992, Jefferson County, Texas.

#6-3-5-5-2-1-1   JAMES MICHAEL KING

James Michael King, born 9 November 1970, Dallas County, Texas,
married Traci Scott Tigert, 8 August 1992, Dallas County, Texas. Traci
was born 21 March 1973, Orange County, Texas.

Child of James Michael King and Traci Scott Tiger

#7-3-5-5-2-1-1-1.   Nicholas Scott King, born 1 January 1993,
Dallas County, Texas.

#6-3-5-6-1-1-1   JAMES WILLIS DOCKERY, JR.

James Willis Dockery, Jr., born 13 October 1929. Bexar County, Texas, married Peggy Jeanne Wilkinson about 1950. Peggy was born 14 September 1935, Red River County, Texas.

Children of James Willis Dockery, Jr. and Peggy Jeanne Wilkinson

#7-3-5-6-1-1-1-1.   Laurie Lea Dockery, born 23 May 1951, Jefferson County, Texas.

#7-3-5-6-1-1-1-2.   Jan Allyn Dockery, born 15 September 1955, Robertson County, Texas.

#7-3-5-6-1-1-1-3.   James Paul Dockery, born 23 February 1961, Bexar County, Texas.

#6-3-5-6-1-1-2   ALLEN DANIEL DOCKERY

Allen Daniel Dockery, born 6 September 1931, Bexar County, Texas, married Laura May Parrish about 1965. Laura was born 27 May 1931, Travis County, Texas.

Children of Allen Daniel Dockery and Laura May Parrish

#7-3-5-6-1-1-2-1.   Daniel Parish Dockery, born 16 November 1967, Bexar County, Texas.

#7-3-5-6-1-1-2-2.   Cynthia Lynn Dockery, born 6 September 1969, Bexar County, Texas.

#6-3-5-6-1-1-3   RICHARD LEE DOCKERY

Richard Lee Dockery, born 28 August 1933, Bexar County, Texas, married Anita Louise Bryant about 1952. Louise was born 3 January 1934, Bexar County, Texas.

Children of Richard Lee Dockery and Anita Louise Bryant

#7-3-5-6-1-1-3-1.   Debra Jane Dockery, born 14 October 1953, Bexar County, Texas.

#7-3-5-6-1-1-3-2.   Richard Lee Dockery, Jr., born 1 May 1956, Bexar County, Texas.

#7-3-5-6-1-1-3-3.   Pamela Gail Dockery, born 17 December 1957, Bexar County, Texas.

#7-3-5-6-1-1-3-4.   Matthew Dale Dockery, born 14 December 1959, Bexar County, Texas.

#7-3-5-6-1-1-3-5.   Wendell Ward Dockery, born 7 August 1961, Bexar County, Texas.

#6-3-5-6-1-1-4   TED EDWIN DOCKERY

Ted Edwin Dockery born 31 December 1935, Bexar County, Texas, married Jo Ann Barbee about 1955. Jo Ann was born 17 November 1935, Bexar County, Texas.

Children of Ted Edwin Dockery and Jo Ann Barbee

#7-3-5-6-1-1-4-1.   Jeffrey Wade Dockery, born 23 February 1957, Kleberg County, Texas.

#7-3-5-6-1-1-4-2.   Kirk Wayne Dockery, born 18 March 1960, Bexar County, Texas.

#7-3-5-6-1-1-4-3.   Gregg Warren Dockery, born 4 December 1961, Bexar County, Texas.

#6-3-5-6-1-4-1   ALLEN WHEELER DOCKERY

Allen Wheeler Dockery, born 12 January 1933, Hays County, Texas, married Charlotte Jacqueline Mills about 1961. Charlotte was born 20 August 1929, Bexar County, Texas.

Children of Allen Wheeler Dockery and Charlotte Jacqueline Mills

#7-3-5-6-1-4-1-1.   Allen Wheeler Dockery, Jr., born 20 October 1962, Bexar County, Texas.

#7-3-5-6-1-4-1-2.   John Brandt Dockery, born 10 May 1966, Tarrant County, Texas.

#6-3-5-6-1-4-2   JO ANN DOCKERY

Jo Ann Dockery, born 10 May 1935, Uvalde County, Texas, married Billy Alton Ward about 1957. Billy was born 31 July 1932, Dimmit County, Texas.

Children of Jo Ann Dockery and Billy Alton Ward

#7-3-5-6-1-4-2-1.   Neal Wheeler Ward, born 14 November 1958, Dimmit County, Texas.

#7-3-5-6-1-4-2-2.   Linda Ann Ward, born 30 January 1961 Dimmit, County, Texas.

#6-3-6-2-3-1-1   BETTY SUE SANDS

Betty Sue Sands, born 5 August 1938, Mississippi County, Missouri, first married James A. Hime, 6 October 1956, Kenton, Mississippi. James was born 28 September 1936, Blencoe, Iowa. After serving four years in the United States Air Force, James worked for an aeronautical engineering firm in California. He later returned to Iowa working for an assembly plant and finally to the United States Post Office where he stayed until retirement. Betty later married Richard J. Campbell, 7 October 1983, Pemiscot County, Missouri. Betty died in Hedley, Donley County, Texas, 23 August 2002.

Children of Betty Sue Sands and James A. Hime

#7-3-6-2-3-1-1-1.   Janna Hime, born 16 February 1959, Mesa, Arizona.

#7-3-6-2-3-1-1-2.   Thomas J. Hime, born 18 February 1957, Aurora, Colorado.

#7-3-6-2-3-1-1-3.   Christopher A. Hime, born 11 January 1971, Orange County, California.

#6-3-6-2-3-5-2   REGENA ELLIOTT

Regina Elliott, born 19 September 1984, Mississippi County, Missouri, married Andy Curlobic, 25 June 1966, Bamberg, Germany. Andy was born 3 June 1946, Alton Illinois. Regina was employer as the Office Manager for a Dental Clinic.

Children of Regena Elliott and Andy Carlobic

#7-3-6-2-3-5-2-1.   Tina Marie Curlobic, born 18 January 1968, Alton, Illinois.

#7-3-6-2-3-5-2-2.   Andrea Curlobic, Born 12 September 1976, Alton, Illinois.

#6-3-6-2-3-7-1   MARGIE ELLEN SANDS

Margie Ellen Sands, born 15 December 1942, Mississippi County, Missouri, first married Paul Lindseyway England 25 November 1960, Batesville, Arkansas and later married Lynn Curtis Lundberg, 7 August 1965, Los Angeles County, California. Lynn was born in 1942 at Anoka, Minnesota.

Child of Margie Ellen Sands and Paul England

#7-3-6-2-3-7-1-1.   Paul Wayne England, born 7 May 1961, Batesville, Arkansas.

Children of Margie Ellen Sands and Lynn C. Lundberg

#7-3-6-2-3-7-1-2.   Marie Ellen Lundberg, born 6 January 1969, Great Lakes, Chicago, Illinois.

#7-3-6-2-3-7-1-3.   Tina Denise Lundberg, born 26 April 1970, San Francisco, California.

#6-3-6-2-3-7-2   LOVACE ANN SANDS

Lovace Ann Sands, born 17 September 1945, Cairo, Illinois, married Harold Lee Johnson Rockford, Winnebago County, Illinois. Harold was born December 1941, Hamilton, Marion County, Alabama. Lovace died 14 August 2000, from a fire. Her and one of her children burned to death in a Trailer House.

Children of Lovace Ann Sands and Harold Johnson

#7-3-6-2-3-7-2-1.   Sheila Ann Johnson, born 15 September 1962, Cairo, Illinois.
#7-3-6-2-3-7-2-2.   Harold Eugene Johnson, born 14 December 1963, Cairo, Illinois.
#7-3-6-2-3-7-2-3.   Lavon Lynn Johnson, born 15 October 1971, Rockford, Illinois.
#7-3-6-2-3-7-2-4.   Christopher Neal Johnson, born 16 November 1974, Rockford, Illinois.

#6-3-6-2-3-7-3   HERBERT HARRISON SANDS

Herbert Sands, born 7 August 1949, Cairo, Illinois, first married Christina Peterson, 14 September 1968, Rockford, Winnebago County, Illinois. Herbert and Christine divorced 15 June 1981. On 15 June 2002, Herbert married Teresa Marie Smiley, Nashville, Tennessee.

Children of Herbert Sands and Christina Peterson

#7-3-6-2-3-7-3-1.   Laura Marie Sands, born 26 July 1969, Rockford, Illinois.
#7-3-6-2-3-7-3-2.   Jennifer Christine Sands, born 26 March 1972, Rockford, Illinois.

#7-3-6-2-3-7-3-3.   Carl Herbert Sands Akre, born 18 April 1977, Rockford, Illinois.

#6-3-6-2-3-7-4   GARY LEE SANDS

Gary Lee Sands, born 21 August 1952, Cairo, Illinois, married Sherry Ann Hampton, 20 March 1973, San Bernardino County, California. Sherry was born 28 August 1958, Kern County, California. Gary later married Linda Diane Nickels Wheeler 25 August 1989, Las Vegas, Nevada.

Children of Gary Sands and Sherry Ann Hampton

#7-3-6-2-3-7-4-1.   Windy Marie Sands, born 25 January 1974, San Bernardino County, California.

#7-3-6-2-3-7-4-2.   Matthew Thomas Sands, born 3 March 1976, Oklahoma City, Oklahoma.

#6-3-6-2-3-8-1   SANDRA LEE QUERTERMOUS

Sandra Lee Quertermous, born 21 March 1945, Cairo, Illinois, married Gary Hartline, 23 December 1960, Jonesboro, Illinois. Gary was born 21 April 1939, Cobden Illinois.

Children of Sandra Lee Quertermous and Gary Hartline

#7-3-6-2-3-8-1-1.   Darrell Lee Hartline, born 11 August 1970, Cape Girardeau, Missouri.

#7-3-6-2-3-8-1-2.   Darla Ann Hartline, born 12 August 1973, Cape Girardeau, Missouri.

#6-3-6-2-3-8-2   LARRY JOE QUERTERMOUS

Larry Joe Quertermous, born 7 January 1947, Cobden, Union County, Illinois married Mildred Crowell in 1965 at Jonesboro, Illinois. Mildred was born 28 June 1947, Cobden, Illinois. Larry farmed near Cobden, Illinois.

Children of Larry Quertermous amd Mildred Crowell

#7-3-6-2-3-8-2-1. Larry Joe Quertermous, born 5 March 1969, Murphysboro, Illinois.

#7-3-6-2-3-8-2-2. Tommy Lee Quertermous, born 29 July 1971, Cape Girardeau, Missouri.

#7-3-6-2-3-8-2-3. Michael Dale Quertermous, born 13 August 1978, Cape Girardeau, Missouri.

#6-3-6-2-3-9-1 THOMAS EUGENE WALDRON

Thomas Eugene Waldron, born 29 October 1948, Hammond, Indiana, married Ann Fue Lavenda, 26 October 1968, Gary, Indiana. Ann was born 1 June 1950, Gary, Indiana.

Children of Thomas Eugene Waldron and Ann Fue Lavenda

#7-3-6-2-3-9-1-1. Ann Marie Waldron, born 8 May 1969, East Chicago, Illinois.

#7-3-6-2-3-9-1-2. Stacy Jean Waldron, born 8 May 1971, East Chicago, Illinois.

#6-3-6-2-3-9-2 ROBERT WALDRON

Robert Waldron, born 28 August 1950, Charleston, Mississippi County, Missouri, married Rebecca Blyth, 5 April 1969, Saint Joseph, Michigan. Rebecca was born 28 February 1951, Merrillville, Indiana.

Children of Robert Waldron and Rebecca Blyth

#7-3-6-2-3-9-2-1. Cassandra Waldron, born 14 December 1969, East Chicago, Indiana.

#7-3-6-2-3-9-2-2.   Robert Waldron, born 27 November 1971, East Chicago, Indiana.

#6-3-6-2-3-9-3   CURTIS WALDRON

Curtis Waldron, born 2 September 1953, Charleston, Mississippi County, Missouri, married Cathy Hensen, 2 October 1971, Saint Soseph, Michigan. Cathy was born 4 December 1955, Merriville. Indiana. Curtis died in 25 March 2006, Indianapolis, Indiana.

Children of Curtis Waldron and Cathy Hensen

#7-3-6-2-3-9-3-1.   Tina Waldron, born 11 August 1972, East Chicago, Indiana.
#7-3-6-2-3-9-3-2.   Curtis Waldron, jr., born 26 February 1973, Richmond, Virginia.
#7-3-6-2-3-9-3-3.   Roy Waldron, born 16 March 1978, Crown Point, Indiana, and died 18 March 1979.
#7-3-6-2-3-9-3-4.   John Waldron, born 31 July 1979, Crown Point, Indiana.

#6-3-6-2-3-9-4   TALBERT WALDRON

Talbert 'Steve' Waldron, born 27 October 1957, East Chicago, Indiana, married Glenda Griffin, 3 July 1976, Merrillville, Indiana. Glenda was born 1 June 1957, Hammond, Indiana.

Children of Talbert Waldron and Glenda Griffin

#7-3-6-2-3-9-4-1.   Christina Waldron, born 12 January 1978, Crown Point, Indiana.
#7-3-6-2-3-9-4-2.   Andrea Waldron, born 12 January 1978, Crown Point, Indiana.
#7-3-5-2-3-9-4-3.   Jenifer Waldron, born 5 May 1980, Munster, Indiana.

#6-3-6-2-7-1-2   WILLIAM CLARENCE BURRIS

William Clarence Burris, born 19 December 1950, Wichita, Kansas, married Debra Hatley, 29 June 1992, De Queen, Arkansas. Debra was born 30 January 1970, Mt Pleasant, Texas. William worked for the United States Post Office.

Child of William Clarence Burris and Debra Hatley

#7-3-6-2-7-1-2-1.   Delbert Burris, born 30 May 1990, Idabel, Oklahoma.

#6-3-6-2-7-1-3   KATHERINE ANN BURRIS

Katherine Ann Burris, born 18 October 1954, Harris County, Texas, married Mark Anthony Burns, 31 January 1973, Tulsa, Oklahoma. Mark was born 5 May 1951, Tulsa, Oklahoma. Mark is a Computer technician and expert. Katherine and Mark make their home in Tulsa, Oklahoma.

Children of Katherine Ann Burris and Mark Anthony Burns

#7-3-6-2-7-1-3-1.   Sonia Ranae Burns, born 21 May 1982, Tulsa, Oklahoma

#7-3-6-2-7-1-3-2.   Shane Gabriel Burns, born 17 April 1984, Tulsa, Oklahoma.

#7-3-6-2-7-1-3-3.   Deanna Faith Burns, born 16 November 1988, Tulsa, Oklahoma.

#6-3-6-2-7-2-1   WILLIAM PAUL LEACH

William Paul Leach, born 5 January 1954, Washington County, Arkansas, married Nancy Hill, 30 June 1973, Mendocino County, California. Nancy was born in 1955. William and Nancy divorced in Mendocino County, California in May of 1975. After the divorce from

Nancy, William engaged in three relationships in which children were born.

Child of William Paul Leach and first spousal relationship

#7-3-6-2-7-2-1-1.   Katherine Elaine Leach, born 31 July 1973, Mendocino County, California.

Children of William Paul Leach and Mckinley

#7-3-6-2-7-2-1-2.   Jason William Leach, born 21 October 1976, Mendocino County, California.

#7-3-6-2-7-2-1-3.   Joshua Paul Leach, born 1 October 1980, Mendocino County, California.

Children of William Paul Leach and Hoy

#7-3-6-2-7-2-1-4.   Monica Rae Leach, born 13 March 1987, Mendocino County, California.

#7-3-6-2-7-2-1-5.   Matthew Aaron Leach, born 20 April 1988, Mendocino County, California.

#6-3-6-2-7-2-2   CAROLYN ISABELL LEACH

Carolyn Isabelle Leach, born 15 May 1955, Mendocino County, California, married Ernest Everett Neves, 9 June 1979, Sacramento County, California. Ernest was born 12 September 1950, Sacramento County, California.

Children of Carolyn Isabelle Leach and Ernest Everett Neves

#7-3-6-2-7-2-2-1.   Amber Rose Neves, born 4 November 1982, Butte County, California.

#7-3-6-2-7-2-2-2.   Autumn Sunshine Neves, born 5 December 1986, Butte County, California.

#6-3-6-2-7-2-3 CHERYL ROSE LEACH

Cheryl Rose Leach, born 30 October 1958, Mendocino County, California, first married Ralph W. Talbot, 31 December 1978, Napa County, California. Ralph was born 6 March 1951, Napa County, California. On November 26 1983, Cheryl married Euclid O. Vieau in Napa County, California. Cheryl next married John Dean Miller. On April 27 1996, Cheryl married Joseph Kneeland, Napa County, California.

Child of Cheryl Rose Leach and Ralph W. Talbott

#7-3-6-2-7-2-3-1.   Jamie Dawn Talbot, born 2 August 1979, Solano County, California.

Child of Cheryl Rose Leach and John Dean Miller

#7-3-6-2-7-2-3-2.   Gabriel Brandon Miller, born 6 October 1992, Napa County, California.

Child of Cheryl Rose Leach and Joseph Kneeland

#7-3-6-2-7-2-3-3.   Joseph Benjamin Kneeland, born 21 November 1997.

#6-3-6-2-7-3-1 JOHN PAUL SARGENT

John Paul Sargent, born 5 June 1954, Washington County, Arkansas, married Debra Sue Stewart, 20 December 1972, Strickler, Washington County, Arkansas. Debra was born 7 November 1959, El Paso, Texas. John Paul Sargent died in a car wreck in Washington County, Arkansas, 26 April 1986.

Children of John Paul Sargent and Debra Sue Stewart

#7-3-6-2-7-3-1-1.   John Paul Sargent, Jr., born 26 May 1954, Fayetteville, Washington County, Arkansas.

#7-3-6-2-7-3-1-2.   Jason Dene Sargent, born 25 April 1978, Fayetteville, Washington County, Arkansas.

#6-3-6-2-7-3-2   JAMES HENRY SARGENT

James Henry Sargent, born 2 February 1956, Washington County, Arkansas, married Betty La Vonne Vickors, 23 June 1979, Prairie Grove, Washington County, Arkansas. Betty was born 19 April 1961, Prairie Grove, Washington County, Arkansas.

Children of James Henry Sargent and Betty La Vonne Vickors

#7-3-6-2-7-3-2-1.   Caramenya Nicole Sargent, born 13 February 1981, Shreveport, Louisiana.
#7-3-6-2-7-3-2-2.   Elizabeth Ann Sargent, born 10 December 1982, Shreveport, Louisiana.

#6-3-6-2-7-3-3   THOMAS LYNN SARGENT

Thomas Lynn Sargent, born 3 September 1961, Washington County, Arkansas, married Debria Ann Runyon, 22 November 1992, Strickler, Washington County Arkansas, Debria was born 8 March 1962, Jefferson City, Missouri.

Child of Thomas Lynn Sargent and Debria Ann Runyon

#7-3-6-2-7-3-3-1.   Russall Edwin Sargent, born 31 December 1985, Roswell, New Mexico.

#6-3-6-2-7-4-1   SHARON KAY EVANS

Sharon Kay Evans, born 10 December 1958, Yakima, Washington, married Keith Guthridge. Keith was born 5 October 1956.

Children of Sharon Kay Evans and Keith Guthridge

#7-3-6-2-7-4-1-1.   Allina Marie Gutrhidge, born 21 July 1984.
#7-3-6-2-7-4-1-2.   Nathan Lee Guthridge, born 15 March 1987.
#7-3-6-2-7-4-1-3.   Keriann Rebecca Guthridge, born 7 July 1989.

#6-3-6-2-7-4-2   KAREN FAY EVANS

Karen Fay Evans, born 11 August 1960, Yakima, Washington, married Timothy Lee Bentz, 21 June 1980. Timothy was born 22 February 1960.

Children of Karen Fay Evans and Timothy Lee Bentz

#7-3-6-2-7-4-2-1.   Amber Dawn Bentz, born 22 September 1981.
#7-3-6-2-7-4-2-2.   Philip Gerald Bentz, born 15 November 1984.
#7-3-6-2-7-4-2-3.   Steven Franklin Bentz, born 16 November 1987.

#6-3-6-2-7-4-3   LEANNA LYNN EVANS

LeAnna Lynn Evans, born 6 January 1963, Yakima, Washington, married Stanley Leroy Douglas, 7 August 1992.

Children of LaAnna Lynn Evans and Stanley Leroy Douglas

#7-3-6-2-7-4-3-1.   Andrew Michael Douglas, born 16 April 1995.
#7-3-6-2-7-4-3-2.   Erica Lynn Douglas, born 29 March 1963.

#6-3-6-2-7-4-4   LADONNA LEE EVANS

LaDonna Lee Evans, born 6 January 1963, Yakima, Washington, married Gerald Mitchell Corbin, 11 September 1982. Gerald was born July 14 1962.

Children of LaDonna Lee Evans and Gerald Mitchell Corbin

#7-3-6-2-7-4-4-1.   Kurtis Phillip Corbin, born 19 October 1991.
#7-3-6-2-7-4-4-2.   Kyle Gerald Corbin, born 19 October 1991.

#6-3-6-2-7-4-5   RACHEL DENISE EVANS

Rachel Denise Evans, born 26 February 1965, Yakima, Washington, married James Lee Erickson. James was born 22 September 1965.

Children of Rachel Denise Evans and James Lee Erickson

#7-3-6-2-7-4-5-1.   Lyndi Elizabeth Erickson, born 10 May 1987.
#7-3-6-2-7-4-5-2.   Mary Mitchell Erickson, born 25 March 1989.
#7-3-6-2-7-4-5-3.   Aaron Lee Erickson, born 14 November 1990.

#6-3-6-2-7-5-1   BRENDA KAY LEACH

Brenda Kay Leach, born 13 September 1954, Yakima, Washington, married Scott Norman Andrew, 22 August 1981, Las Vegas, Nevada. Scott was born 22 November 1954.

Children of Brenda Kay Leach and Scott Norman Andrews

#7-3-6-2-7-5-1-1.   Jason Ryan Andrews, born 22 October 1982.
#7-3-6-2-7-5-1-2.   Jeremy Christopher Andrews, born 23 May 1985.

#6-3-6-2-7-5-2   LARRY 'DEAN' LEACH

Larry 'Dean" Leach, born 14 November 1955, Yakima, Washington, married Sheryl Lynn Tolar, 27 December 1974, Yakima, Washington. Sheryl was born 21 April 1955.

Children of Larry 'Dean' Leach and Sheryl Lynn Tolar

#7-3-6-2-7-5-2-1.   Erin Dean Leach, born 7 September 1977, Seattle, Washington.

#7-3-6-2-7-5-2-2.   Justin Thomas Leach, born 16 June 1979, Redmond, Washington.

#6-3-6-2-8-1-1   PHYLLIS JEAN HANES

Phyllis Jean Hanes, born 25 August 1943, Mississippi County, Missouri, married Harrison Beasley, 15 January 1961, Charleston, Mississippi County, Missouri. Harrison was born 24 January 1940, Charleston, Missouri.

Child of Phyllis Jean Hanes and Harrison Beasley

#7-3-6-2-8-1-1-1.   Tim Beasley, born 15 January 1962, Kingman, Arizona.

#6-3-6-2-8-2-1   BETTY LOU HILL

Betty Lou Hill, born 9 January 1943, Mississippi County, Mississippi, married William L. Getz, 18 June 1960, San Bernardino County, California. William was born 8 August 1937, Aurora, Illinois and died 12 July 1992, Apple Valley, California.

Children of Betty Lou Hill and William L. Getz

#7-3-6-2-8-2-1-1.   William Todd Getz, born 17 July1966, Los Angeles County, California.

#7-3-6-2-8-2-1-2.   Brian S. Getz, born 18 April 1967, San Bernardino County, California.

#6-3-6-2-8-2-2   GARY MICHAEL HILL

Gary Michael Hill, born 18 March 1947, Mississippi County, Missouri, married Lois Vinega, Ontario, California. Lois was born in Colorado.

Children of Gary Michael Hill and Lois Vinega

#7-3-6-2-8-2-2-1.   Gary Michael Hill, born 14 December 1973, Fort Lauderdale, Florida.

#7-3-6-2-8-2-2-2.   Edward Daniel Hill, born 18 July 1978, Fort Lauderdale, Florida.

#6-3-6-2-8-2-3   CHARLES ALFORD HILL

Charles Alford Hill, born 26 January 1948, Mississippi County, California, married Ruby J. Menix, 25 November 1967, San Bernardino County, California. Ruby was born in 1948.

Children of Charles Alford Hill and Ruby J. Menix

#7-3-6-2-8-2-3-1.   Charles Alford Hill, born 28 May 1968, San Bernardino County, California.

#7-3-6-2-8-2-3-2.   Dustin Michael Hill, born 4 February 1973, San Bernardino County, California.

#7-3-6-2-8-2-3-3.   Shelly Leanne Hill, born 23 December 1978, San Bernardino County, California.

#6-3-6-2-8-3-1   EDWARD DELANE MORGAN, JR.

Edward Delane Morgan, Jr., born 11 April 1946, Sikeston, Mississippi County, Missouri married Barbara Dobbs. Barbara was born 5 September 1948.

Children Of Edward Delane Morgan, Jr. and Barbara Dobbs

#7-3-6-2-8-3-1-1. Michelle Morgan, born 7 December 1967, California.

#7-3-6-2-8-3-1-2. Kenny Morgan, born 1968, California.

#7-3-6-2-8-3-1-3. Edward Delane Morgan, born 29 May 2001, California.

#6-3-6-2-8-3-2   DENNIS MORGAN

Dennis Morgan, born 30 June 1947, Sikeston, Mississippi County, Missouri. Fathered three children out of wedlock.

Children of Dennis Morgan

#7-3-6-2 8-3-2-1. Kevin Lasiter Morgan, born 1969, Sikeston, Missouri.

#7-3-6-2-8-3-2-2. Windy Morgan, born 1980, Sikeston, Missouri.

#7-3-6-2-8-3-2-3. Wesley Morgan, born in Sikeston, Missouri.

#7-3-6-2-8-3-3   DANNY GENE MORGAN

Danny Gene Morgan, born 30 September 1949, Sikeston, Mississippi County, Missouri, married Margaret McClain.

Children of Danny Gene Morgan and Margaret McClain

#7-3-6-2-8-3-3-1. Danny Gene Morgan, Jr., born 13 February 1969, Sikeston, Missouri. Danny died 20 January 1970.

#7-3-6-2-8-3-3-2. Timmy Morgan, born 1973, Sikeston, Mississippi County, Missouri.

#7-3-6-2-8-3-3-3. Tammy Morgan, born 1975, Sikeston, Mississippi County, Missouri.

#6-3-6-2-8-3-4   DAVID MORGAN

David Morgan, born 30 July 1954, Sikeston, Mississippi County, Missouri, married Marjorie Blasingaim, 25 January 1975, Charleston, Mississippi County, Missouri. Marjorie was born 31 December 1956, East Prairie, Mississippi County, Missouri. David is a Maintenance engineer for Business Equipment and Lives in Florissant, Missouri.

Children of David Morgan and Marjorie Blasingaim

#7-3-6-2-8-3-4-1.   Michael Shawn Morgan, born 22 July 1975, Charleston, Missouri. Died 25 August 2005 Florissant, Missouri.
#7-3-6-2-8-3-4-2.   Korey Dale Morgan, born 20 July 1979, US Navy, Guam US Territory.
#7-3-6-2-8-3-4-3.   Joushua Cole Morgan, born 22 December 1984, Sikeston, Missouri.

#6-3-6-2-8-3-5   DIANA MORGAN

Diana Morgan, born 2 September 1955, Sikeston, Mississippi County, Missouri, married Roger Cain, 13 June 1953, Charleston, Mississippi County, Missouri. Roger was born 13 June 1953, Mississippi County, Missouri.

Children of Diane Morgan and Roger Cain

#7-3-6-2-8-3-5-1.   Sarah Lula Cain, born 4 September 1986 Sikeston, Missouri.
#7-3-6 2-8-3-5-2.   Stacy Cain, born September 1989 Sikeston, Missouri.

#6-3-6-2-8-3-6   DALE MORGAN

Dale Morgan, born 30 December 1956, Sikeston, Mississippi County, Missouri, married Huffer.

#7-3-6-2-8-3-6-1.   Samuel Delenerichar Morgan, born 19 March 1993, Riverside County, California.

#6-3-6-2-8-3-7   DEBORAH MORGAN

Deborah Morgan, born 14 December 1957, Sikeston, Mississippi County, Missouri, married Larry Mc Curter. Larry was born 1959, East Prairie, Missouri

Children of Deborah Morgan and Larry Mc Curter

#7-3-6-2-8-3-7-1.   Laurie Mc Curter, born 3 August 1973, Sikeston, Missouri.
#7-3-6-2-8-3-7-2.   Terry Mc Curter, born 1977, Kansas City, Missouri.
#7-3-6-2-8-3-7-3.   Harley Mc Curter, born 1979, Kansas City, Missouri.

#6-3-6-2-9-1-1   JEFFREY ALAN LOCKWOOD

Jeffrey Alan Lockwood, born 6 June 1949, Hennepin County, Minnesota, first married Luann Renee Bursaw, 26 November 1971, Hennepin County, Minnesota. Luann was born in 1953. Jeffrey And Luann were divorced 27 July 1976, Hennepin County, Minnesota. Jeffrey later married Janice Dorene Bebault. Janice was born in 1957. Jeffrey and Janice were divorced 1 December 1981, at Hennepin County, Minnesota. They later re-married 6 June 1987. Jeffrey later married Mercedes N. Grilley. They were divorced 9 November 1993, Hennepin County, Minnesota.

Child of Jeffrey Alan Lockwood and Luann Renee Bursaw

#7-3-6-2-9-1-1-1.   Lulia Ann Lockwood, born 9 February 1975, Hennepin County, Minnesota.

Child of Jeffrey Alan Lockwood and Janice Dorene Bebault

#7-3-6-2-9-1-1-2. Shawn Mathew Lockwood, born 4 June 1978, Hennepin County, Minnesota.

#6-3-6-2-9-1-2 CHERYL CHRISTINE LOCKWOOD

Cheryl Christine Lockwood, born 4 July 1953, Hennepin County, Minnesota, had one child out of wedlock.

Child of Cheryl Christine Lockwood born out of wedlock

#7-3-6-2-9-1-2-1. April Lockwood, born Hennepin County, Minnesota.

#6-3-6-2-9-1-5 PATRICIA ARLEVA LOCKWOOD

Patricia Arleva Lockwood, born 16 October 1954, Hennepin County, Minnesota, married Russell Alan Kampa, 24 October 1987, Sherburne County, Minnesota. Russell was born in 1959. Patricia and Russell were divorced 13 March 1992, Sherburne County, Minnesota.

Child of Patricia Arleva Lockwood and Russell Alan Kampa

#7-3-6-2-9-1-5-1. Sara Bethena Kampa, born 3 October 1990, Hennepin County, Minnesota.

#6-3-6-2-9-3-1 LINDA PHARR

Linda Pharr, born 8 April 1952, Washington County, Arkansas, married Robert Philip Reese, 16 January 1977, Washington County, Arkansas. Robert was born 11 March 1952, Berry County, Missouri. Linda Works as a Nurse in Springfield, Missouri. She and Robert make their home in Neosho, Jasper County, Missouri.

Children of Linda Pharr and Robert Philip Reese

#7-3-6-2-9-3-1-1. Clayton Reese, born 12 November 1979, Washington County, Arkansas.
#7-3-6-2-9-3-1-2. Clifton Reese, born 8 February 1984, Springfield, Missouri.

#6-3-6-2-9-3-2   MICHAEL WAYNE PRARR

Michael Wayne Pharr, born 22 May 1953, Washington County, Arkansas, married Beverly Pennell, 22 May 1980, Fayetteville, Washington County, Arkansas. Beverly was born 21 December 1951, Washington County, Arkansas. Michael was employed in the Poultry Business. He and Beverly make their home in Gentry, Benton County, Arkansas.

Children of Michael Wayne Pharr and Beverly Pennell

#7-3-6-2-9-3-2-1. Asa Pharr, born 12 March 1984, Washington County, Arkansas.
#7-3-6-2-9-3-2-2. Micah Pharr, born 10 September 1990, Washington County, Arkansas.

#6-3-6-2-9-3-3   MARSHA PHARR

Marsha Pharr, born 20 January 1957, Washington County, Arkansas, first married Douglas M. Wenzel, about 1978 Washington County, Arkansas. Douglas was born in August of 1955. Marsha Later married Brian Hash. Brian was born about 1960.

Children of Marsha Pharr and Douglas M. Wenzel

#7-3-6-2-9-3-3-1.   Sean Wenzel, born 12 July 1979, Little Rock, Arkansas.

#7-3-6-2-9-3-3-2.   Brandon Wenzel, born 18 July 1984, Fort Myers, Florida.

#6-3-6-2-9-4-1   DENISE BIGGS

Denise Biggs, born 24 April 1957, Washington County, Arkansas, first married Mickey Joe Hudgens, 6 September 1975, Lincoln, Washington County, Arkansas. Mickey was born 20 August 1954, Socorro, New Mexico and died 20 May 1982, Westville, Adair County, Oklahoma. Denise and Mickey grew chickens in Adair County, Oklahoma. Denise later married Kenneth Brian Power, 28 July 1990, Fayetteville, Washington County, Oklahoma. Denise and Kenneth operated a Sporting Goods Store in Springdale, Arkansas.

Child of Denise Biggs and Mickey Joe Hudgens

#7-3-6-2-9-4-1-1.   Kenli Rhea Hudgens, born 16 March 1978, Washington County, Arkansas.

Child of Denise Biggs and Kenneth Brian Power

#7-3-6-2-9-4-1-2.   Patton Elizabeth Power, born 5 May 1993, Washington County, Arkansas.

#6-3-6-2-9-4-2   CARL BIGGS

Carl Biggs, born 8 February 1959, Washington County, Arkansas, married Wanda Haegele, 30 May 1980, Cane Hill, Washington County, Arkansas. Wanda was born 30 March1942, Arlington Heights, Illinois. Carl and Wanda farmed and raised Turkeys in Washington County, Arkansas.

Children of Carl Biggs and Wanda Haegelle

#7-3-6-2-9-4-2-1. Jared Biggs, born 19 March 1983, Washington County, Arkansas.

#7-3-6-2-9-4-2-2. Caylan Biggs, born 22 March 1986, Washington County, Arkansas.

#6-3-6-2-9-4-3 CURTIS PAUL BIGGS

Curtis Paul Biggs, born 26 March 1963, Washington County, Arkansas, married Machiel Dawn Kegley, 8 November 1994, Washington County, Arkansas. Machiel was born 11 March 1972, Reno, Nevada. Paul and Machiel farmed and grew Turkeys in Washington County, Arkansas.

Child of Curtis Paul Biggs and Machiel Dawn Kegley

#7-3-6-2-9-4-3-1. Treyton Biggs, born 8 April 1994, Washington County, Arkansas.

#6-3-6-2-10-1-1 SHARON ANN LEACH

Sharon Ann Leach, born 6 August 1951, Oakland, Alameda County, California, married Jeffrey Bruce Davidson, 15 April 1973, Alameda County, California. Jeffrey was born 16 June 1949, Oakland, Alameda County, California.

Children of Sharon Ann Leach and Jeffrey Bruce Davidson

#7-3-6-2-10-1-1-1. Michael Richard Davidson, born 2 March 1975, Monterey County, California.

#7-3-6-2-10-1-1-2. Jodi Lynn Davidson, born 21 June 1976, Monterey County, California.

#6-3-6-2-10-1-2   PAULA JO LEACH

Paula Jo Leach, born 3 October 1957, Redwood City, California, married Kenneth Edward Gatewood, 18 October 1980, Orange County, California. Kenneth was born 2 November 1951, Orange County, California.

Children of Paula Jo Leach and Kenneth Edward Gatewood

#7-3-5-2-10-1-2-1.   Jessica Marie Gatewood, born 31 December 1981, Los Angeles county, California.
#7-3-6-2-10-1-2-2.   Janice Lee Gatewood, born 28 October 1986, Santa Clara County, California.
#7-3-6-2-10-1-2-3.   Marshall Bryan Gatewood, born 26 July 1988, Santa Clara County, California.
#7-3-6-2-10-1-2-4.   Kenneth Gatewood, Jr., born 24 July 1991, Santa Clara County, California.

#6-3-6-2-11-1-1   JOHNNY RAY ETHERIDGE, JR.

Johnny Ray Etheridge, Jr., born 13 April 1954, Prairie Grove, Washington County, Arkansas, first married Sherry Lafern McLaughlin, 29 November 1974, Potter County, Texas. Sherry was born 12 June 1957, Hutchinson County, Texas. After a divorce, Johnny married Debra A. Frazier, 12 December 1980, Potter County, Texas. Debra was born 15 December 1959, Portsmouth, Virginia. Johnny has been employed and successful in several Jobs, Iowa Beef, Swan Foods, Car Salesman and now a Truck Driver.

Children of Johnny Ray Etheridge, Jr. and Sherry Lafern McLaughlin

#7-3-6-2-11-1-1-1.   Frankye Shannon Etheridge, born 11 September 1977, Potter County, Texas.
#7-3-6-2-11-1-1-2.   Catherine Ann Etheridge, born 4 February 1979, Potter County, Texas.

Child of Johnny Ray Etheridge, Jr. and Debra A. Frazier

#7-3-6-2-11-1-1-3.   Johnny Ray Etheridge, lll, born 19 October 1984, Potter County, Texas.

#6-3-6-2-11-1-3   PATRICIA GAIL ETHERIDGE

Patricia Gail Etheridge, born 26 June 1959, Norman, Cleveland County, Texas, first married Kenneth E. Laird, 15 October 1977, Potter County, Texas. Kenneth was born in 1956. Patricia later married James Warren Copeland, 14 February 1991, Nueces County, Texas. James was born in 1958.

Child of Patricia Gail Etheridge and Kenneth E. Laird

#7-3-6-2-11-1-3-1.   Katricia Samon Laird, born 17 December 1981, Oklahoma City, Oklahoma.

Child of Patricia Gail Etheridge and James Warren Copeland

#7-3-6-2-11-1-3-2.   James Christopher Copeland, born 18 December 1991, Nueces County, Texas.

#6-3-6-2-11-2-1   PATRICK EUGENE BROWN LL

Patrick Eugene Brown, ll, born 23 March 1963, Oklahoma City, Oklahoma. Married Jeane Marie Walsh, 3 August 1991, Tulsa, Tulsa County, Oklahoma. Jeane was born 10 June 1969 and grew up in the area of Chicago, Illinois. Rick was a Car Salesman and stay at home dad. Jeane worked replacing fuel sells in Atomic Energy Plants.

Children of Patrick Eugene Brown ll and Jeane Marie Walsh

#7-3-6-2-11-2-1-1.   Sareta Marie Brown, born 16 January 1995, Albuquerque, New Mexico.

#7-3-6-2-11-2-1-2.   Denali Frances Brown, born 5 May 2005, Denver, Colorado.

#6-3-6-2-11-2-2   MICHAEL LEACH BROWN

Michael Leach Brown, born 31 August 1963, Oklahoma City, Oklahoma, married Leeann McCormick, 10 August 1985, Moore, Oklahoma. Leeann was born 13 February 1863, Kansas City, Missouri, and grew up in the area of Chicago, Illinois. Michael is an Attorney. He and Leeann make their home in the Village, a suburb of Dallas, Texas.

Children of Michael Leach Brown and Leeann McCormick

#7-3-6-2-11-2-2-1.   Kirsten Michelle Brown, born 25 January 1989, Norman, Oklahoma.
#7-3-6-2-11-2-2-2.   Hannah Lee Brown, born 27 December 1991, Norman, Oklahoma.

#6-3-6-2-11-2-3   SARITA FRANCES BROWN

Sarita Frances Brown, born 29 July 1965, Oklahoma City, Oklahoma, first married Jay Allen Williamson, June of 1986 Moore, Oklahoma. Jay was an Annapolis Graduate and Navy Pilot. He was born 15 July 1963, Oklahoma City, Oklahoma. He was killed in a plane crash off the west Coast of California, 21 March 1991. On August 25 1998, Sarita married Todd Smith. Todd is a Doctor. He and Sarira make their home near Hoover, Alabama. Todd was born 25 July 1965, Oscoda, Michigan.

Children of Sarita Frances Brown and Jay Allen Williamson

#7-3-6-2-11-2-3-1.   Samantha Danielle Williamson, born 14 February1987, Pensacola, Florida.
#7-3-6-2-11-2-3-2.   Jacob Patrick Williamson, born 24 December 1989, Oklahoma City, Oklahoma.

Child of Sarita Frances Brown and Todd Smith

#7-3-6-2-11-2-3-3.   Allison Smith, born 11 September 1995, Norman, Oklahoma

#6-3-6-2-11-3-1   GEORGE HARRISON LEACH III

George Harrison Leach, III, born 6 July 1961, Plainview, Hale County, Texas, married Melissa Osborne, 23 March 1985, Oklahoma City, Oklahoma. Lisa was born 23 September 1963, Dallas, Texas. George is an Attorney and at present is the First Assistant District Attorney of the First Judicial District of the State of Oklahoma.

Children of George Harrison Leach III and Melissa Osborne

#7-3-6-2-11-3-1-1.   George Harrison Leach, IV, born 4 October 1988, Liberal, Kansas.

#7-3-6-2-11-3-1-2.   Tiffany Leach, born 30 March 1991, Liberal, Kansas.

#6-3-6-2-11-3-2   DEBRA LYNN LEACH

Debra Lynn Leach, born 2 March 1963, Fayetteville, Washington County, Arkansas, married Tere Clay Williams, 5 June 1982, Keyes, Cimarron County, Oklahoma. Tere was born 28 May 1963, Cimarron County, Oklahoma. Tere is an Accountant and Bookkeeper. She and Tere make their home in Oklahoma. Debra is a Bank Vice President and loan officer.

Children of Debra Lynn Leach and Tere Clay Williams

#7-3-6-2-11-3-2-1.   Shandi Williams, born 17 February 1984, Boise City, Oklahoma

#7-3-6-2-11-3-2-2.   Keyton Williams, born 3 October 1986, Boise City, Oklahoma.

#6-3-6-2-13-1-1 CARL SPRATT

Carl Spratt, born 15 February 1952, Carbondale, Illinois, married Wanda Elizabeth Warren, 13 January 1973, Arcata, California. Wanda was born 2 April 1948, Arcata, California.

Child of Carl Spratt and Wanda Elizabeth Warren

#7-3-6-2-13-1-1-1.   Katherine Spratt, born 30 October 1987, Fortuna, California.

#6-3-6-2-13-1-2 KATHY SPRATT

Kathy Spratt, born 10 September 1954, Salem, Illinois, married Adrian Lee "Joe" Timmerman, 16 February 1974, Fortuna, California. Joe was born 26 July 1953, Scotia, Humboldt County, California.

Children of Kathy Spratt and Adrian Lee "Joe" Timmerman

#7-3-6-2-13-1-2-1.   Brian L. Timmerman, born 17 February 1976, Fortuna, California.
#7-3-6-2-13-1-2-2.   Greg Michael Timmerman, born 11 August 1978, Fortuna, California.
#7-3-6-2-13-1-2-3.   Brad Andrew Timmerman, born 21 April 1980, Fortuna California.

#6-3-6-2-13-4-1 TRACY KAY SPRATT

Tracy Kay Spratt, born 28 January 1959, Carmi, Illinois, first married John K. Nilz, 7 August 1978, Mountain Home, Arkansas. John was born in August 1958 Conway, Faulkner County, Arkansas. On 1 May 1982, Tracy married Daniel John Hawkins. Daniel was born 1 November 1949.

Child of Tracy Kay Spratt and John G. Nilz

#7-3-6-2-13-4-1-1.   Shannon Krista Nilz, born 18 November 1979, Mountain Home, Arkansas.

Children of Tracy Kay Spratt and Daniel John Hawkins

#7-3-6-2-13-4-1-2.   Robert Aaron Hawkins, born 17 February 1983, Mountain Home, Arkansas.
#7-3-6-2-13-4-1-3.   Ashley Michelle Hawkins, born 29 May 1984, Mountain Home, Arkansas.

#7-3-6-2-13-4-2   WILLIAM WALTER SPRATT, JR.

William Walter Spratt, Jr., born 8 March 1963, New Iberia, Louisiana, married Janell Kunert, 19 June 1989, Mountain Home, Arkansas.

Child of William Walter Spratt, Jr. and Janell Kunert

#7-3-6-2-13-4-2-1.   Danielle Nicole Spratt, born 1 October 1991, Little Rock, Arkansas.

#6-3-6-2-13-4-3   ELSIE ANNE SPRATT

Elsie Anne Spratt, born 20 January 1967, New Iberia, Louisiana, married Michael Biggs, 30 November 1991, Little Rock, Arkansas.

Children of Elsie Anne Spratt and Michael Biggs

#7-3-6-2-13-4-3-1.   Ian Michael Biggs, born 31 May 1992, Little Rock, Arkansas.
#7-3-6-2-13-4-3-2.   Patrick Leonard Biggs, born 20 October 1994, Little Rock, Arkansas.

#6-3-7-1-1-2-1   BRENDA CHRISTINE GUTHREY

Brenda Christine Guthrey, born 15 April 1952, Tulsa, Oklahoma, married Michael Sterling Cook, 7 August 1971, Ardmore Carter County, Oklahoma. Michael was born 23 February 1948.

Children of Brenda Christine Guthrey and Michael Sterling Cook

#7-3-7-1-1-2-1-1.   Michelle Renee Cook, born 15 April 1976.
#7-3-7-1-1-2-1-2.   Kristin Casey Cook, born 23 June 1985.

#6-3-7-1-1-2-2   MARCIA ELSIE GUTHREY

Marcia Elsie Guthrey, born 19 February 1955, Searcy, Arkansas, married Robert Terrell (Terry) Wheeler, 31 December 1976, Ardmore, Oklahoma. Terry was born 11 July 1953, Stuttgart, Germany. Marcie is a School Teacher.

Children of Marcia Elsie Guthrey and Robert Terrell (Terry) Wheeler

#7-3-7-1-1-2-2-1.   Erwin Elizabeth Wheeler, born 2 December 1985, Clinton, Oklahoma.
#7-3-7-1-1-2-2-2.   Sarah Catherine Wheeler, born 2 February 1991, Clinton, Oklahoma.

#6-3-7-1-1-3-1   ANDY THOMAS MARTS

Andy Thomas Marts, born 2 March 1961, Clarksville, Arkansas, married Tammie Milligan, 9 August 1986, Baxter County, Arkansas. Tammie was born 19 July 1961, Abilene, Texas.

Children of Andy Thomas Marts and Tammie Milligan

#7-3-7-1-1-3-1-1.   Alan Thomas Marts, born 11 June 1988, Mountain Home, Arkansas.

#7-3-7-1-1-3-1-2.   Christopher Andrew Marts, 2 September 1990, Mountain Home, Arkansas.

#6-3-7-1-1-3-2   KENT MICHAEL MARTS

Michael Kent Marts, born 17 March 1963, Clarksville, Arkansas, married Natalie Gardner, 31 May 1986, Harrison, Arkansas. Natalie was born 6 January 1964, Harrison, Arkansas.

Children of Kent Michael Marts and Natalie Gardner

#7-3-7-1-1-3-2-1.   Jeffrey McClinton Marts, born 11 May 1989, Rogers, Arkansas.
#7-3-7-1-1-3-2-2.   Sarah Elizabeth Marts, born 23 August 1990, Rogers, Arkansas.
#7-3-7-1-1-3-2-3.   Laura Catherine Marts, born 10 February 1995, Rogers, Arkansas.
#7-3-7-1-1-3-2-4.   David Mart, born 12 September 2001, Rogers, Arkansas.

#6-3-7-1-1-4-2   SUZANNE LEA SCHOMBERG

Suzanne Lea Schomberg, born 23 February 1971, St Louis, Missouri married Paul Cox in June of 1996, Holstein, Missouri. Paul was born 9 June 1964, Virginia.

Children of Suzanne Lea Schomberg and Paul Cox

#7-3-7-1-1-4-2-1.   Sara Ealise Cox, born 28 January 2005, Richmond, Virginia.
#7-3-7-1-1-4-2-2.   Anna Elizabeth Cox, born 2 July 2008, Richmond, Virginia.

#6-3-7-5-2-1-1   KENNETH JERALD RICH

Kenneth Jerald Rich, born 24 January 1960, Las Vegas, Nevada, first married Jacquelin D. Willis, 26 May 1981, St George, Utah. Jacquelin was born 21 March 1963, Henderson, Nevada. Kenneth divorced Jacquolin, 2 October 1986, Clark County, Nevada. Kenneth later married Alice Marie Barton, 11 April 1992, Las Vegas, Clark County, Nevada. Alice was born 17 January 1966, Columbus, Ohio. Kenneth is a fork lift operator in Las Vegas, Nevada.

Children of the marriage of Kenneth Jerald Rich and Jacquelin D. Willis

#7-3-7-5-2-1-1-1.   Travis Rich, born 21 September 1982, Henderson, Nevada.
#7-3-7-5-2-1-1-2.   Matt Rich, born 26 July 1984, Las Vegas, Nevada.
#7-3-7-5-2-1-1-3.   Josh Rich, born 25 November 1985, Las Vegas, Nevada.
#7-3-7-5-2-1-1-4.   John Rich, born 3 December 1977, Henderson, Nevada.

Children of Kenneth Jerald Rich and Alice Marie Barton

#7-3-7-5-2-1-1-5.   Brandi Rich, born 9 August 1986, Las Vegas, Nevada.
#7-3-7-5-2-1-1-6.   Levy Rich, born 14 June 1993, Henderson, Nevada

#6-3-7-5-2-1-2   MICHAEL ALAN RICH

Michael Alan Rich, born 19 October 1971, Las Vegas, Nevada, married Patricia Barnes. Patricia was born 24 June 1971, Gore, Oklahoma. Michael and Patricia make their home in Muskogee, Oklahoma.

Children of Michael Alan Rich and Patricia Barnes

#7-3-7-5-2-1-2-1.   Dakota Rich, born 4 August 1995, Muskogee, Oklahoma.
#7-3-7-5-2-1-2-2.   Autum Lorna Rich, born 14 November 2002, Muskogee, Oklahoma.
#7-3-7-5-2-1-2-3.   Snowie Rich, born 1 February 2007 Muskogee, Oklahoma.

#6-3-7-5-2-2-1   VIRGINIA MURRAY

Virginia Murray, born 30 April 1955, Stilwell, Adair County, Oklahoma, married Dean Kirk.

Children of Virginia Murray and Dean Kirk

#7-3-7-5-2-2-1-1.   Shelly Kirk, born.
#7-3-7-5-2-2-1-2.   Debbie Kirk, born.

#6-3-7-5-2-4-1   PAMELA SUE RICH

Pamela Sue Rich, born 20 October 1956, Muskogee, Oklahoma, married Jim Grisham.

Children of Pamela Sue Rich and Jim Grisham

#7-3-7-5-2-4-1-1.   Mindy Grisham, born 29 October 1979, Tulsa, Oklahoma.
#7-3-7-5-2-4-1-2.   Holly Grisham, born 13 July 1982, Tulsa, Oklahoma.

#6-3-7-5-2-4-2   SHARON LANETT RICH

Sharon Lanett Rich born 6 November 1962, Muskogee, Oklahoma, married Steve Cowen.

Child of Sharen Lanette Rich and Steve Cowen

#7-3-7-5-2-4-2-1.   Samantha Cowen, born 3 November 1993, Tulsa, Oklahoma.

#6-3-7-5-2-6-2   FINCHER BURL RICH

Fincher Burl Rich, born 8 April 1968, Muskogee, Oklahoma, married Machelle Replogle in 1998, Muskogee, Oklahoma. Machelle was born 16 October 1971, Coeta, Oklahoma.

Children of Fincher Burl Rich and Machelle Replogle

#7-3-7-5-2-6-2-1.   Brenda Machelle Rich, born 9 October 1998, Tulsa, Oklahoma
#7-3-7-5-2-6-2-2.   Mary Rose Rich, born 7 August 1999, Grove, Oklahoma.
#7-3-7-5-2-6-2-3.   William Burl Rich, born 18 March 2004, Tulsa, Oklahoma.

#6-3-7-5-6-1-1   WESLEY CLEO WORLEY

Wesley Cleo Worley, born 28 May 1967, King County, Washington, married Angela Kay Marble, 13 September 1989, Long Beach, San Bernardo County, California. Angelia was born 5 February 1971, Pocattello, Idaho.

Children of Wesley Cleo Worley and Angela Kay Marble

#7-3-7-5-6-1-1-1.   Kristi Elizabeth Worley, born 11 December 1988, Reedsport, Douglas County, Oregon.
#7-3-7-5-6-1-1-2.   Timothy Cameron Worley, born 2 December 1992, Los Angeles County, California.

#6-3-7-5-6-2-1   JULIE JO BORN

Julie Jo Born, born 3 November 1973, Apple Valley, San Bernardino, California married Helms.

Child of Julie Jo Born and Helms

#7-3-7-5-6-2-1-1.   Thomas Joshua Helms, born 11 December 1976, Salem, Marion County, Oregon.

#6-3-9-2-5-1-3   KRISTI ANN YOCUM

Kristi Ann Yocum, born 2 September 1964, Fresno, Fresno County, California, married Jeffrey Adam Bain. Jeffrey was born in 1961.

Child of Kristi Ann Yocum and Jeffrey Adam Bain

#7-3-9-2-5-1-3-1.   Jacob Roy Bain, born 1994.

#6-3-9-2-5-9-1   STEPHANI ANN HOLMES

Stephani Ann Holmes, born 15 February 1974, Fresno County, California, married Anthony Newton Moreno. Anthony was born 29 September 1971, Fresno County, California.

Children of Stephani Ann Holmes and Anthony Newton Moreno

#7-3-9-2-5-9-1-1.   Ryan Anthony Moreno, born 21 January 1992, Fresno County, California.
#7-3-9-2-5-9-1-2.   Sierra Rianne Moreno, born 27 February 1993, Mendocono County, California.

EIGHTH GENERATION

#7-3-1-3-2-1-3-1 JERROD MILES BARTLETT

Jerrod Miles Bartlett, born 16 January 1983, Oklahoma City, Oklahoma, married Lindsey.

Child of Jerrod Miles Bartlett and Lindsey

#8-3-1-3-4-1-3-1-1.   Mary Jordon Bartlett, born 1 September.

#7-3-1-3-2-1-3-2 TYLER LEE BARTLETT

Tyler Lee Bartlett born 2 August 1895 Oklahoma Coty, Oklahoma, married Jenifer.

Child of Tyler Lee Bartlett and Jenifer

#8-3-1-3-2-1-3-2-1.   Maddox Bartlett, born 29 July 2006.

#7-3-1-5-3-4-1-1 MITCHELL EDWARD MULHALL

Mitchell Edward Mulhall, born 15 September 1960, Ft Carson, Colorado married Karen Marjorie Buchanan, 17 September 1994, Redstone, Colorado. Karen was born in 1963.

Child of Mitchell Edward Mulhall and Karen Marjorie Buchanan

#8-3-1-5-3-4-1-1-1.   Liam Edward Mulhall, born.

#7-3-1-5-3-4-1-2 JILL ELIZABETH MULHALL

Jill Elizabeth Mulhall, born 2 June 1962, Ft Carson, Colorado, married John Robert Obereiner, 16 September 1989, Glenwood Springs, Colorado. John was born 3 September 1960, Evanston, Illinois.

Child of Jill Elizabeth Mulhall and John Robert Obereiner

#8-3-1-5-3-4-1-2-1.   Annabel Kate Obereiner, born.

#7-3-1-6-4-4-1-1 KARL DEAN ERIKSON

Karl Dean Erikson, born 28 November 1968, Los Angeles County, California, married Carol Elizabeth Emerson, 4 September 1993, Glendale, California. Carol was born 22 March 1966, Glendale, California.

Child of Karl Dean Erikson and Carol Elizabeth Emerson

#8-3-1-6-4-4-1-1-1.   Sean Alexander Erikson, born 28 May 1995, San Bernardino County, California.

#7-3-1-6-4-4-1-2 CRAIG ADAM ERIKSON

Craig Adam Erikson, born 19 August 1970, Los Angeles County, California, married Kimberley Kay Wallace, 31 October 1990. Kimberly was born 9 December 1969, Indiana.

Children of Craig Adam Erikson and Kimberley Kay Wallace

#8-3-1-6-4-4-1-2-1.   Chadwick Craig Erikson, born 21 March 1992, Granada Hills, California.
#8-3-1-6-4-4-1-2-2.   Ashley Kimberline Erikson, born 16 February 1993, Indiana.

#7-3-2-2-9-2-2-1 KAREN LYNN BLASIER

Karen Lynn Blasier, born 1 July 1954, Sulphur, Murrah County, Oklahoma, married Gerald Franklin, 24 August 1974, Oklahoma City, Oklahoma. Gerald was born 28 September 1954, Oklahoma City, Oklahoma.

Children of Karen Lynn Blasier and Gerald Franklin

#8-3-2-2-9-2-2-1-1.　Sarah Jean Franklin, born 4 January 1977, Norman, Cleveland County, Oklahoma.

#8-3-2-2-9-2-2-1-2.　Will Blasier Franklin, born 11 November 1979, Norman, Cleveland County, Oklahoma.

#8-3-2-2-9-2-2-1-3.　Katherine Elizabeth Franklin, born 28 June 1983, Enid, Garfield County, Oklahoma.

#7-3-2-2-9-2-2-2 TONY RALPH BLASIER

Tony Ralph Blasier, born 22 October 1956, Ardmore, Carter County, Oklahoma, married Melissa Holland, 6 August 1979. Melissa was born 11 July 1958, Tahlequah, Cherokee County, Oklahoma.

Children of Tony Ralph Blasier and Melissa Holland

#8-3-2-2-9-2-2-2-1.　Meagan Ann Blasier, born 1 July 1986 Oklahoma City, Oklahoma.

#8-3-2-2-9-2-2-2-2.　Emma Nicole Blasier, born 19 December 1991, Oklahoma City, Oklahoma.

#7-3-2-5-1-1-2-1 ALICE LEE KECK

Alice Lee Kech, born Washington County, Arkansas married Don Gumm.

Children of Alice Lee Keck and Don Gumm

#8-3-2-5-1-1-2-1-1.   Jeanette Gumm, born.
#8-3-2-5-1-1-2-1-2.   Donna Gumm, born.

#7-3-2-5-1-1-3-1   BOB HOWARD

Bob Howard, born 27 February 1936, Washington County, Arkansas, married Bertha Dean Shannon. Bob died in 1982, Tulsa, Oklahoma.

Child of Bob Howard and Bertha Dean Shannon

#8-3-2-5-1-1-3-1-1.   Vicki Dean Howard, born 19 May 1958, Tulsa, Oklahoma.

#7-3-2-5-1-1-3-2   THEDA JEAN HOWARD

Theda Jean Howard, born 22 February 1938, Los Angeles, California, married Ray Braly, 9 March 1957, Lincoln, Washington County, Arkansas. Ray was born about 1936, Washington County, Arkansas. Theda later married Jim York, 25 November 1964, Sallisaw, Oklahoma.

Children of Theda Jean Howard and Ray Braly

#8-3-2-5-1-1-3-2-1.   Glenn Ray Braly, born 13 December 1957, Fayetteville, Arkansas.
#8-3-2-5-1-1-3-2-2.   Howard Paul Braly, born 21 June 1960, Siloam Springs, Arkansas.

#7-3-2-5-1-1-7-1   BOBBY GENE GLIDEWELL

Bobby Gene Glidewell, born 1 May 1954, Berea, Ohio. (wife unknown).

Children of Bobby Gene Glidewell

#8-3-2-5-1-1-7-1-1.   Michael Glidewell, born Washington County, Arkansas.
#8-3-2-5-1-1-7-1-2.   Luke Glidewell, born Washington County, Arkansas.

#7-3-2-5-1-1-7-2 JANET FAY GLIDEWELL

Janet Fay Glidewell, born 15 August 1957, Washington County, Arkansas. (Husband Unknown)

Children of Janet Fay Glidewell

#8-3-2-5-1-1-7-2-1.   Vicky, born Washington County, Arkansas.
#8-3-2-5-1-1-7-2-2.   Brenda Lee, born in Oklahoma.

#7-3-2-5-1-3-2-1 GALE RODGERS

Gale Rogers, born 3 May 1939, Washington County, Arkansas, married Ronnie Allen

Children of Gale Rodgers and Ronnie Allen

#8-3-2-5-1-3-2-1-1.   Rhonda Allen, born Washington County, Arkansas.
#8-3-2-5-1-3-2-1-2.   Jonothan Allen, born Washington County, Arkansas.

#7-3-2-5-1-3-2-2 PAMELA RODGERS

Pamela Rodgers, born 19 September 1949, Washington County, Arkansas, married Richard Watson.

Children of Pamela Rodgers and Richard Watson

#8-3-2-5-1-3-2-2-1.   Kara Watson, born Washington County, Arkansas.

#8-3-2-5-1-3-2-2-2.   Mathew Richard Watson, born Washington County, Arkansas.

#7-3-2-5-1-3-3-1 JAMES RICHARD BUTZBACK

James Richard Butzback, born 27 January 1953, Los Angeles County, California, marrird Kathlene E. Crandall, 18 March 1961, Los Algeles County, California. Kathlene was born in 1944.

Children of James Richard Butzback and Kathlene E. Crandall

#8-3-2-5-1-3-3-1-1.   Lisa M. Butzback, born 2 September 1961, Los Angeles County, California.

#8-3-2-5-1-3-3-1-2.   Elizabeth M. Butzback, born 2 September 1962, Los Angeles County, California.

#8-3-2-5-1-3-3-1-3.   James S. Butzback, born 15 April 1963, Los Angeles County, California.

#7-3-2-5-1-3-4-1 JUDITH GLIDEWELL

Judith Glidewell, born in 1948, married Arnold Stanton, 20 February 1970, Orange County, California. Arnold was born in 1941.

Child of Judith Glidewell and Arnold Stanton

#8-3-2-5-1-3-4-1-1.   Kari N. Stanton, born 18 September 1970, Orange County, California.

#7-3-2-5-1-3-4-2 JANE ANN GLIDEWELL

Jane Ann Glidewell, born 17 March 1953, Los Angeles County, California, married Douglas T. Munroe, 18 December 1976, Orange County, California. Douglas was born in 1947.

Children of Jane Ann Glidewell and Douglas T. Munroe

#8-3-2-5-1-3-4-2-1.　James Philip Munroe, born 20 April 1979, Orange County, California.

#8-3-2-5-1-3-4-2-2.　Hayley Jane Munroe, born 18 December 1982, Orange County, California.

#7-3-2-5-1-3-4-3 LISA GAYE GLIDEWELL

Lisa Gaye Glidewell, born 17 September 1958, Los Angeles County, California, married Clayton K. Boyer, 10 May 1985, Orange County, California. Clayton was born in 1930.

Child of Lisa Gaye Glidewell and Clayton K. Boyer

#8-3-2-5-1-3-4-3-1.　Grayson Maxwell Boyer, 22 September 1987, Orange County, California.

#7-3-2-5-1-3-5-1 TIMOTHY GENE GLIDEWELL

Timothy Gene Glidewell, born 31 July 1951, Los Angeles County, California, married Susan F. Wine, 28 June 1974, Stanislaus County, California. Susan was born in 1952.

Children of Tomothy Gene Glidewell and Susan F. Wine

#8-3-2-5-1-3-5-1-1.　Christopher E. Glidewell, born 4 April 1975, Stanislaus County, California.

#8-3-2-5-1-3-5-1-2.　Heather Lillian Glidewell, born 12 January 1978, Stanislaus County, California.

#8-3-2-5-1-3-5-1-3.   Timothy Arthur Glidewell, born 13 March 1986, Stanislaus County, California.

#7-3-2-5-1-3-5-2   MICHAEL E. GLIDEWELL

Michael E. Glidewell, born 22 January 1956, Orange County, California, married Julia B. Barker, 23 May 1981, Stanislaus County, California. Julia was born in 1960.

Children of Michael E. Glidewell and Julia B. Barker

#8-3-2-5-1-3-5-2-1.   Benjamin Lee Glidewell, born 22 January 1984, Stanislaus County, California.
#8-3-2-5-1-3-5-2-2.   Collin Adams Glidewell, born 3 April 1986, Stanislaus County, California.

#7-3-2-5-4-2-2-1   SUZANNA LEACH

Suzanna Leach, born 27 January 1978, Tulsa, Tulas County, Oklahoma, married Jimmy Cross. Jimmy was born in 1971, Nicklosville, Kentucky

Children of Suzanne Leach and Jimmy Cross

#8-3-2-5-4-2-2-1-1.   Breanna Cross, born 23 December 1997, Lexington, Kentucky.
#8-3-2-5-4-2-2-1-2.   James Bennett Cross, born 19 October 1999, Sherman, Texas.

#7-3-2-5-7-1-1-2   BOBBY DEAN RINEHART

Bobby Dean Rinehart, born 26 May 1972, Washington County, Arkansas, married Cathleen Colene Simpson, 26 May 1972, Stilwell, Oklahoma. Cathleen was born 11 January 1954, Atoka, Oklahoma.

Children of Bobby Dean Rinehart and Cathleen Colene Silpson

#8-3-2-5-7-1-1-2-1.   Bobby K. Rinehart, born 1 September 1973, Tahlequah, Oklahoma.

#8-3-2-5-7-1-1-2-2.   Bryan Dean Rinehart, born 26 February 1976, Tahlequah, Oklahoma.

#7-3-2-5-7-2-1-1 JAMI DEE-ANNE RINEHART

Jami Dee-Anne Rinehart, born 10 February 1960, Tulsa, Oklahoma, married Basil L. Pelton, 7 November 1980. Basil was born in February 1956. Jami and Basil make their home in Owassa, Tulsa County, Oklahoma.

Child of Jami Dee-Anne Rinehart and Basil L. Pelton

#8-3-2-5-7-2-1-1-1.   Britni Dee-Anne Pelton, born 29 September 1986, Tulsa County, Oklahoma.

#7-3-2-5-7-3-1-1 GAYE LYNN RINEHART

Gaye Lynn Rinehart, born 24 August 1955, Ft Worth, Tarrant County, Texas, married Gordon Jones. Lynn later married Garry Warner.

Child of Gaye Lynn Rinehart and Gordon Jones

#8-3-2-5-7-3-1-1-1.   Taylor Thomas Jones, born 15 February 1993.

#7-3-2-5-7-3-1-2 KELLYE JANETTE RINEHART

Kellye Janette Rinehart, born 2 November 1960, Hollywood, California, first married Lester Stone. Kellye later married Richard Carlton.

Child of Kellye Janette Rinehart and Lester Stone

#8-3-2-5-7-3-1-2-1.   Jennifer Dawn Stone, born 1 September 1984.

#7-3-2-5-7-3-2-1 PAUL DON REED

Paul Dean Reed, born 4 December 1958, Washington County, Arkansas, married Jamie Rennea Sturdy, 1 July 1978, Washington County, Arkansas. Jamie was born 28 June 1960, Washington County, Arkansas.

Children of Paul Don Reed and Jamie Rennea Sturdy

#8-3-2-5-7-3-2-1-1.   Carrie Marie Reed, born 22 May 1981, Tahlequah, Oklahoma, married Christian Seaton, 13 July 2002, Washington County, Arkansas.

#8-3-2-5-7-3-2-1-2.   Donald Neal Reed, born 9 June 1984, Tahlequah, Oklahoma, married Amber Renae Stokes, 10 December 2005, Benton County, Arkansas.

#7-3-2-5-7-3-2-2 CLARK NEAL REED

Clark Neal Reed, born 25 March 1962, Washington County, Arkansas, first married Laconna Kay Fowler, 14 July 1980, Missouri. Later Clark married Jacqueline Lea Page, 14 October 1983. Jacqueline was born 27 August 1964.

Child of Clark Neal Reed and Laconna Kay Fowler

#8-3-2-5-7-3-2-2-1.   Christy Reanae Reed, born 6 March 1981, Tahlequah, Oklahoma.

Child of Clark Neal Reed and Jacqueline Lea Page

#8-3-2-5-7-3-2-2-2.   Nicole Lea Reed, born 13 January 1986, Benton County, Arkansas.

#8-3-2-5-7-3-2-2-3.   Randi Jo Reed, born 30 January 1990, Benton County, Arkansas.

#7-3-2-5-7-3-2-3   TIMOTHY GENE REED

Timothy Gene Reed, born 17 April 1965, Washington County, Arkansas, married Charla Kay Washington, 23 November 1984, Washington County, Arkansas. Charla was born 19 October 1965, Washington County, Arkansas.

Children of Timothy Gene Reed and Charla Kay Washington

#8-3-2-5-7-3-2-3-1.   Timothy Mathew Reed, born 31 October 1990, Washington County, Arkansas.

#8-3-2-5-7-3-2-3-2.   Cody Edward Reed, born 7 April 1994, Washington County, Arkansas.

#7-3-2-5-7-5-1-1   STEPHEN CLINTON PAINTER

Stephen Clinton Painter, born 29 July 1953, married Jenny Keturak Cox.

Children of Stephen Clinton Painter and Jenny Keturak Cox

#8-3-2-5-7-5-1-1-1.   Benjamin Isaac Painter, born 24 October 1978.

#8-3-2-5-7-5-1-1-2.   Aran Reed Painter, born 30 May 1980.

#8-3-2-5-7-5-1-1-3.   Misty Lurae Painter, born 16 June 1982.

#7-3-2-5-7-5-1-2 MELISSA DEAN PAINTER

Melissa Dean Painter, born 29 September 1957, first married Ronnie Hill. After Ronnie's death Melissa married Lloyd Cole, 28 September 1996.

Children of Melissa Dean Painter and Ronnie Hill

#8-3-2-5-7-5-1-2-1. Clay Hill, born 15 October 1983.
#8-3-2-5-7-7-1-2-2. Cole Hill, born 8 February 1988.

#7-3-3-1-3-1-1-1 DEBORAH L. SHACKLEFORD

Deborah L. Shackelford, born 19 July 1956, Tulare County, California, married Rocky D. Montgomery, 29 May 1976, Tulare County, California. Rocky was born 19 July 1956, Tulare County, California.

Children of Deborah L. Shackelford and Rocky D. Montgomery

#8-3-3-1-3-1-1-1-1. Daniel Dean Montgomery, born 21 November 1978, Tulare County, California.
#8-3-3-1-3-1-1-1-2. William Dean Montgomery, born 20 March 1980, Tulare County, California.

#7-3-3-1-3-1-1-2 DIANE G. SHACKLEFORD

Diane G. Shackelford, born 24 October 1958, Tulare County, California, married Timothy D. Denton, 4 August 1979, Tulare County, California. Timothy was born 29 March 1956, Tulare County, California.

Children of Diane G. Shackelford and Timothy D. Denton

#8-3-3-1-3-1-1-2-1. Heather Alissa Denton, born 7 December 1980, Tulare County, California.
#8-3-3-1-3-1-1-2-2. Melodyann Marie Denton, born 16 December 1983, Tulare County, California.

#8-3-3-1-3-1-1-2-3.	Ryan Timothy Denton, born 26 August 1985, Tulare County, California.
#8-3-3-1-3-1-1-2-4.	Amy Michelle Denton, born 1 April 1987, Tulare County, California.
#8-3-3-1-3-1-1-2-5.	Jeremiah Michelle Denton, born 9 July 1989, Tulare County, California.
#8-3-3-1-3-1-1-2-6.	Jonathan Daniel Denton, born 28 February 1991, Tulare County, California.
#8-3-3-1-3-1-1-2-7.	Mathew Henry Denton, born 23 July 1993, Tulare County, California.

#7-3-3-1-3-1-1-3 DENISE L. SHACKLEFORD

Denise L. Shackelford, born 31 December 1961, Tulare County, California, married Glen A. Thomas, 2 August 1980, Tulare County, California. Glen was born in 1956.

Children of Denise L. Shackelford and Glen A Thomas

#8-3-3-1-3-1-1-3-1.	Christopher Glen Thomas, born 27 December 1980, Tulare County, California.
#8-3-3-1-3-1-1-3-2.	Michael Anthony Thomas, born 25 May 1983, San Bernardino County, California.
#8-3-3-1-3-1-1-3-3.	Tiffany Antionettere Thomas, born 9 June 1984, Tulare County, California.
#8-3-3-1-3-1-1-3-4.	Brooke Lorenfaith Thomas, born 3 August 1989, Tulare County, California.
#8-3-3-1-3-1-1-3-5.	Cody Mathew Thomas, born 17 August 1991, Tulare County, California.

#7-3-5-2-2-3-1-2 KRISTI LEE WILLIAMSON

Kristi Lee Williamson, born 10 January 1960, Hays County, Texas, married Michael Renee Bira, 9 June 1984, Hays County, Texas. Michael was born, 4 October 1958, Hays County, Texas

Children of Kristi Lee Williamson and Michael Renee Bira

#8-3-5-2-2-3-1-2-1. Lindsay Michelle Bira, born 20 December 1985,
                     Dallas County, Texas.
#8-3-5-2-2-3-1-2-2. Lauren Danielle Bira, born 22 June 1989 Dallas
                     County, Texas.

#7-3-5-2-2-3-1-3 KATHI ANN WILLIAMSON

Kathi Ann Williamson, born 14 April 1963, Hays County, Texas,
married Michael Henry Snell, 13 August 1989.

Children of Kathi Ann Williamson and Michael Henry Snell

#8-3-5-2-2-3-1-3-1. Samantha Snell, born 9 September 1990, Dallas
                     County, Texas.
#8-3-5-2-2-3-1-3-2. Mikayla Marie Snell, born 6 July 1993, Dallas
                     County, Texas.

#7-3-5-4-2-4-1-1 WILLIAM MILBURN JENKINS

William Milburn Jenkins, born 16 April 1962, Travis County, Texas,
married Christie Lynne Boosa, 16 December 1983, Tarrant County,
Texas. Christie was born 13 May 1964, Tarrant County, Texas.

Children of William Milburn Jenkins and Christie Lynne Boosa

#8-3-5-4-2-4-1-1-1. Preston William Jenkins, born 26 April 1988,
                     Dallas County, Texas.
#8-3-5-4-2-4-1-1-2. Courtney May Jenkins, born 22 August 1991,
                     Dallas County, Texas.
#8-3-5-4-2-4-1-1-3. Tara Christine Jenkins, born 17 September
                     1996, Tarrant County, Texas.

#7-3-5-4-2-4-1-2 BARBARA MARIE JENKINS

Barbara Marie Jenkins, born 12 May 1970, Dallas County, Texas, married Anthony Edward McDaniel, 9 March 1991, Dallas County, Texas. Anthony was born 12 February 1969, Dallas County, Texas.

Child of Barbara Marie Jenkins and Anthony Edward McDaniel

#8-3-5-4-2-4-1-2-1.   Austin Reid McDaniel, born 2 January 1993, Tarrant County, Texas.

#7-3-5-5-1-2-1-2 DEANNA KIM DRIVER

Deanna Kim Driver, born 30 December 1963, Reeves County, Texas, married Gus Ralph Hoff, lll, 22 June 1985, La Salle County, Texas. Gus was born 28 November 1960, Bexar County, Texas.

Children of Deanna Kim Driver and Gus Ralph Hoff, lll

#8-3-5-5-1-2-1-2-1.   Gus Ralph Hoff, IV, born 12 October 1988, Bexar County, Texas.

#8-3-5-5-1-2-1-2-2.   Dustin Fayne Hoff, born 18 May 1990, Bexar County, Texas.

#7-3-5-5-1-2-3-2 MERIDITH NICOLE RANKIN

Meridith Nicole Rankin, born 5 September 1979, Denton County, Texas, married Randy Alfred Evans, 11 July 1998, Wise County, Texas. Randy was born 9 September 1979, Dallas County, Texas.

Child of Meridith Nicole Rankin and Randy Alfred Evans

#8-3-5-5-1-2-3-2-1.   MacKenzie Jean Evans, born 17 September 1996, Denton County, Texas.

#7-3-5-6-1-1-1-1 LAURIE LEA DOCKERY

Laurie Lea Dockery, born 23 May 1951, Jefferson County, Texas, married Carl Edwin Gulley, 17 July 1971, McLennan County, Texas. Edwin was born 20 December 1949, McLennan County, Texas.

Children of Laurie Lea Dockery and Carl Edwin Gulley

#8-3-5-6-1-1-1-1-1. Carl Edwin Gulley, Jr., born 12 April 1975, McLennan County, Texas.

#8-3-5-6-1-1-1-1-2. James Mark Gulley, born 14 November 1977, McLennan County, Texas.

#8-3-5-6-1-1-1-1-3. Jonathan David Gulley, born 14 April 1980, McLennan County, Texas.

#8-3-5-6-1-1-1-1-4. Jeffrey Michael Gulley, born 26 September 1984, McLennan County, Texas.

#7-3-5-6-1-1-1-2 JAN ALLYN DOCKERY

Jan Allyn Dockery, born 15 September 1955, Robertson County, Texas, married Chester Stanley Stanzeski, Jr. 10 March 1979, Harris County, Texas. Chester was born 25 July 1955, Bexar County, Texas.

Children of Jan Allyn Dockery and Chester Stanley Stanzeski, Jr.

#8-3-5-6-1-1-1-2-1. Caitlyn Paige Stanzeski, born 13 May 1985, Harris County, Texas.

#7-3-5-6-1-1-1-3 JAMES PAUL DOCKERY

James Paul Dockery, born 23 February 1961, Bexar County, Texas, married Katherine Eileen Leas, 23 August 1986, Bexar County Texas. Katherine was born in 1960.

Children of James Paul Dockery and Katherine Eileen Leas

#8-3-5-6-1-1-1-3-1.   James Braden Dockery, born 3 November 1987, Bexar County, Texas.

#8-3-5-6-1-1-1-3-2.   Shelbilea Nicole Dockery, born 19 April 1994, Bexar County, Texas.

#7-3-5-6-1-1-3-2 RICHARD LEE DOCKERY

Richard Lee Dockery, born 1 May 1956, Bexar County, Texas, married Debra Kay Kroll, 22 October 1977, Bexar County, Texas. Debra was born 24 February 1958, Bexar County, Texas.

Children of Richard Lee Dockery and Debra Kay Kroll

#8-3-5-6-1-1-3-2-1.   Denise Kay Dockery, born 6 March 1980, Bexar County, Texas.

#8-3-5-6-1-1-3-2-2.   Kyle Richard Dockery, born 22 February 1983, Bexar County, Texas.

#8-3-5-6-1-1-3-2-3.   Lyndsey Kristine Dockery, born 16 March 1990, Bexar County, Texas.

#7-3-5-6-1-1-3-3 PAMELA GAIL DOCKERY

Pamela Gail Dockery, born 17 December 1957, Bexar County, Texas, married Linden Keith Vance, 11 August 1979, Bexar County, Texas. Linden was born 11 November 1958, Bexar County, Texas.

Child of Pamela Gail Dockery and Linden Keith Vance

#8-3-5-6-1-1-3-3-1.   Pamela Nicole Vance, born 14 November 1983, Brazos County, Texas.

#7-3-5-6-1-1-3-4 MATTHEW DALE DOCKERY

Matthew Dale Dockery, born 14 December 1959, Bexar County, Texas, married Donna Lee Green, 24 October 1986, Bexar County, Texas. Donna was born in 1964.

Children of Matthew Dale Dockery and Donna Lee Green

#8-3-5-6-1-1-3-4-1. Cassie Lee Dockery, born 18 May 1987, Bexar County, Texas.

#8-3-5-6-1-1-3-4-2. Matthew Dale Dockery, Jr., born 29 May 1990, Bexar County, Texas.

#7-3-5-6-1-1-3-5 WENDELL WARD DOCKERY

Wendell Ward Dockery, born 7 August 1961, Bexar County, Texas, married De Ann Marie Dugie, 17 November 1984, Bexar County, Texas. De Ann was born 23 June 1963, Bexar County, Texas.

Children of Wendell Ward Dockery and Jo Ann Marie Dugie

#8-3-5-6-1-1-3-5-1. Joshua Anton Dockery, born 28 January 1987, Bexar County, Texas.

#8-3-5-6-1-1-3-5-2. Travis Wendell Dockery, born 24 July 1990, Bexar County, Texas.

#7-3-5-6-1-1-4-1 JEFFREY WADE DOCKERY

Jeffrey Wade Dockery, born 23 February 1957, Kleberg County, Texas, married Anne Conley, 7 June 1978, Bexar County, Texas. Anne was born in 1959.

Child of Jeffrey Wade Dockery and Anne Conley

#8-3-5-6-1-1-4-1-1. Sara Nila Dockery, born 3 August 1980, Bexar County, Texas.

#7-3-5-6-1-1-4-2 KIRK WAYNE DOCKERY

Kirk Wayne Dockery, born 18 March 1960, Bexar County, Texas, married Sarah Nan Brumlow, 1 August 1981, Wilson County, Texas. Sarah was born 31 March 1959, Ector County, Texas.

Children of Kirk Wayne Dockery and Saran Nan Brumlow

#8-3-5-6-1-1-4-2-1. Robert Gordon Dockery, born 26 August 1984, Lubbock County, Texas.
#8-3-5-6-1-1-4-2-2. Kris Willis Dockery, born 12 September 1986, Bexar County, Texas.
#8-3-5-6-1-1-4-2-3. Kathy Lee Dockery, born 19 November 1990, Bexar County, Texas.

#7-3-5-6-1-4-1-2 JOHN BRANDT DOCKERY

John Brandt Dockery, born 10 May 1966, Tarrant County, Texas, married Kimberly Evans about 1975.

Child of John Brandt Dockery and Kimberly Evans

#8-3-5-6-1-4-1-2-1. Makenzie Lee Dockery, born 10 July 1997, Bexar County, Texas.

#7-3-5-6-1-4-2-2 LINDA ANN WARD

Linda Ann Ward, born 30 January 1960, Dimmit County, Texas, married John Paul McNair, 15 July 1978, Dimmit County, Texas. John was born 10 November 1959, Walker County, Texas.

Children of Linda Ann Ward and John Paul McNair

#8-3-5-6-1-4-2-2-1. John Neal McNair, born 12 August 1980, Maverick County, Texas.

#8-3-5-6-1-4-2-2-2.   Sherry Ann McNair, born 12 August 1980, Maverick County, Texas.

#7-3-6-2-3-1-1-1 JANNA HIME

Janna Hime, born 16 February 1959, Mesa, Arizona, married Michael Hanson, November 26 1982, Jefferson, South Dakota. Michael was born 30 December 1961, Sioux City, Iowa. Michael was a Farmer.

Children of Janna Hime and Michael Hanson

#8-3-6-2-3-1-1-1-1.   Vance Hanson, born 17 April 1984, Glendale, Arizona.
#8-3-6-2-3-1-1-1-2.   Kati Elisabeth Hanson, born 13 October 1987, Sioux City, Iowa.
#8-3-6-2-3-1-1-1-3.   Lucas James Hanson, born 21 January 1993, Sioux City, Iowa.

#7-3-6-2-3-1-1-2 THOMAS J. HIME

Thomas J. Hime, born 18 February 1957, Aurora, Colorado, married Anna Kluver, 16 December 1999, Onawa, Iowa. Anna was born in 1957, Onawa, Iowa.

Children of Thomas J. Hime and Anna Kluver

#8-3-6-2-3-1-1-2-1.   Joey Hime, born 13 November 1974, Onawa, Iowa.
#8-3-6-2-3-1-1-2-2.   Tommy Hime, born 5 June 1992, Onawa, Iowa.

#7-3-6-2-3-5-2-1 TINA MARIE CURLOBIC

Tina Marie Curlobic, born 18 January 1968, Alton, Illinois, married John David Lasater, 27 August 1994, Alton, Illinois. John was born 24 April 1967, Poplar Bluff, Missouri. John is a Medical Doctor.

Children of Tina Marie Curlobic and John David Lasater

#8-3-6-2-3-5-2-1-1.   Dustin Lasater, born 15 July 1993, Alton, Illinois.

#8-3-6-2-3-5-2-1-2.   Mason Lasater, born 24 March 1998, Salem, Oregon.

#8-3-6-2-3-5-2-1-3.   Tyson Lasater, born 9 July 1999 Salem, Oregon.

#7-3-6-2-3-5-2-2 ANDREA CARLOBIC

Andrea Carbolic, born 12 September 1976, Alton, Illinois, married Gene Stevenson in the Bahamas'

Children of Andrea Carbolic and Gene Stevenson

#8-3-6-2-3-5-2-2-1.   Darian Stevenson, born 12 May 1998, Alton, Illinois.

#8-3-6-2-3-5-2-2-2.   Tyler Stevenson, born 10 March 2000, Alton, Illinois.

#7-3-6-2-3-7-1-1 PAUL WAYNE ENGLAND

Paul Wayne England, born 7 May 1961, Batesville, Arkansas, married Joann Satterwhite, 27 November 1981, Batesville, Arkansas. Joann was born 6 May 1961, Batesville, Arkansas.

Children of Wayne England

#8-3-6-2-3-7-1-1-1.   Kristy Ann England, born 20 July 1987, Newport, Arkansas.

#8-3-6-2-3-7-1-1-2.   Tiffany Dawn England, born 21 December 1990, Newport, Arkansas.

#8-3-6-2-3-7-1-1-3.   Patrick Wayne England, born 23 April 1995, Newport, Arkansas.

#7-3-6-2-3-7-1-2 MARIE ELLEN LUNDBERG

Marie Ellen Lundberg, born 6 January 1969, Great Lakes, Chicago, Illinois, married Anthony Moore, 20 June 1993, San Diego, California.

Child of Marie Ellen Lundberg and Anthony Moore

#8-3-6-2-3-7-1-2-1.   Tribecca Cherise Moore, born 26 February 26 1977, Yakasaki, Japan.

#7-3-6-2-3-7-1-3 TINA DENISE LUNDBERG

Tina Denise Lundberg, born 26 April 1970, San Francisco, California, gave birth to three children out of wedlock.

Child of Tina Denise Lundberg and Dondwell Gooding

#8-3-6-2-3-7-1-3-1.   Marcus Dondwell Lundberg Gooding, born 13 February 1988, San Diego County, California.

Child of Tina Denise Lundberg and Maurice Cuellar

#8-3-6-2-3-7-1-3-2.   Murice Alendria Lundberg Cuellar, born 1 May 1995, San Diego County, California.

Child of Tina Denise Lundberg and Keith Brown

#8-3-6-2-3-7-1-3-3.   Sage Monique Lundberg Brown, born 15 November 1996, San Diego County, California.

#7-3-6-2-3-7-2-1 SHEILA ANN JOHNSON

Sheila Ann Johnson, born 15 September 1962, Rockford, Illinois, first married Kenneth McCarley, 1 April 1978, Hamilton, Marion County, Alabama. Kenneth was born 29 October 1958, Hamilton, Marion

County, Alabama. Sheila later married Rick Ross, 13 March 1999. Rick was born 24 May 1958, Shelby, Cleveland County, North Carolina.

Children of Sheila Ann Johnson and Kenneth McCarley

#8-3-6-2-3-7-2-1-1.   Deannea Marie McCarley, born 20 May 1979, Rockford, Illinois.
#8-3-6-2-3-7-2-1-2.   Michael Allen McCarley, born 30 April 1983, Hickory, North Carolina.

Child of Sheila Ann Johnson and Rick Ross

#8-3-6-2-3-7-2-1-3.   Catherine Lavace Ross, born 11 July 2003, Hickory, North Carolina.

#7-3-6-2-3-7-2-4 CHRISTOPHER NEAL JOHNSON

Christopher Johnson, born 16 November 1974, Cairo, Alexander County, Illinois, married Wanda Spencer, 21 February 1999, Hickory, Catawba County, North Carolina. Wanda was born 4 November 1970, Gaffney, North Carolina. Christopher and Frances Hawkins also had a child.

Child of Christopher Neal Johnson and Frances Hawkins

#8-3-6-2-3-7-2-4-1.   Angela Hawkins, Johnson, born 23 February 1993, Hickory, Catawba County, North Carolina.

Children of Christopher Neal Johnson and Wanda Spencer

#8-3-6-2-3-7-2-4-2.   Christopher Aaron Johnson, born 31 August 2000, Hickory, Catawba County, North Carolina.

#7-3-6-2-3-7-3-1 LORI MARIE SANDS

Lori Marie Sands, born 26 July 1969, Cairo, Illinois, married Brian Zwiger, 9 April 1988, Rockford, Illinois. Brian was born 30 June 1966, Rockford, Winnebago County, Illinois.

Child of Lori Marie Sands and Brian Zwiger

#8-3-6-2-3-7-3-1-1.　　Danyiel Vwiger, born 13 April 1990, Rockford, Illinois.

#7-3-6-2-3-7-3-2 JENNIFER SANDS

Jennifer Sands, born 26 March 1972, Rockford, Winnebago County, Illinois, married Thomas Cagle, 11 June 1994, Rockford, Winnebago County, Illinois. Thomas was born 20 July 1968, Fort Worth, Texas.

Child of Jennifer Sands and Thomas Cagle

#8-3-6-2-3-7-3-2-1.　　Emily Christine Cagle, born 24 March 1999, Fort Worth, Texas.
#8-3-6-2-3-7-3-2-1.　　Adam Thomas Cagle, born 29 May 2003, Fort Worth, Texas.

#7-3-6-2-3-7-3-3 CARL HERBERT SANDS AKRE

Carl Herbert Sands akre, born 18 April 1977, Rockford, Winnebago County, Illinois, married Bethany Eytalis. Carl's sir name was changed to Akre after his mother and father divorced and before he was 18 years of age.

Children of Carl Herbert Sands Akre and Bethany Eytalis

#8-3-6-2-3-7-3-3-1.　　Tyler Jacob Sands Akre, born 22 March 1977, Rockford, Illinois.

#8-3-6-2-3-7-3-3-2.   Bailey William Sands Akre, born 15 July 1999, Rockford, Illinois.

#8-3-6-2-3-7-3-3-3.   Lily Grace Sands Akre, born 23 December 2002, Rockford, Illinois.

#7-3-6-2-3-7-4-1   WINDY MARIE SANDS

Windy M. Sands, born 25 January 1974, San Bernardino County, California, killed with her daughter by a drunk driver in an automobile accident, 10 June 2000. Unmarried.

Child of Windy Marie Sands

#8-3-6-2-3-7-4-1-1.   Kimberly Annmarie Sands, born 4 January 1994, San Bernardino County, California. Died in car accident 10 June 2000.

#7-3-6-2-3-7-4-2   MATTHEW THOMAS SANDS

Matthew Thomas Sands, born 3 February 1976, in Oklahoma City, Oklahoma, married Annie Kate Brite, 12 July 1997, Oklahoma City, Oklahoma. Annie was born 21 April 1975, Oklahoma City, Oklahoma. Matthew and Annie were married in the Capital Rotunda in the Capital building in Oklahoma City, Oklahoma.

Child of Matthew Thomas Sands and Annie Kate Brite

#8-3-6-2-3-7-4-2-1.   Kaylie Alaxenderia Sands, born 14 August 2005, Victorville, California.

#7-3-6-2-3-8-1-1   DARLA ANN HARTLINE

Darla Ann Hartline, born 12 August 1973, Cape Girardeau, Missouri, married James Peterman, 3 January 1993, Cobden, Illinois. James was born 13 October 1973, Germany.

Children of Darla Ann Hartline and James Peterman

#8-3-6-2-3-8-1-1-1.   Alexis Danielle Peterman, born 12 December 1994, Cape Girardeau, Missouri.

#8-3-6-2-3-8-1-1-2.   Makynzie Ray Peterman, born 28 June 1999, Cape Girardeau, Missouri.

#7-3-6-2-3-8-1-2 DARRELL LEE HARTLINE

Darrell Lee Hartline, born 11 August 1970, Cape Girardeau, Missouri, married Teri McCann. Terry was born in Alto Pass, Illinois.

Child of Darrell Lee Hartline and Teri McCann

#8-3-6-2-3-8-1-2-1.   Bobby Joe Hartline, Born 10 October 2001.

#7-3-6-2-7-3-1-1 JOHN PAUL SARGENT, JR.

John Paul Sargent, Jr., born 26 May 1975, Fayetteville, Washington County, Arkansas.

Child of John Paul Sargent, Jr.

#8-3-6-2-7-3-1-1-1.   Sierra Nicole Sargent, born 3 September 1995, Fayetteville, Washington County, Arkansas.

#7-3-6-2-7-3-1-2 JASON DENE SARGENT

Jason Dene Sargent, born 25 April 1978, Fayetteville, Washington County, Arkansas, married Donna H. Faison, 19 September, 1999, Strickler, Washington County, Arkansas. Donna was born 29 June 1979, Richmond, Virginia.

Children of Jason Dene Sargent and Donna H. Faison

#8-3-6-2-7-3-1-2-1.   John Ralston Sargent, born 24 January 2000, Jacksonville, North Carilina.
#8-3-6-2-7-3-1-2-2.   Dale Michael Sargent, born 29 April 2001, Camp LeJeune, North Carolina.
#8-3-6-2-7-3-1-2-3.   Mathew Denish Sargent, born 6 June 2004, Camp LeJeune, North Carolina.

#7-3-6-2-7-3-2-1   CARAMENYA NICHOLE SARGENT

Caramenya Nichole Sargent, born 13 February 1981, Shreveport, Louisiana, married Mark Thomas Burnett, 7 August 2004, Prairie Grove, Washington County, Arkansas. Mark was born 15 December 1981, Newport News, Virginia.

Child of Caramenya Nicole Sargent and Mark Thomas Burnett

#8-3-6-2-7-3-2-1-1.   Calloway Elizabeth Burnett, born 29 December 2007, Ft Worth, Texas.

#7-3-6-2-7-3-2-2   ELIZABETH ANN SARGENT

Elizabeth Ann Sargent, born 10 December 1982, Shreveport, Louisiana, married Wyatt Jonathon Wagner, 6 September 2008, Owasso, Oklahoma. Wyatt was born 12 September 1974, Dallas, Texas.

#7-3-6-2-8-2-1-1   WILLIAM TODD GETZ

William Todd Getz, born 17 July 1966, Los Angeles, California, married Melinda Lee Hughes, 3 August 1992, Salt Lake City, Utah. Melinda was born 20 September 1971, Salt Lake City, Utah.

Children of William Todd Getz and Melinda Lee Hughes

#8-3-6-2-8-2-1-1-1.   Morgan Bailey Getz, born 13 September 1992, Salt Lake City, Utah.

#8-3-6-2-8-2-1-1-2.   William Cody Getz, born 20 February 1996, Phoenix, Arizona.

#7-3-6-2-8-2-1-2 BRIAN S. GETZ

Brian S. Getz, born 18 April 1967, San Bernardino County, California, married Laura Molly Rodriquez, 3 October 1990, Las Vegas, Nevada. Laura was born 13 February 1970, Riverside, California.

Children of Bryan S. Getz and Laura Molly Rodriquez

#8-3-6-2-8-2-1-2-1.   Meghan Ramy Getz, born 6 May 1996, Salt Lake City, Utah.

#8-3-6-2-8-2-1-2-2.   Dallas Sebastian Getz, born 21 November 2003, Corona, California.

#8-3-6-2-8-2-1-2-3.   Austyn Scott Getz, born 8 August 2005, Corona, California.

#7-3-6-2-9-4-1-1 KENLI RHEA HUDGENS

Kenli Rhea Hudgens, born 16 March 1978, Washington County, Arkansas, married James Craig Dunham, 27 November 2004, Prairie Grove, Washington County, Arkansas.

Children of Kenli Rhea Hudgens and James Craig Dunham

#8-3-6-2-9-4-1-1-1.   James Rylin Dunham, born 22 August 2006, Washington County, Arkansas.

#8-3-6-2-9-4-1-1-2.   Zaley Ray Dunham, born 29 April 2008, Washington County, Arkansas.

#7-3-6-2-11-1-1-1 FRANKYE SHANNON ETHERIDGE

Frankye Shannon Etheridge, born 11 September 1977, Potter County, Texas, married William J. Warren, 17 August 2002, Potter County, Texas. William was born 26 February 1977, Colorado.

Children of Frankye Shannon Etheridge and William J. Warren

#8-3-6-2-11-1-1-1-1. Sebastain Gabriel Warren, born 27 January 2001, Potter County, Texas.
#8-3-6-2-11-1-1-1-2. Syndel Skye Warren, born 22 January 2003, El Paso County, Texas.

#7-3-6-2-11-1-1-2 CATHERINE ANN ETHERIDGE

Catherine Ann Etheridge, born 4 February 1979, Potter County, Texas, married Kenneth Boatright, 2003, Amarillo, Texas. Kenneth was born 2 December 1969, Amarillo, Texas.

Children of Catherine Ann Etheridge and Kenneth Boatright

#8-3-6-2-11-1-1-2-1. Nathaniel Ray Boatright, born 4 August 1997, Potter County, Texas.
#8-3-6-2-11-1-1-2-2. Jessie Jaden Boatright, born 21 January 2006, Potter County, Texas.

#7-3-6-2-11-1-3-1 KATRICIA SAMON LAIRD

Katricia Samon Laird, born 17 December 1981, Oklahoma City, Oklahoma, married Marcus Presas, 11 March 2005, Nueces, Texas.

Children of Katricie Samon Laird and Marcus Presas

#8-3-6-2-11-1-3-1-1. Jacob Ryan Presas, born 25 October 2005, Nueces County, Texas.

#8-3-6-2-11-1-3-1-2. Makayla Gail Presas, born 19 July 2007, Nueces County, Texas.

#7-3-6-2-11-3-2-1 SHANDI WILLIAMS

Shandi Williams, born 17 February 1984, Boise City, Cimarron County, Oklahoma, first married Joseph Thane Holick, 5 October 2002, Oklahoma City, Oklahoma. Shandi Later married Sam Lionelli at Ponca City, Kay County, Oklahoma.

Child of Shandi Williams and Joseph Thane Holick

#8-3-6-2-11-3-2-1-1. Conner Riley Holick, born 16 April 2003, Kay County, Oklahoma.

Child of Shandi Williams and Sam Lionelli

#8-3-6-2-11-3-2-1-2. Breckyn Noel Lionelli. born 20 August 2010, Payne County, Oklahoma.

#7-3-7-5-2-4-1-1 MINDY GRISHAM

Mindy Grisham, born 29 October 1979, Tulsa, Tulsa County, Oklahoma, married Mathew Smith.

Children of Mindy Grisham and Mathew Smith

#8-3-7-5-2-4-1-1-1. Bryce Smith, born 30 March 2001, Tulsa, Oklahoma.
#8-3-7-5-2-4-1-1-2. Shaeli Smith, born 1 July 2004, Tulsa, Oklahoma.

NINTH GENERATION

#8-3-2-5-1-1-3-2-1 GLENN RAY BRALY

Glenn Ray Braly, born 13 December 1957, Fayetteville, Washington County, Arkansas, unknown wife.

Child of Glenn Ray Braly

#9-3-2-5-1-1-3-2-1-1. Bobby Braly, born 18 July 1984.

#8-3-2-5-1-1-3-2-2 HOWARD PAUL BRALY

Howard Paul Brawly, born 21 June 1960, Siloam Springs, Benton County, Arkansas, unknown wife.

Child of Howard Paul Braly

#9-3-2-5-1-1-3-2-2-1. Allison Braly, born 18 July 1984, Fayetteville, Arkansas.

#8-3-2-5-1-3-2-1-1 RHONDA ALLEN

Rhonda Allen, born Washington County, Arkansas, married Mark Precer.

Children of Rhonda Allen and Mark Precer

#9-3-2-5-1-3-2-1-1-1. Caroline Precer, born Washington County, Arkansas.

#9-3-2-5-1-3-2-1-1-2. Kimberly Precer, born Washington County, Arkansas.

#8-3-2-5-1-3-2-2-1 KARA WATSON

Kara Watson, born Washington County, Arkansas, married Brett Cunningham.

Children of Kara Watson and Brett Cunningham

#9-3-2-5-1-3-2-2-1-1. McKenna Cunningham, born Washington County, Arkansas.

#9-3-2-5-1-3-2-2-1-2. Allison Cunningham, born Washington County, Arkansas.

#8-3-2-5-7-1-1-2-1 BOBBY K. RINEHART

Bobby K. Rinehart born, 1 September 1973, Tahlequah, Cherokee County, Oklahoma, married Shala Hudson.

Children of Bobby K. Rinehart and Shala Hudson

#9-3-2-5-7-1-1-2-1-1. Jordan Rinehart, born 13 February 1996.

#9-3-2-5-7-1-1-2-1-2. Ray Ann Rinehart, born 13 February 1996.

#9-3-2-5-7-1-1-2-1-3. Tyler Borean Rinehart, born 9 September 1998.

#8-3-2-5-7-1-1-2-2 BRYAN DEAN RINEHART

Bryan Dean Rineheart, born 26 February 1976, Tahlequah, Cherokee County, Oklahoma, first married Lena Beaver and later unknown wife.

Child of Bryan Dean Rinehart and Lena Beaver

#9-3-2-5-7-1-1-2-2-1. Darren Nicklaus Rinehart, born 29 April 2001.

Child of Bryan Dean Rinehart and unknown

#9-3-2-5-7-1-1-2-2-2. Brinley Catalin Rinehart, born 16 July 2005.

#8-3-2-5-7-3-2-2-1   CHRISTY REANAE REED

Christy Reanea Reed, born 13 January 1986, Benton County, Arkansas married David Erin Rackley, 19 November 2007, Sherwood, Arkansas. David was born 2 February 1978.

Child of Christina Reanae Reed and David Erin Rackley

#9-3-2-5-7-3-2-2-1-1.   Joshua David Rackley, born 3 March 2008, North Little Rock, Arkansas.